mastodon

Art by Theresa Deeter

Keweenaw

Houghton

Ontonagon

Baraga

gebic

Marquette

Iron

Dickinson

Alger

Schoolcraft

Luce

Chippewa

Mackinac

Delta

Menominee

lumberjack

Petoskey stone

Emmet

Cheboygan

Charlevoix

Presque Isle

Montmorency

Antrim

Otsego

Alpena

Leelanau

Benzie

Grand Traverse

Kalkaska

Crawford

Oscoda

Alcona

Manistee

Wexford

Missaukee

Roscommon

Ogemaw

Iosco

French explorer

Mason

Lake

Osceola

Clare

Gladwin

Arenac

Huron

Oceana

Newaygo

Mecosta

Isabella

Midland

Bay

Tuscola

Sanilac

Muskegon

Montcalm

Gratiot

Saginaw

Ottawa

Kent

Ionia

Clinton

Shiawassee

Genesee

Lapeer

St. Clair

Allegan

Barry

Eaton

Ingham

Livingston

Oakland

Macomb

Van Buren

Kalamazoo

Calhoun

Jackson

Washtenaw

Wayne

Berrien

Cass

St. Joseph

Branch

Hillsdale

Lenawee

Monroe

Native American chief

Art by Aaron Zenz

Meet Michigan

by David B. McConnell

The students on the cover are using their talents to learn and share about Michigan. Two are making a big state map. This is for a Michigan History Day project. One is practicing a Native American dance for a Pow Wow. The third is entering his drawing of Kirtland's Warbler in an art contest. How can you share with others what you learn about Michigan ?

This book is dedicated to the memory of
Mr. Mel Miller, a tireless advocate of
teaching about Michigan and its history.

Acknowledgments

This book would not have been possible without the assistance and suggestions of many Michigan educators. Special thanks to each of you! My apologies if I failed to include anyone's name.

Educators

Maggie Bilby, Nancy Flory, Mary Foulke, Kelly Gaideski, Julie Garrison, Marty Mater, Robert Palmer, Mary Palmer, Sheryl Sanford, Karen Todorov, Anita Weirich

Illustrators

Theresa Deeter, Don Ellens, Mark Koenig, Robert Morrison Tim Pickell, George Rasmussen, Aaron Zenz

Thanks to the following students at Hillsdale College who submitted illustrations for this book: Cassandra Bacon, Jessica Bastian, Carly Gosine, Rachel Moir, Maggie O'Connor, Jodi Olthouse, Tricia Schoon, Amy Scott, Brita Thompson

Family

It takes many hands to finish a project of this size. Besides the comments from educators, my wife and parents have been a great help too, especially my mother. They all contributed to this book.

Additional thanks to the various archives and Michigan corporations who provided photos.

Printed in Canada by Friesens

Hillsdale Educational Publishers, Inc.

**39 North Street, Hillsdale, Michigan 49242
fax 517-437-0531   phone 517-437-3179
www.hillsdalepublishers.com**

ISBN 978-1-931466-12-7

*My encouragement to those educators who take the time
to present Michigan to their students in spite
of a crowded curriculum. Keep up the good work!*

About the Author

David McConnell has a lifelong interest in history and teaching. For many years he has been a member of the Michigan Council for Social Studies, the Michigan Council for History Education and the Historical Society of Michigan. He is also a member of the National Council for Social Studies and Association for Supervision and Curriculum Development. Dave lives with his wife Janice in their country home near Hillsdale. For the past 30 years he has written and developed Michigan studies textbooks and teaching resources. These include—

Discover Michigan, 1981, 1985
Explore Michigan A to Z, 1993
Forging the Peninsulas: Michigan Is Made, 1989, 2001, 2008
A Little People's Beginning On Michigan, 1981, 2002
Michigan Activity Masters, 1985, 1999
Michigan's Story, 1996, 2002
Our Michigan Adventure, 1998, 2002, 2005, 2008
A Puzzle Book For Young Michiganians, 1982

Also served as editor and contributor for
    Computer Games On Michigan, 1996, 2004
    Michigan Student Desk Map and associated lessons
    Michigan Government and You
    Michigan Map Skills and Information Workbook

Awards:
Our Michigan Adventure
    Award of Merit, Historical Society of Michigan.
Forging the Peninsulas: Michigan Is Made -
    Award of Merit, Historical Society of Michigan.
Discover Michigan -
    Michigan Product of the Year, non consumer division.
Listed in *Michigan Authors* 1993, 2001

The author at Lincoln Elementary School talking with Jonathan Huhta and his class about Michigan's logging days .

CONTENTS

CONTENTS

ECONOMICS

You will meet some new ideas in this book. Some will be about our past- our history. Some will be about money and economics. Others will be about values. These are important values. They make our state and our country great. We call them core democratic values. These values are like building blocks. Our state and our country are built on them.

These ideas and values tie in with our past. They also tie in with our present.

There are special pictures to guide you to these ideas. Look for them as you read. You will find important thoughts next to each one.

For money and economics, we will use...

For core democratic values, we will use...

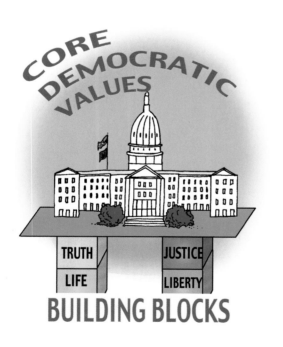

CORE DEMOCRATIC VALUES

TRUTH   JUSTICE

LIFE   LIBERTY

BUILDING BLOCKS

Teachers want you to start to think like historians. Historians study the past. You should ask and answer the kinds of questions historians use. What questions would they ask? Here are some.

What happened? When did it happen?
Who was there?   Why did it happen?

When you see this picture you know it is time to think about these questions.

Teachers also want you to start to think like a geographer. Geographers study the land and the water. They look at rivers, lakes and oceans. They want you to understand maps. They want you to see how geography shaped our state. Here are some questions geographers ask.

Where is it?
What is it like there?
How is it connected to other places?
How did the land or the water affect
what happened there?

GEOGRAPHY

When you see this picture you know it is time to think about geography.

Teachers also want you to know when events took place. They want you to know what happened first and what happened next.

We use time lines to help do this. Here is a time line.

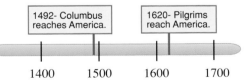

| 1492- Columbus reaches America. | | 1620- Pilgrims reach America. | |
| 1400 | 1500 | 1600 | 1700 |

The picture with the clock and dates will let you know you should think about time and what came first.

Chapter 1 - Meet Michigan

Chapter 1 Lesson 1

the big,
bright ideas

Ideas To Explore
What is a state?
What gives Michigan its shape?
How did our state get the name Michigan?

Places To Discover
Great Lakes
Michigan (mish eh gan)
peninsula (pen in su la)
Lower Peninsula
Upper Peninsula

Words to Welcome
borders (bor ders)
government (gov ern ment)

Michigan
Social
Studies
GLCEs
3G1.0.2
3C3.0.2

Welcome
to Meet
Michigan!

viii

Chapter 1

Meet Michigan

Think about this question while you read.

What is a state?

Luis is checking out
our state stone.

Welcome to Michigan. This is where you live. Your hometown is here. This is your state. Michigan is full of fun and exciting things. Let's learn about them.

Read about its Indian tribes. Listen to a chief tell you a legend. See the old forts from long ago. Some of our first towns began as forts.

Go back in time. See how our pioneer men and women lived. Learn why they came to Michigan and how they got here. Discover how Michigan became a state. Find out how it has grown and changed.

<u>What would YOU like to learn about Michigan?</u>

The fort at Mackinaw City.

THIS IS MICHIGAN!

Mainland United States
without Alaska, Hawaii & the Commonwealth of Puerto Rico

What is Michigan?

It is one of our 50 states. It is part of the United States of America. Each state is different from the others. Some states have much land. Some have less land. Some have many people. Other states have fewer people.

Have you ever wondered what a state is?

*Each state has three parts. A state is its **land**, its **people** and its **government**.*

First, a state is land. When we say land, do not leave out its lakes and water. Each state has its own shape.

1 Land

2 People

3 Government

Each state has its own **borders**. *A border is where one state ends and the next state begins.* Has your family driven across Michigan's border?

A state is also the people who live there. You and I are each a little bit of Michigan. The things we do are all a part of our state.

People need rules. They need help doing some things. *Government does things for us we cannot do by ourselves. It helps people. It builds highways. It pays for the police. It makes laws. It helps people protect their rights.* Government is the third part of what a state is.

Our Shape

Some states have square shapes. Some are long. Some are tall. Michigan has a very different shape. No other state has a shape like ours. Our shape is quite interesting!

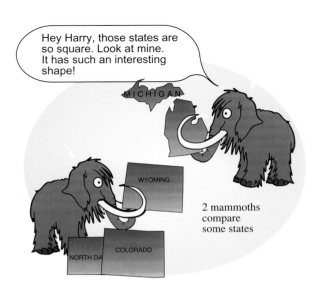

Hey Harry, those states are so square. Look at mine. It has such an interesting shape!

MICHIGAN

WYOMING

2 mammoths compare some states

NORTH DA

COLORADO

3

A photo of Lake Superior. A large ship sails by. This ship carries coal to a power plant. Courtesy David McConnell

We are not like any other state. We are different in two ways. First, we are in the middle of the **Great Lakes**! The Great Lakes are HUGE lakes. You cannot see across them. Each of them holds a lot of water. Big ships sail on them. No other state has so much fresh water around it. The Great Lakes give our land its shape. You can spot Michigan quickly, even from outer space!

A photo taken from outer space. The photo was taken in the winter. There is ice on some of the Great Lakes.

Courtesy Liam Gumley, Space Science and Engineering Center, University of Wisconsin-Madison

Next, Michigan is divided into two big parts. It is the only state that is this way. We have the **Upper Peninsula**. It is the northern part. We have the **Lower Peninsula**. It is the southern part. Have you heard the word **peninsula** before? *A peninsula is land with water on three sides.* The Great Lakes are around our two peninsulas. Check it out on a map.

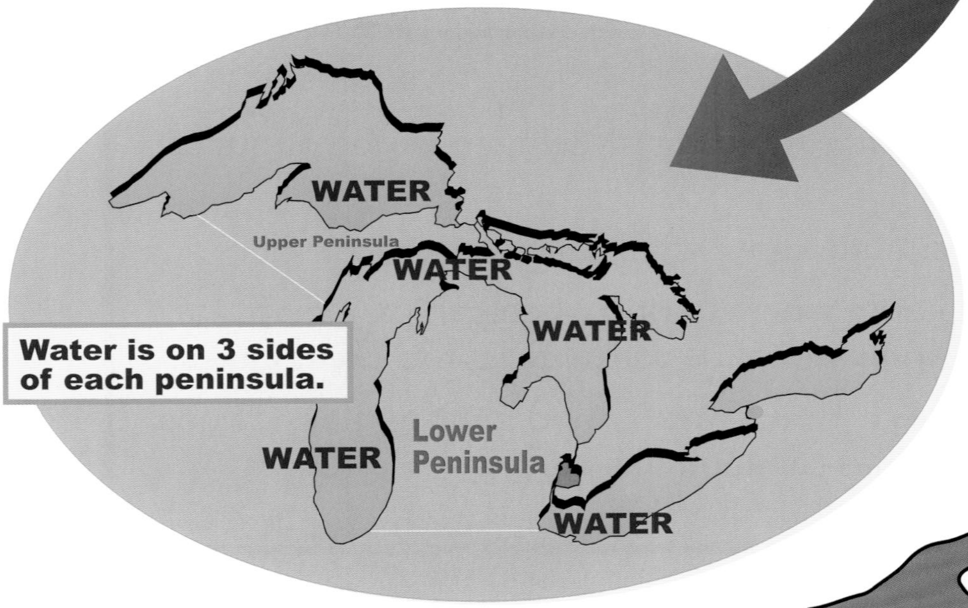

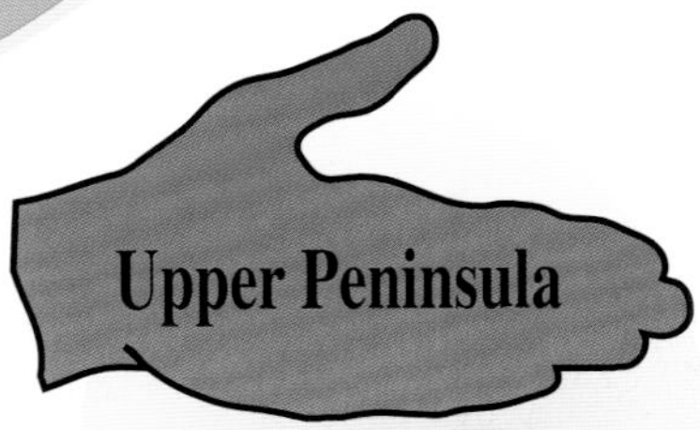

WATER

Upper Peninsula

WATER

WATER

Water is on 3 sides of each peninsula.

WATER

Lower Peninsula

WATER

N

W · E

S

Upper Peninsula

The Lower Peninsula looks like a hand or a mitten. Some people also say the Upper Peninsula has a hand shape too. Put the two shapes together. The Upper Peninsula is the left hand. The Lower Peninsula is the right hand. Now your hands look like Michigan!

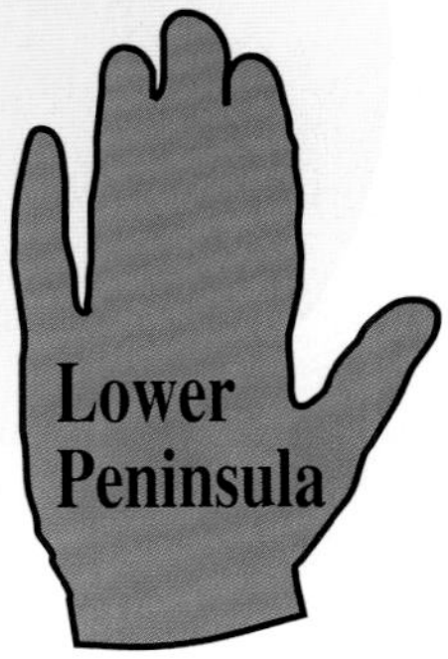

Lower Peninsula

5

Picture drawn
by George
Rasmussen.

Our Name

What does the name of our state mean? The name Michigan comes from Native American words! It means big lake or great lake. That fits our state. It has so much water around it!

Remember ....

You have learned that Michigan is one of our 50 states.

You should know what a state is.

You know where to find Michigan on a map. You know its shape comes from the Great Lakes.

We have two parts called peninsulas. Those peninsulas can look like hands.

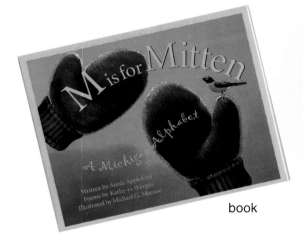

book

There are many ways to learn more about Michigan. You may want to read a book about Michigan. There are also videos about our state.

video

Think About It. Write About It!

1. Tell what you know about the shape of Michigan.

2. What is a peninsula?

3. What does the name Michigan mean?

4. What is a state?

5. Name one thing state government does for us.

Brain Stretchers

What makes Michigan different from other states in the United States?

Words In Action!

Imagine you have a pen pal in another state. Write an e-mail telling about Michigan. Use facts you learned from this lesson.

Chapter 1 Lesson 2

Ideas To Explore

common good: what is best for *everyone*, not just yourself.

state flag: Each state has a state flag. What does ours look like?

state symbols: Which symbols (SIM bols) stand for Michigan?

Places To Discover

Isle Royale (sounds like- eye l • roy al)

Lansing (lan sing)

Words to Welcome

coral (KOR al)

deposit (dee pos it)

fossil (fos el)

Kalkaska (kal KAS ka)

Latin (LAT n)

human characteristic (hu man • kar ak ter iz tik)

natural characteristic

nature

opinion

state game mammal

state seal

Tuebor (TOO-a-bor) a Latin word

Michigan
Social
Studies
GLCEs
3G1.0.2
3G5.0.1
3C1.0.1
3C5.0.1
3P3.1.1
3P3.3.1
3P4.2.1
3P4.2.2

OUR STATE SYMBOLS

Think about this question while you read.
How do our state symbols help people learn about Michigan?

Check out our **state symbols** (SIM bols)! The symbols are things which are special to Michigan. Here are some examples.

The **robin** is the *state bird*. People said it is the best known and most loved bird here.

Our *state flower* is the **apple blossom**. It has been the state flower since 1897. In the spring the apple blossoms are beautiful on the trees. Our climate helps this tree grow well here.

The **white pine** is our *state tree*. It is an evergreen. Many were used for lumber long ago. The lumber helped to build lots of homes. Michigan does not have nearly as many white pine trees today. Our climate and soil help this tree grow well here. It grows best in the north part of the state.

The colorful **brook trout** is our *state fish*. It is about eight to ten inches long. Blue, green and red spots cover its sides.

Our state symbols are natural characteristics of Michigan. They are a part of nature - the outdoors.

The *state stone* is the **Petoskey stone**. Many are found on the beaches near the city of Petoskey. This stone is very old. Each stone is a piece of ancient **coral**. Coral grows in seas and oceans.

You may wonder how pieces of coral got here. It means a sea once covered this land! That was a very long time ago. Without that great sea, there would be no Petoskey stone today. Look closely. You can see the coral pattern in the stone.

How do we get a state symbol? Our state government in **Lansing** votes and says so. In 1973 it voted to have a *state gem*. They chose the **greenstone**. You can find these little green stones on **Isle Royale** (eye l roy al). This is an island in Lake Superior. The stones are often on the beaches there.

We even have a *state soil*. This is the **Kalkaska** (kal KAS ka) **soil**. The state government chose this special soil. That was in 1990. This helps people remember how important soil is to all of us. Without soil there would be no farms. We could not grow our food.

A while ago some students felt we should have a *state reptile*. The students thought about it. Then they said the painted turtle would be the best choice. In 1995 the **painted turtle** became Michigan's state reptile!

The **whitetail deer** is Michigan's *state game mammal.* Over a million deer live here. They are found in every part of the state. Many of you have seen one.

Our *state wildflower* is the **dwarf lake iris**. This kind of flower is hard to find. It is very small.

Dwarf Lake Iris- Courtesy Dr. Dennis Albert

We also have a *state fossil.* What is a **fossil**? *A fossil was once a living thing that has changed to stone.* It takes a very long time to make a fossil. Most fossils are found in the ground.

a mastodon

Mastodon bones are often found here. Those animals lived here a very long time ago. They looked like hairy elephants. The mastodon was voted the *state fossil* a few years ago.

Made by Nature or by People?

Each state symbol is special to us. Each is found here. Each one is made by **nature**. It is a **natural characteristic** of our state. The robin is made by nature. The apple blossom is made by nature. The Kalkaska soil is made by nature.

Hillsdale College student Chase Beck holds two bones from a mastodon. The bones were found in Hillsdale county.

11

Michigan has **human characteristics** too. These are things made by humans. Men and women made them. Buildings and bridges are human characteristics. A road is a human characteristic. People made it. Another example is a school. On the other hand, a river is a natural characteristic. It was made by nature.

Michigan's Flag

Michigan has its own **state flag**. Have you ever seen it? Most of the flag is bright blue. In the middle is the Michigan **State Seal**.

The state seal is a picture. This picture is used by our state government. You may see it on government papers or at state offices.

The seal has an eagle holding arrows and an olive branch. There is an elk and a moose too. There is also a man with one hand raised. This means peace. In his other hand is a rifle. This means we will

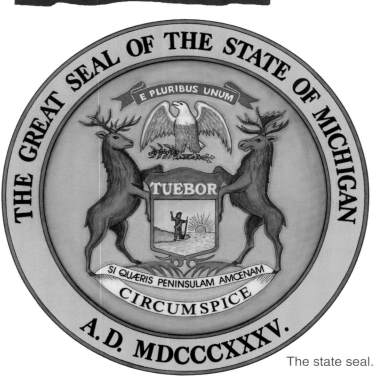

The state seal.

defend our state. There is also a rising sun and a lake on the state seal.

COMMON GOOD

Thinking about the **COMMON GOOD** is a lot more than thinking about just yourself.

It is thinking about what is good for everyone!

The seal has several words on it. These words are from an old language called **Latin** (LAT n). One of the Latin words on the flag is "**Tuebor**" (sounds like- TOO-a-bor). It means "I will defend."

How can you defend Michigan? Have you ever thought about it? One way is to help keep it clean. Do not leave litter along the sidewalk or play-ground. Pick up after yourself. Do not drop gum and candy wrappers on the ground. Do not leave pop cans at the park. Recycle them instead.

Not just

Keeping Michigan clean is good for everyone. It is thinking about the **common good**! Thinking about the common good is thinking about what is good for everyone. It is not thinking just about yourself. It is not being selfish. Helping to keep Michigan clean is helping to defend it. It is also working for the common good.

The Bottle Bill

Once there were lots of bottles and cans thrown along our roads. It was a mess! People said this made Michigan ugly.

Our state did something. It made a new law in 1976. This is often called the "Bottle Bill." It put a **deposit** on soda pop and other fizzy beverages. *A deposit is money paid up front and given back when the item is returned.* Today the deposit on each bottle or can is 10 cents. People pay an extra 10 cents each. They get it back when they return the bottles and cans to the store. It was felt the deposit would help people take the bottles and cans back.

Over four billion bottles and cans go back to Michigan stores each year. Wow! The bottle bill is one reason for this. The deposit helps people do what they should do anyway. Our state was one of the first to have deposits. Eleven states now have this kind of deposit law.

There is still trash on our roads, but not as many bottles or cans. Should we have laws to get rid of other kinds of trash? Why don't more states have deposit laws? What do you think?

States that have bottle and can deposits.

Think About It. Write About It!

1. Name three of our state symbols.

2. The Petoskey stone is interesting. What does it tell us about Michigan a very long time ago?

3. Think about a road and a river. Which one is a natural characteristic? Which one is a human characteristic?

4. How can you help defend or protect Michigan?

Brain Stretcher
Draw a picture of a new state flag for Michigan. Include at least one human characteristic and at least one natural characteristic.

Think Like a historian
Use the Internet to learn more about how the state seal was made. Who made it? When was it made? Was it made with ideas borrowed from other places?

Take a Stand!
How can we have less litter at our parks and playgrounds? Explain your **opinion**.

Make a Plan
Make a "do not litter plan." What will you say? What is the best way to share your ideas with others?

Chapter 1 Lesson 3

Ideas To Explore
climate (kli mit)
lake effect (ee fect)
glacier (glay sher)
persuasive essay (per sway siv • es say)
public policy issue
    (pub lick • pol eh see • ish shoe)
rivers: Where does the water from Michigan's
    rivers go?

Places To Discover
Canada (KAN uh duh) -
    the large country next to us
Houghton Lake (ho ton)
Lake Erie (EAR ee)
Lake Huron (hYOUR on)
Lake Michigan
Lake Ontario (ON tair ee oh)
Lake Superior (SUP EAR ee or)
Tahquamenon Falls (TAH KWA meh non)
Wisconsin (wes con sin)

Michigan
Social
Studies
GLCEs
3G1.0.2
3G5.0.1
3C5.0.1
3P3.1.1
3P3.1.3
3P3.3.1
3P4.2.1
3P4.2.2

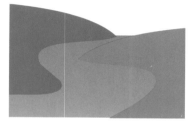

Rivers To Remember
Grand River - Michigan's longest river
Menominee (meh NOM eh nee) River

The Water Around Us

Think about these questions while you read.
How are lakes and rivers important to Michigan?
What made the Great Lakes?

Carly and Mike are on a family trip. They pull off the road and the car stops. Mom and Dad tell them, "Come out and look around!"

They walk over a big hill of sand and Mike says, "Wow! That is a lot of water! What is the name of this river?"

Carly quickly says, "That's not a river. It's a lake."

Mike wants to know how she can tell the difference.

Carly explains, "Rivers do not look the same as lakes. Rivers are long and narrow. Lakes tend to be like big, wide circles. The water in rivers flows. It moves from one end to the other."

"So, what is the name of this lake?" Mike asks.

Carly smiles and says, "It is Lake Michigan. It gives our state part of its shape."

photo courtesy of retired teacher Nancy Hanatyk

LAKE SUPERIOR

LAKE HURON

LAKE MICHIGAN

LAKE ONTARIO

LAKE ERIE

Enjoy the Great Lakes!

The Water Around Us

How does water help give our state its shape? We have the Great Lakes around us. The Great Lakes also split our state into two peninsulas.

Lake **H** uron
Lake **O** ntario
Lake **M** ichigan
Lake **E** rie
Lake **S** uperior

There are five Great Lakes. To remember their names, think HOMES. Each letter in HOMES starts the name of a Great Lake. The lakes are: Huron, Ontario, Michigan, Erie and Superior. Michigan is our home, so do not forget HOMES! **Lake Ontario** is the only one that does not touch our state. Find it on a map.

Largest and Deepest

Lake Superior is huge. It is the deepest Great Lake. It has more area than any other fresh water lake in the world! Only the salty oceans and seas are bigger. Lake Superior is north of the Upper Peninsula. It's water is cold all year. Many ships have sunk in it. What would it be like to see one – down in the dark, cold water?

Superior

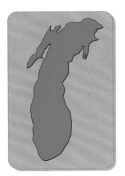

Michigan

All in the U.S.A.

The only Great Lake that is all inside the United States is **Lake Michigan**. We share the rest with **Canada** (KAN uh duh). Canada is the country next to us.

On the East Side

Lake Huron is the second largest Great Lake. This lake is east of Michigan. It was named after one of the tribes who lived on its shores.

Not Very Deep

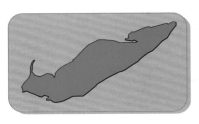

Erie

Lake Erie does not get the prize as the biggest lake. It does win for being the most shallow of the Great Lakes. It is also further south than the others.

Huron

The Great Lakes and Our Climate

The Great Lakes help our **climate**. We call this the "**lake effect**." Here is how it works. In the summer, the cool lakes keep the air from being so hot. It is cooled when it blows over the water. In the winter the lakes keep us a bit warmer. The water does not cool as fast as the land.

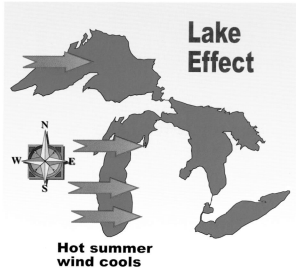

Hot summer wind cools over the water.

Our rivers flow into the Great Lakes.

Rivers Fill the Great Lakes

How do the Great Lakes get their water today? It comes from rain. Some rain falls right into the Lakes. Other rain falls on the land and runs into **rivers**. *Rivers drain the low places and take the water to the Lakes.* All Michigan rivers flow into one of the Great Lakes.

How Did We Get the Great Lakes?

They started with lots and lots of ice. If you had been there, you would have to look up and up to see the top. You would shiver. Sure the ice made it cold, but it was also a cold time on earth. It was too cold for the ice to melt in the summer. This ice was called a **glacier.**

A glacier is a thick cover of ice that does not melt in the summer. It gets thicker and thicker for many years. It is squeezed down from the North Pole. It slowly moves over the earth.

As the great glacier moved over Michigan, it dug up the softer land. The glacier made low places. When it melted, its water filled in the low places. They became the Great Lakes. At the same time, the dirt it had carried with it was left behind. This dirt made hills in the southern part of our state.

Our Longest River

Michigan's longest river is the **Grand River**. It begins in the south of Michigan. It is very small where it starts. It runs west to reach Lake Michigan. All of the state's longest rivers go into Lake Michigan. As the Grand River crosses the state, it grows wider and deeper. It goes through some big cities, like Lansing and Grand Rapids.

The Grand River
near Grand Rapids

The Menominee
River

The **Menominee River** is in the Upper Peninsula. It makes part of our border with **Wisconsin**. Wisconsin is a state west of us.

The Detroit River is over 2,000 feet wide. That makes it our widest river. Can you guess where it is? It goes by Detroit, of course! Our largest city has the widest river.

The Detroit River

Many cities started on rivers. People often traveled on rivers. Before good roads, it was easier to go by canoe or boat.

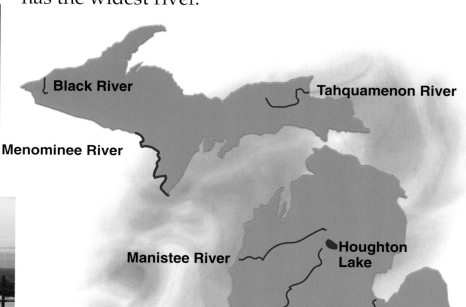

Black River

Tahquamenon River

Menominee River

Manistee River

Houghton Lake

Muskegon River

Saginaw River

Grand River

Kalamazoo River

Grand Rapids

Lansing

Detroit

Detroit River

St. Joseph River

Waterfalls

The Lower Peninsula has most of the long rivers. The Upper Peninsula has most of the waterfalls.

Michigan's biggest waterfall is in the eastern Upper Peninsula. Its name is **Tahquamenon Falls** (tah KWAH meh non). It has two parts. At the tallest part, the water falls 48 feet. That is like five classrooms stacked on top of each other!

Tahquamenon Falls-
Photo Courtesy
Janice McConnell

Many Small Lakes!

Michigan has thousands of small lakes. These lakes are great for fishing. People also like to sail their boats on them. Visitors come here from far away to enjoy these lakes.

The state's largest lake inside Michigan is **Houghton Lake** (HO ton). Can you find it on a map? It is in the Lower Peninsula. People enjoy boating there in the summer. They like to ice fish there in the winter. Some also ride snowmobiles on it when it is frozen.

Be Careful and Keep It Clean

Our lakes and rivers are wonderful things. They give us water to drink. They give us places to use our boats and to fish. They can be places to swim or have picnics. They can supply water used to make products we buy. All of this water is a wonderful resource for our state.

Be careful.

So, we need to be careful with our lakes and rivers. Do not waste the water. Keep the water clean. We should not throw junk and garbage into them. We want to have lots of good water for a long time.

How lakes and rivers are used can be a **public policy issue**. All the people, the public, are concerned. An issue is something important to people. An issue has at least two sides to it. Some people may want to build homes around a lake. Other people may want no homes around a lake. They think it is pretty and peaceful without homes. People must decide which is best. Then they can make a policy or law about it.

When we talk about issues, we need to explain our stand. Often we can talk to others to do this. Sometimes we need to write our ideas. We need to do this with care so people know what we mean. We need to *persuade* them. *This means we want them to see things our way.* We will write down our stand clearly. We will write an essay- a ***persuasive essay***.

Think About It. Write About It!

1. Name the five Great Lakes. Underline the ones touching Michigan.

2. Name the world's largest freshwater lake in area.

3. How is our climate affected by the Great Lakes?

4. Name Michigan's longest river.

5. Which peninsula has our biggest waterfalls?

6. How did a glacier give Michigan its shape?

GEOGRAPHY

Be a Geographer

Study a map of Michigan. Find the Grand River and follow its path. Find another long river. Write its name and the name of one large city along it.

Take a Stand!

Here is a public policy issue. Other states do not have as much water as Michigan. Should we give them water from the Great Lakes? Write a persuasive essay. Explain your stand.

Think about sharing your stand with others. What is the best way to do this? Where is the best place to do it? When is the best time to share it?

Should we let it go to other places?

MICHIGAN

MICHIGAN

Chapter 1 Lesson 4

Ideas To Explore
Compare our two peninsulas.

Neighbors To Know
Indiana (IN dee AN ah)
Ohio (OH hi oh)
Wisconsin (wes con sin)

Places To Discover

Ann Arbor
Dearborn
Detroit (dee TROYt)
Escanaba (ES can ah ba)
Flint
Grand Rapids
Livonia (liv own ee uh)
Marquette (mar KETT)
Monroe (mun row)
Mt. Arvon (mount, like mountain) (ar von)
Porcupine Mountains (por kyou pine)
Sault Ste. Marie (soo SAYnt ma ree) - Ste. stands for Saint
St. Ignace (SAYnt IG ness) - St. stands for Saint
Sterling Heights (stir ling • hites)
Warren (war in)

Michigan
Social
Studies
GLCEs
3G1.0.1
3G1.0.2
3G2.0.1
3G2.0.2
3G5.0.1

Words to Welcome

capital
copper
counties (KOUN tees)
feature
iron
region (REE jun)

Be Michigan Map Smart

Think about this question while you read.
**How has Michigan's geography affected
the way people live?**

Suzy says, "I want to be a geographer someday!"

Luke asks, "What on earth is a geographer?"

"Well, Luke, you have part of the answer already," Suzy says.

Luke asks, "What do you mean, Suzy?"

Suzy adds, "Geographers study the earth. They like to read maps and learn about the land. I really like maps. I can learn a lot from maps. I can see where to find cities. I can learn where to find the high places- the mountains. I can find the low places- the valleys. I can see lakes and discover islands."

"Okay, Suzy, I want to learn more about geography too. I want to look at a map and find where we are," says Luke.

Suzy points to a map, "See, Michigan is in the northern part of the United States. It is not in the far west. It is not on the east side. It is near the middle. What else do you see?"

Michigan has four neighbors. Three of them are other states. These states touch Michigan. **Ohio** (OH hi oh) and **Indiana** (IN dee AN ah) are to the south. The third is **Wisconsin**.

Michigan's Neighbors

The fourth neighbor is Canada. Canada is a country like the United States. It is north and east of us. Find it on a map. What do these two countries share? Canada and the United States share the Great Lakes!

Three rivers form the border between Canada and us. To reach Canada you must cross a river. Bridges make this easy to do. The land of our state and Canada do not touch.

The bridge to Canada at Port Huron.

The flag of Canada

Michigan and Canada are friends. You can cross the border any time. Some people go on trips to Canada. Many products are shipped between us.

Our Big Cities

Most people in our state live in cities. The largest city is **Detroit** (dee TROYt). Over 800,000 people live there. It is the 11th largest city in the

United States. Detroit began over 300 years ago, but it is not our oldest city. It is in the Lower Peninsula. Detroit is near Canada. Find it on a map.

Downtown Detroit.

Our second largest city is not as big as Detroit. It is much smaller. This is **Grand Rapids**. It is west of Detroit. Almost 200,000 people live in Grand Rapids. It is in the western part of the Lower Peninsula. Grand Rapids was started about 170 years ago.

Check out the map that shows our state at night. The light seen from space lets you see where people live. You can see much light around Detroit. Many of Michigan's people live nearby. There are other large cities within a few miles. One of these is **Warren.** It is our third largest city. Some other big cities are **Ann Arbor, Dearborn, Livonia and Sterling Heights.** They are all near Detroit. Can you find them on the map? Why do you think so many people live near Detroit?

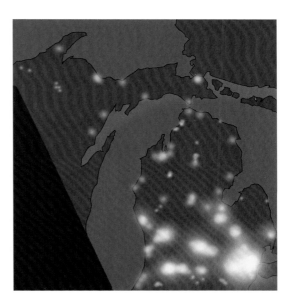

A picture of Michigan at night from outer space. Lights show where people live and where our cities are.

Do not forget Lansing. It has about 120,000 people. Lansing is our state **capital**. *This is the city where our state laws are made.* The governor's office is in Lansing.

We love our city!!

Michigan has the oldest city in the Midwest. It is Sault Ste. Marie!

Flint is also a large city. Flint is almost the same size as Lansing. For a long time Flint has been known for making cars and trucks.

Look at the Upper Peninsula. The cities are much smaller there. The largest is **Marquette** (mar KETT). It started in 1850. About 20,000 people live there. It is near the center of the peninsula. South of Marquette is **Escanaba** (ES can ah ba). Head to the east. You will find another large city. It is **Sault Ste. Marie** (soo SAYnt ma ree).

Which is the oldest city in Michigan? This is Sault Ste. Marie. It began in 1668. That was a long time ago! Nearby is **St. Ignace** (SAYnt IG ness), the second oldest Michigan city. It began in 1671.

Compare Our Peninsulas

CLIMATE:

The Upper Peninsula is colder. This is because it is farther north. It has much snow. There might be 20 feet of snow in one winter! That is almost enough to cover a house! Most of the Lower Peninsula has less than five feet each winter. The Upper Peninsula also has a short season to grow crops. Some crops will not grow well there because it can get so cold. Corn does not grow very well there.

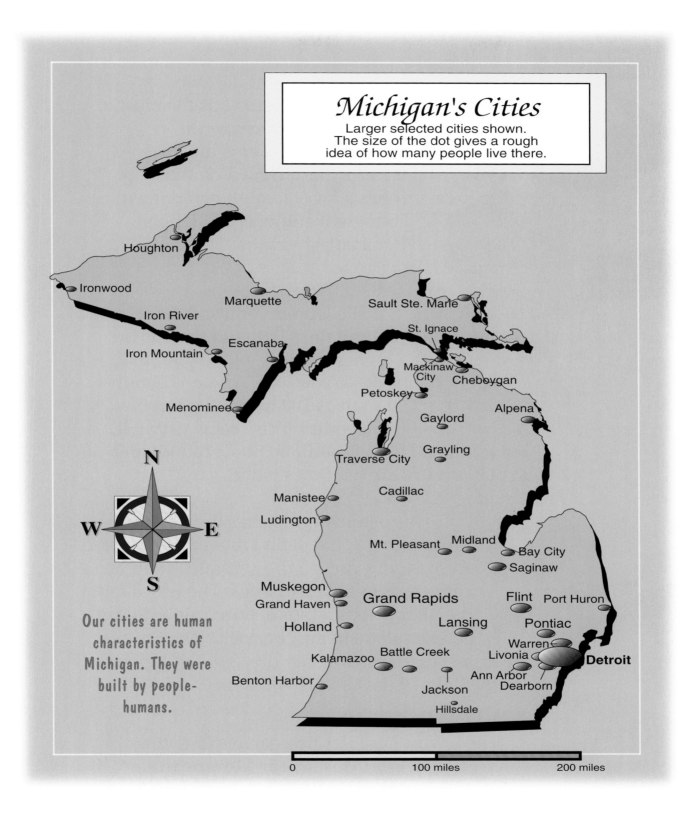

Michigan's Cities
Larger selected cities shown.
The size of the dot gives a rough
idea of how many people live there.

Houghton

Ironwood

Marquette

Iron River

Sault Ste. Marie

St. Ignace

Escanaba

Iron Mountain

Mackinaw City

Cheboygan

Petoskey

Menominee

Alpena

Gaylord

Grayling

Traverse City

Cadillac

N

W **E**

S

Manistee

Ludington

Mt. Pleasant   Midland

Bay City

Saginaw

Muskegon

Grand Haven

Grand Rapids

Flint   Port Huron

Our cities are human
characteristics of
Michigan. They were
built by people—
humans.

Holland

Lansing

Pontiac

Warren

Battle Creek

Livonia

Detroit

Kalamazoo

Ann Arbor

Dearborn

Benton Harbor

Jackson

Hillsdale

0   100 miles   200 miles

31

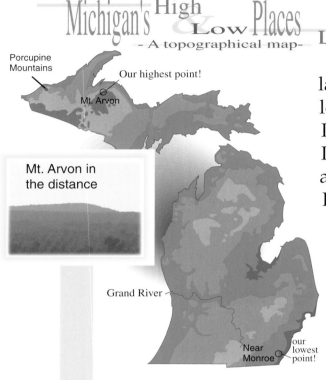

Michigan's High & Low Places
- A topographical map-

Porcupine Mountains

Our highest point!

Mt. Arvon

Mt. Arvon in the distance

Grand River

Near Monroe

our lowest point!

LAND:

Which peninsula has the most land? Is it the upper or the lower? The answer is the lower. It looks like a mitten on the map. It has a lot of land. It could make about two and one-half Upper Peninsulas!

MOUNTAINS:

The Upper Peninsula has the mountains! The land there is the highest. This is where you find **Mt. Arvon**. Mt. Arvon is about as tall as 100 houses on top of each other. This seems very tall, but it is small for a mountain. Some mountains in our country are ten times taller!

This peninsula also has the **Porcupine Mountains**. You will find them about as far west as you can go in our state. They are very close to Lake Superior. The tribes felt the shape looks like a porcupine. Some people call them the "Porkies." The Porkies are in a state park. You can drive to the top and see the Lake of the Clouds.

The Lake of the Clouds

THE LOWEST PLACE:

The lowest land in Michigan is along the shore of Lake Erie. This is near **Monroe** (mun row). Which part of the state has that area?

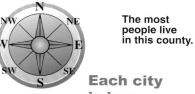

Wayne

The most people live in this county.

Each city is in a county. The map shows Michigan's 83 counties.

Check a map. You will find it far to the southeast (SE).

CITIES:

The Lower Peninsula has more cities and some of them are quite large. More people live in the Lower Peninsula. Look at the green map chart. Can you think of reasons so many people live in that part of the state?

USEFUL METALS:

The Upper Peninsula is known for two metals. It has **copper** and **iron**. Copper is used to make wire to carry electric power. Your house has copper wire. It goes to the plugs where you get power. For a long time much copper was mined there. The copper brought a lot of people to the area. They started towns around the copper mines. The mines are closed now. The copper is buried deep in the earth. It costs less to mine it in other places.

Oakland

Macomb
Genesee

Kent

WHERE people live *in Michigan*

copper wire

Iron is still mined there. Iron is used to make frying pans, cars and other products. Your bike is probably made of iron. Nails are made from iron. Many people came to get jobs because there was iron. They worked in the iron mines. Towns grew up around the iron mines.

iron pans

33

Men and boys on a pile of rocks outside a Michigan mine. Photo from Library of Congress.

Jobs in the mines brought people north. They went to the Upper Peninsula. They moved there to find work. Without the copper and iron, they would not have gone. No metals are mined in the Lower Peninsula.

What Is A Region?

Some people like geography. They study it. They think about the earth. They think about its land and water. They may study a **region** (REE jun). *A region is an area of land or sometimes water. All parts of a region share a **feature**. The feature can be a natural one or a human one.* A road is a human feature. A river is a natural one.

A river is a natural feature.

A road is a human feature.

Toaster from the kitchen "region."

Tire from the garage "region."

Think of regions this way. At home, your kitchen is one region. Your garage is another. All the things in the kitchen are about food or eating. The garage is for your car. The main feature of the kitchen is food. The main feature of the garage is cars.

All of the states that touch the Great Lakes can be part of the same region- **the Great Lakes region**. These states share the Great Lakes. Which states do you think are in the Great Lakes Region? They are Michigan, Ohio, Indiana, Illinois and Wisconsin. The Great Lakes are a natural feature. Each state has some of the same features due to the Great Lakes. As an example, they all have beaches.

Meet Reggie Region. He has 4 parts to his body. Each one shares his heart. This is like the states that touch Michigan sharing the Great Lakes. All parts of a region share something.

Let's Split Michigan Into Regions

Can we split our state into two regions? Yes, we can. Each peninsula can be its own region. Each one is quite different. The Upper Peninsula has many natural features. It has miles and miles of forests. There are also dozens of lakes. The whole peninsula shares these features. All of the Lower Peninsula shares big cities and busy highways. It has many human features. This is how our state can be split into two regions.

Michigan As 2 Regions

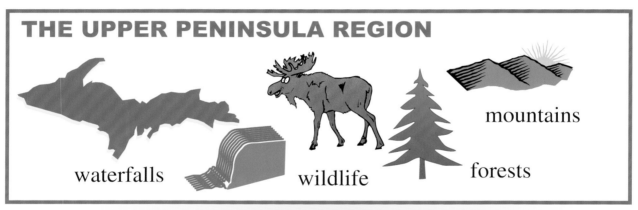

THE UPPER PENINSULA REGION

waterfalls   wildlife   forests   mountains

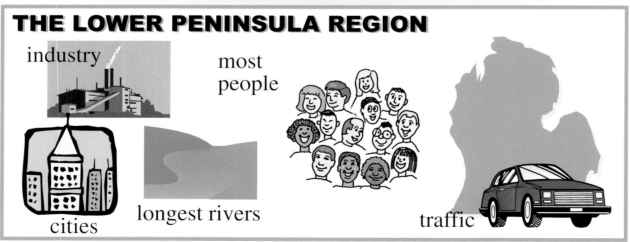

THE LOWER PENINSULA REGION

industry   most people

cities   longest rivers   traffic

Think About It. Write About It!

1. Name the three states that touch Michigan.

2. Name the country that is next to Michigan.

3. Name the two largest cities in our state. Which is nearest to you?

4. Why did people move to the Upper Peninsula?

5. What is a region?

6. How can our state be split into two regions?

7. What do the states in the Great Lakes Region share?

Brain Stretchers

Compare Michigan's two largest cities. Make a graph. Show about how many people live in each place. Be sure to label your graph.

Think like a Geographer

Make a map of Michigan. Show two human characteristics (things made by people). Also show two natural characteristics (things made by nature).

Explain this. How has Michigan's geography affected the way people live?

GEOGRAPHY

Think Like a historian

Make a timeline. Show when three Michigan cities started. Label each city. Write the date by each city on your timeline.

See Our State !

3. Pictured Rocks

2. Tahquamenon Falls

1. Mackinac Bridge

4. An old copper
mine near Ontonagon

The red lines in the Great
Lakes show Michigan's
borders. Large parts of the
Great Lakes are in Michigan.

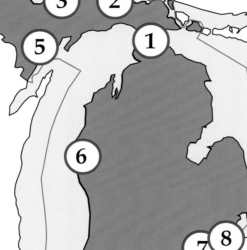

5. A lighthouse at Escanaba

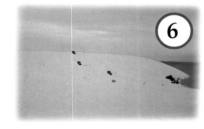

7. A train at The Henry
Ford in Dearborn

8. Comerica Park- a
baseball park in Detroit

6. A sand dune at Pentwater-
the little dots are cars!

5 Themes of Geography

GEOGRAPHY

Location: Where is it?

Place: What is it like there?

Each place has natural characteristics. These are part of nature. They can be rocks, rivers, sand dunes or beaches. Each place has human characteristics. These are things made by people. They can be roads or bridges. They can be lighthouses or stadiums.

People- Nature Interaction: How have people interacted with nature there? Did people make changes? Did they build a road? Did people use what nature provided there? Did they cut down trees to make a house? Did they catch fish? Did people change or adapt because of what nature had there?

Movement: How did people, goods or ideas move to or from this place?

Region: Do other places have things in common with this place? These could be made by nature. These could be made by people.

Have you visited any place on page 38? Where is that place? What did you see that nature put there? What did you see that people put there? How did you get there? How is that place like your town or city?

Michigan's First People

Chapter 2 Lesson 1

People to Meet
Native Americans (nay tiv • am air uh kins)
Hopewell people (hope well)

Words to Welcome
artifact (art eh fact)
diversity (dih VER seh tee)
dugouts (dug outs)
historians (hiss tor ee ans)
mound
ornaments (orn ah ments)

Michigan
Social
Studies
GLCEs
3H3.0.1
3H3.0.5
3H3.0.10
3G4.0.2
3G5.0.2
3E1.0.3
3P3.3.1

Thinking Like a Historian
Look back into the past. Ask what happened?
When did it happen? Who was there? Why did
it happen?

When was it?
In this lesson we will go back about 2,000 years!

Hopewell People live here.

1492 Columbus reaches America.

Today

0   1000   1500   2000

A time line shows *key events* in the order they took place. They are shown from earliest to latest.

Interesting People from Long Ago

Think about this while you read:
**Did early Native Americans trade
for things from far away?**

Indian Mounds

At school Linda and Josh were looking at maps. They looked at a map of their city. Linda asked Josh, "I see a road called Indian Mounds Drive. What is that?"

"I never heard of it. Let's ask our teacher, Ms. Ortiz," says Josh.

Their teacher said, "That is the road which goes by the old Indian mounds."

"What is an **Indian mound**, Ms. Ortiz?"

She said, "It is a place where some Native Americans buried their dead. They are along the shore of the Grand River."

Here is a Hopewell mound. This one is not in Michigan.

Josh and Linda's eyes went very wide. They both said, "There are dead people there?"

Ms. Ortiz went on, "Yes, there are old, old bones. There are also clay pots, arrowheads and spear-points. Fancy **ornaments** were buried too. Suppose you wanted to study these people. What could you learn from these things?

Here is what one artist thinks a Hopewell man may have looked like.

Ornaments are things like earrings and necklaces.

Art by George Rasmussen.

"The spearpoints may tell how they hunted. We may learn which animals they hunted. Maybe we can see how they made the points. What kind of stone was it? These are some of the things we can learn. All the things from the mounds are **artifacts**. *Artifacts are things left behind by people who lived long ago*.

"The people who made the mounds were called the **Hopewell** (HOPE well). This group lived here before the **Native Americans** we hear of today. We do not know what these people called themselves. Hopewell is the name of a farmer. Some mounds were found on his land.

"The Hopewell had villages in many states. Grand Rapids and Muskegon are about as far north as they went. There were mounds near Detroit too.

"The Hopewell probably farmed. They never moved too far north. We think they lived where their crops grew best.

"Most often the Hopewell lived along rivers. Perhaps they used the rivers to go to other places and trade. They may have made **dugouts**. *Dugouts are logs hollowed out into boats.* There are things in their mounds from far away. Some mounds have sea shells. Where is the nearest sea? Some have things made from copper. Where is the nearest copper? Some of these came from places over 1,000 miles away. Trade was important to the Hopewell.

This is a sea shell from Florida.

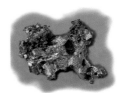

This is copper from the Upper Peninsula.

Here is some flint stone from Indiana.

A Hopewell made this hand from mica. The mica may have come from Tennessee.

The Hopewell Traded with Faraway Places

This glass from a volcano in Idaho is called obsidian. It can be made into arrowheads and other things.

This is a Hopewell clay bowl. It is supposed to be a beaver with a stick in its mouth.

"They were good artists and metal workers. They made things from copper and sometimes silver. They carved pipes from stone and used them for smoking. They made clay pots and baked them until they were hard. All we know about them we learned from their mounds. The Hopewell people disappeared hundreds of years ago.

"The Hopewell did not live here by themselves. Other groups were here too. Michigan had **diversity** a long time ago. *Diversity is a core democratic value. It means different kinds of people living and working together.* The Hopewell worked with their trading partners.

"Now most Hopewell mounds are gone. People made room for farms and homes. The mounds were removed. That is sad. Once special features like these are gone, we cannot get them back. They are lost forever."

Linda said, "Wow, the Hopewell sound interesting!"

Ms. Ortiz went on, "You can see things found in the mounds. They are in the museum downtown. You can also go to web sites on the internet. Keep in mind the Hopewell lived in other places. Michigan was just a small part of the area where they lived. They lived so long ago **historians** can only know a little about them."

Historians are detectives. They try to solve mysteries from the past. They study clues people like the Hopewell left behind. They do this to learn what really happened. They try to put the puzzle of the past together. Historians may need to make guesses. The longer back in time, the more they have to guess. Some facts may always be unknown.

The Hopewell were not the first people here. They came and went. Other groups came after them. All of these early people may be called Native Americans.

Think About It. Write About It!

1. What clues did the Hopewell leave behind? How do these clues help us know about them?

2. Did the Hopewell trade for things far away? Explain your answer.

3. What did the Hopewell do with their dead?

Brain Stretchers

Compare and contrast the Hopewell with people now. Make a chart showing trade, travel and taking care of the dead. Label each part of your chart.

Take a Stand!

Historians want to learn more about the Hopewell. Should they dig up their mounds to do this? Is this respectful of the dead in the mounds? Give reasons to support your stand.

Chapter 2 Lesson 2

Ideas To Explore
adapting to the environment - changing the way you
live to use what nature provides.

People To Meet
Anishnabeg (ah NISH nAH beg) - the people
Gijikens or Giji (gij eh kins)
Nabek (na bek)
Odawa or Ottawa (oh DA wa), (ott uh wa)
Ojibway, Ojibwa or Chippewa (oh jib way)
Potawatomi (POT a WAT oh me)
tribe

Places to Discover
Alaska (ah las ka) -a state in the United States
Asia -a large region across the Pacific Ocean
China (chy nuh) -a large country in Asia
Europe (YOUR up) -an area of land across the
    Atlantic Ocean (France is a country in Europe.)
India (in dee uh)- another large country in Asia
North America -the land where Canada, the
    United States and Mexico are found

Michigan
Social
Studies
GLCEs
3H3.0.1
3H3.0.5
3H3.0.7
3G4.0.2
3G5.0.2

Words to Welcome
birchbark
canoe (cuh new)
moccasin (mock uh sin)
sap
wigwam (wig wam)
wild rice

Michigan's Tribes

Think about these questions while you read:

**Where did the first people in Michigan
live before they came here?
About when did they arrive?**

What I Found At the Farm

It was April and I was ready for spring. I
was restless. School was getting on my nerves.
I liked my teacher, but you can only take so
much sitting in a classroom. I had forgotten all
about the field trip Mrs. Sanford had planned.
We were going to a farm, but this was not a
modern farm. On this farm they used horses as
they did over 100 years ago. Mrs. Sanford
thought it would be good for us to learn about
the old ways farmers once used.

Finally the bus stopped and they let us out.
Now we could stretch our legs. There were two
horses on the other side of the fence. They were
the biggest horses I had ever seen. I
mean HUGE! Mrs. Jackson came to help
keep an eye on us. She parked her car
next to the fence. You will not believe
what happened. One of those horses
walked over by it and licked her
window. Gross! Mrs. Jackson let out a
little squeal. She ran over and shooed the
horse away. That was funny.

The farmer hitched the horses to a plow. He explained why it was important to plow a field before planting the seeds. He told us it was hard work for the horses to pull the plow. Then they went to work. They slowly moved across the ground. The metal plow turned the dirt over as it went. He said using horses is much, much slower than using a tractor. He had to stop and let the horses rest. You could see they were all sweaty. While they were resting, he asked the class to come over and see how the plow worked.

You had to be careful as you walked. The dirt was soft after it was plowed. There were also some big stones in the dirt. So I was watching when I saw something in the ground. It just caught my eye. It did not look like a normal stone, but it was made of stone. I picked it up. It was thin and pointed. I held it up and asked, "What is this?"

The farmer spoke. He said, "Young lady, what you have there is a spearpoint. It is something made by the Native Americans probably hundreds or thousands of years ago. It is made of a kind of stone called flint."

I stood and gave it to him. He told me, "You keep this artifact and take it to school. Your class can study it. Maybe it will get all of you excited to learn about the people who lived here a very long time ago."

Picture drawn by George Rasmussen.

Back on the bus I passed the spear point around. Everyone got to hold it and look at it. We were all excited and we did want to learn more. We had many questions for Mrs. Sanford by the time we returned to school. Who exactly made the spearpoint? How long ago did they live here? What was life like for those people? What sort of homes did they have?

A wigwam.

The wooden frame
for a wigwam.

Go Back in Time

Let's answer some of those questions. What was happening hundreds of years ago right where you are sitting? What would you see? You might see **wigwams**. Wigwams are made of birchbark. The bark goes over a frame of wood. The birch bark was peeled off birch trees.

The people you see speak differently. They dress differently too. Who are they? They are Native Americans. They were the first people here. Native means first. These people may also be called Indians. The name Indians was used by people who were lost. Those people came here from far away and thought they had found **India**!

Let's meet the people who first lived where you live now. They lived in **tribes**. *A tribe is like a big, big group of relatives all living in the same neighborhood.*

They may be called **Odawa**. This sounds like oh DA wa. They might be **Ojibway**. This sounds like oh JIB way. Others were the **Potawatomi**. This sounds like POT a WAT o me. These are the names of three tribes. Each tribe had its own ways of doing things. Each had its own beliefs and language.

They Lived Close to Nature

Most of us live very differently than these first people. They lived very close to **nature**. If they needed something, they found it or made it. They **adapted to the environment**. *They changed the way they lived to use what nature provided.* Today, we depend on a store having it. We use money to pay for it.

When they were hungry, the tribes hunted or fished for food. They could not open the freezer to get something for supper. If they needed a plant, they grew it or knew where to find it. Almost every day they saw the sun rise. They saw the sun go down. They saw the stars at night. You are probably watching TV when the sun goes down. Most nights you do not see the stars because you are indoors.

They understood that all things are connected. Each plant and animal is a part of a bigger picture. The tribes did not kill more animals than they needed for food. They knew each animal gave up its life so they could use it for fur or food.

How Did They Get Here?

Have people always lived here? Most who study history do not think so. These historians think there were no people in **North America** at first. *North America includes three nations. They are*

All living things are connected.

Canada, the United States and Mexico. They think the first groups moved from **Asia**. To help you find Asia, look for **China** on a map. China is a nation in Asia. These groups crossed a strip of land to reach **Alaska**. That land is now covered by part of an ocean. We call this area of water the Bering (BEAR ing) Strait. Some historians think they may have moved from other places instead. The first people here may have come from South America. Historians are still searching for the final answer.

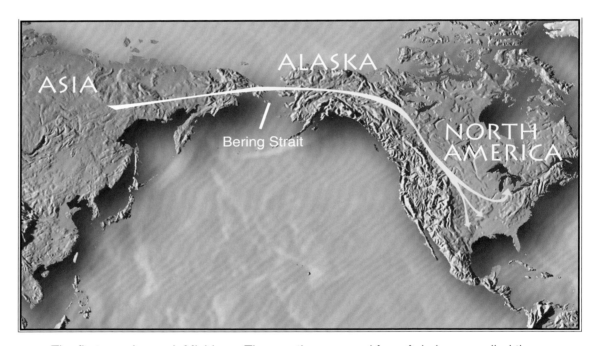

The first people reach Michigan. The gap they crossed from Asia is now called the Bering Strait. DNA from some Hopewell teeth tells us they had ancestors in Asia and South America.

If no one lived here, why did they come? People move for different reasons. Perhaps there was not enough food in Asia. This would push people away. Maybe the hunting was better in

North America. This would pull them here. Maybe they wanted to explore. Maybe they wanted to escape a war. That would push them away. Once in North America, they spread out. Finally, some of them reached Michigan.

When Did They Arrive?

How long ago did the first people come here? We think it was about 12,000 years ago! They reached southern Michigan first. Why?

Before that time, this land was covered with ice! Yes, it was covered with a glacier of ice. Thousands of years ago this ice began to melt. It melted first in the south where it was warmer. People could live in the south while it was still icy in the north.

How do we know these things? People who study the past tell us. These historians look for clues buried in the ground. Sometimes they dig up things left behind by the first people. They may find arrowheads, stone tools and other clues. Do you know anyone who has found an arrowhead or spear point?

How Many Were There?

Going back 400 years, when the tribes lived here alone, there were fewer people. Maybe 35,000 to

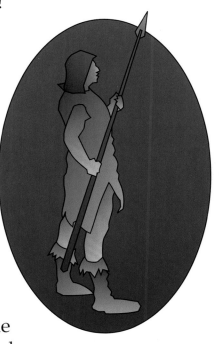

The first people who lived in Michigan probably came here about 12,000 years ago.

A stone arrowhead is an artifact from the past.

45,000 people lived in Michigan then. It is hard to know for sure. Historians make the best guess they can.

More About the Ojibway

Let's walk into the woods and meet a brother and sister. They are your age. They are Native Americans. The girl's name is **Gijikens** (sounds like- GIJ eh kens), which means small cedar tree. Those in her family call her Giji. Her brother's name is **Nabek** (sounds like- nah beck) and it means a boy bear. They are members of the Ojibway tribe. Their home is in the Upper Peninsula.

Learn more about the Native Americans. Read **Life in an Anishinabe Camp** by Niki Walker from Crabtree Publishing Company.

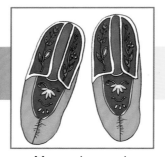

Moccasins made from deer hide.

They want to tell you about their tribe. The word Ojibway is a kind of **moccasin** (mock uh sin). Ojibway is a name used by nearby tribes. The Ojibway called themselves **Anishnabeg** (ah NISH nAH beg). *It means the people*. Each tribe had a word in its language meaning 'the people.' That is the name they usually called themselves.

Nabek says, "Our tribe is a large one. It does not just live in Michigan. We live all across the area of the northern Great Lakes."

Giji says, "Our people have lived in other places at different times. Our legends say we moved from the East long ago."

Do Not Be Confused

The names of tribes often have different spellings. This is because the tribes did not use written words. People from **Europe** wrote the same word, but often spelled it differently. Ojibway is the same as Ojibwa, or even Chippewa. *They all mean the same tribe.*

Clothes and Food

Furs and animal skins were used to make most clothes. Everything used was found in nature.

Finding food was very important. There were no stores. There were few ways to keep food from spoiling. The tribes had to hunt or fish almost every day.

The tribes often lived along the lakes and rivers. Nabek enjoyed fishing with his father. They went out in a **birchbark canoe**.

Native Americans had clothes made from animals. Their shirts, pants and moccasins may be made from deer hides. This man is standing by a birch tree.
Art by Dirk Gringhuis.

A canoe covered with birch bark.

55

Wild rice was important food for some tribes. It grew in swampy places. Giji and Nabek used a canoe to harvest the rice. Nabek paddled through the tall rice. Giji pulled the plants over the canoe and shook them. The dark ripe grains of rice fell into the canoe.

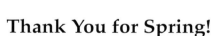

School?

Ojibway boys and girls learned by being with dad and mom. They watched what their parents did. Soon they could hunt or make clothes too. They did not spend time in classrooms. They learned by watching and doing.

Winter Could Be Hard

When Giji and Nabek were very young, winter was an adventure. They thought the snow was fun. As they grew older, they realized winter was not an easy time. It was hard to hunt in the deep snow. Food became hard to find and there was less to eat.

In the springtime, Indians collected the sap from the sugar maple trees. They often used birchbark containers. Art by Aaron Zenz.

Thank You for Spring!

Wow! Spring! Warmer weather meant more to eat. It was also the time to make maple sugar! The Ojibway went into the forests to collect **sap** from the maple trees. They boiled away the water in the sap. Finally it became maple syrup or maple sugar. The warm sticky sweet was a treat! The tribes used maple sugar and honey to sweeten their food.

Maple trees can live to be two hundred years old. Maybe your maple syrup came from the same tree used by the tribes long ago! You can learn more about maple sugar in the next lesson.

A bottle of maple syrup and a maple leaf.

Think About It. Write About It!

1. What did Native American homes in Michigan look like?

2. How were Native American children educated?

3. What does the word Anishnabeg mean?

4. Name three things from nature used by the tribes. Tell how each was used.

5. Give one reason Native Americans moved from place to place.

6. What did the Michigan tribes eat and what kind of clothes did they wear?

Brain Stretchers

Explain how important nature was to the tribes. How did this affect their beliefs?

Words In Action!

Imagine you are an Ojibway boy or girl from long ago. Tell about a day in your life.

Chapter 2 Lesson 3

Ideas To Explore
migrate (mi grate)
scarce

People To Meet
Huron (hYOUR on) tribe or Wyandotte (wine dot)
Menominee (meh NOM eh nee) tribe
Miami (my AM ee) tribe
Three Fires tribes

Places to Discover
Mishi Gami (means a big lake)
Wyandotte (wine dot)

Michigan
Social
Studies
GLCEs
3H3.0.4
3H3.0.10
3G1.0.1
3G5.0.2

Words to Welcome
customs (kus tums)
legend (lej und)
longhouse
trade

YEAR 1492

Columbus reaches America in 1492.

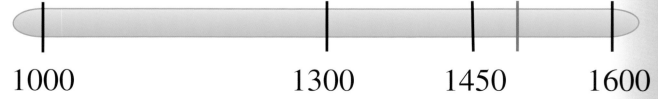

1000   1300   1450   1600

As far as historians know, the Native Americans lived alone in Michigan for all this time.

Who Were the Three Fires Tribes?

Think about this while you read.
Which tribe lived where you live now?
What did they call themselves?

Who were Giji and Nabek's neighbors? The Ojibway shared the land with the Odawa and the Potawatomi.

The Odawa may also be called Ottawa or Odawe. All these names mean the same people. This tribe lived in the northwest Lower Peninsula. Odawa comes from the word "adawa" or "adawe," *which means to **trade**.* The Odawa traded corn, sunflower seeds and tobacco with other tribes. Trading has always been important here. People still trade or exchange things with each other.

People trade something they have plenty of for something that is **scarce**. *If it is scarce, they do not have much of it.* A Michigan tribe might have copper nearby. They might trade it for a buffalo robe from a tribe in the west.

The Tribes Traded

Copper for weapons or ornaments

Tobacco to smoke

Sunflower seeds to eat.

Flint stone for arrowheads

Buffalo hides for blankets

Some tribes in Michigan may have copper, but not buffalo hides. They may have sunflower seeds, but not flint stone for arrowheads.

Once the Odawa and the Huron lived to the east in Canada. Then they moved when other tribes attacked them. Moving to escape war is one reason to **migrate** (MY great) or move. People may migrate to find food. People may migrate to avoid disease. Some things push people away from one place. These things make them want to leave. Other things may pull them to a new place. These things make them want to move there.

Moving from place to place is migration.

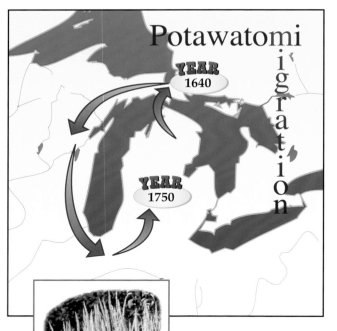

Potawatomi Migration

YEAR 1640

YEAR 1750

Burning fields before planting crops is changing or modifying the environment.

The Potawatomi (POT a WAT o me)

The Potawatomi also moved from place to place. By 1750 they settled in southern Michigan. The Potawatomi name comes from Ojibway words for fire. It may mean "people of the place of the fire." They often burned their fields before planting crops. This may be why they have that name.

This tribe lived farther south than the Ojibway and Odawa. Since they lived in a warmer area, the Potawatomi could farm more. The land where they lived also had better soil. This helped their crops grow. They planted corn,

A digging stick used by the tribes for planting crops. Art by Aaron Zenz.

squash, beans, tobacco, melons and sunflowers. Because of their crops, the Potawatomi did not move their villages often. They did not need to always look for food.

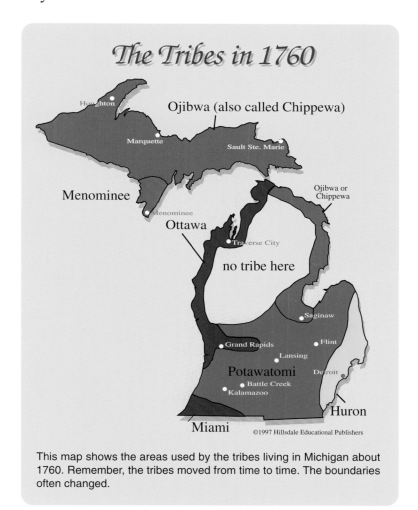

The Tribes in 1760

Ojibwa (also called Chippewa)

Houghton

Marquette

Sault Ste. Marie

Menominee

Menominee

Ottawa

Ojibwa or Chippewa

Traverse City

no tribe here

Saginaw

Grand Rapids

Flint

Lansing

Potawatomi

Detroit

Battle Creek

Kalamazoo

Huron

Miami

©1997 Hillsdale Educational Publishers

This map shows the areas used by the tribes living in Michigan about 1760. Remember, the tribes moved from time to time. The boundaries often changed.

Which tribe lived where you do?

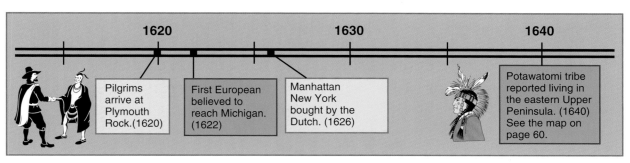

1620

1630

1640

Pilgrims arrive at Plymouth Rock.(1620)

First European believed to reach Michigan. (1622)

Manhattan New York bought by the Dutch. (1626)

Potawatomi tribe reported living in the eastern Upper Peninsula. (1640) See the map on page 60.

This is a time line. It shows what happened and when.

Who were
the 3 fires?

The Three Fires

The Potawatomi, Ojibway and Odawa are related. These tribes are sometimes known as the "**Three Fires**." The three tribes all spoke a similar language. They could talk to each other. They lived in the same kind of homes. They did things the same way. Sometimes the three tribes worked together. They might do this to protect themselves from an enemy. These are the reasons they are grouped together.

In the 1700s and 1800s, the Three Fires were the main tribes living in Michigan. They were not the only tribes though.

Other Tribes in Michigan

The **Menominee** (meh NOM eh nee) lived in the Upper Peninsula. The Menominee River is named after them. Menominee is an Ojibway word for "wild rice people." Wild rice was an important food for them. Their **customs** were much like those of the Ojibway who lived nearby. *Customs mean ways of doing things. It includes foods, habits and holidays.*

The **Miami** (my am ee) lived in the Lower Peninsula near Niles. This was in the southwest corner of Michigan. Their area was quite small. Their tribe did not have many people.

The **Huron** (hYOUR on) tribe once lived in Canada. Later, other tribes attacked them. This forced them to move. The Huron tried different places in Michigan for a new home. They moved near Mackinac Island. Next they tried Detroit. The tribe was also known as the Wendat or **Wyandotte** (wine dot). The city of Wyandotte is named after them.

The Huron spoke a language that was different from those of the Three Fires. They also had a different kind of home. The Three Fires tribes lived in wigwams. The Huron lived in **longhouses**. Longhouses were larger than wigwams. Several families lived in each one. The Huron sometimes built walls around their villages. They made their villages into small forts.

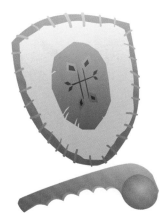

When fighting their enemies, some tribes used war clubs and shields covered with hide. Art by Aaron Zenz.

A Huron longhouse. Art by Tim Pickell

The Legend of the First Maple Sugar

What is a **legend**? A legend is an old story. Legends have been told over and over for a long time. A legend may have some make-believe parts.

Let me tell you of a time from long ago. Come to **Mishi Gami** the land between the great waters. Springtime was beginning. The last of the snow had melted. Meet an Ojibway boy called **Wasagesick** (was uh gee sik). He enjoyed helping his mother. He was too young to join the men when they went hunting. That would come later.

Today his mother asked him to bring water she needed for cooking. Their camp was far from the river. It was a long walk for a young boy. Still, Wasagesick liked walking through the woods. He did not mind it. He watched the birds and listened for deer along the way.

Pictures on these pages by Maggie O'Connor. Hillsdale College student.

Wasagesick filled his birchbark container with water. It was now quite heavy. He could see camp when a rabbit jumped across his path. He looked at the rabbit and tripped. He did not see a big tree root and it caught his foot. He cried out in surprise. All the water spilled. He fell and hurt his knee.

His mother heard him and ran to him. "Are you all right?" she asked. He ran to her forgetting his container by the tree.

Wasagesick said, "Yes, Mother, I am fine. I am so sorry I spilled all of the water you needed."

"That is all right, son. We will have stew another night," his mother said.

The next day, Laughing Water was walking in the woods. She saw her son's container where it rested against a big maple tree. It was almost half full of water. She said to herself, "Wasagesick did not spill as much as he thought." She took it home and used it to make deer stew.

As the stew cooked it had a pleasing smell. She had never known her stew to smell like this. At that moment, her husband came home. He

smelled the stew. He took a twig and got a sample and tasted it. A big smile came to his face. He smacked his lips and told Laughing Water how good it was. Now she tested the stew. It was really good! She shared how Wasagesick left his container next to the maple tree. Maybe it had sap from the tree, not water as she thought.

Her husband told everyone in the camp about the sweet water from the maple tree. Now when it is early spring, the Ojibway gather the maple sap. They boil it down. They make maple sugar that they store in birchbark containers. Now they can enjoy a sweet treat all year long.

Collecting maple sap and making maple syrup is still fun.

It is something we have been doing in Michigan for a long, long time.

If you have a chance to do it, think of the Ojibway, Odawa and Potawatomi boys and girls who did it first.

Photo by the author.

Think About It. Write About It!

1. Which tribe lived in your part of the state during the 1700s?

2. Which tribes were the Three Fires?

3. What does scarce mean? Name something that is scarce today.

4. What does the word migrate mean?

5. Tell something that could push a tribe to move to a new place. Tell something that may pull a tribe to a new place.

6. How did the tribes get maple sugar?

7. What is a legend? Why did the tribes tell legends?

Brain Stretchers

Draw a map showing where Michigan's main tribes lived. Use your left hand as a guide to make the two peninsulas. Show where each tribe lived. Be sure to label your map.

Are scarce things usually more valuable? Explain how being scarce relates to being valuable.

Words In Action!

Explain why the Three Fires tribes are grouped together. How are they alike? How are they different?

If it was scarce, they did not have much of it.

SCARCE

67

Chapter 2 Lesson 4

People To Meet

Hiawatha (HI eh WA tha)
Henry Schoolcraft
Jane Schoolcraft
Henry Wadsworth Longfellow

Places To Discover

Kalamazoo (kal ah mah zoo)
Mackinac Island (MACK in aw • EYE land)
Menominee (meh NOM eh nee)
Muskegon (mus KEE gon)
Pontiac (PON tee ak)
Saginaw (SAG en aw)

Words to Welcome

Words to Welcome

invention (in ven shun)
snowshoe
toboggan (tah BOG an)
wisdom (wiz dum)

Michigan
Social
Studies
GLCEs
3H3.0.2
3H3.0.4
3H3.0.8

Gifts From The Tribes

Think about this while you read:
**Do the tribes still
touch our lives today?**

Stories and Legends

Do you like a good story? The tribes do! They give us some fine stories and legends. They tell legends and history to their children. This way they keep facts and stories about their past alive. Long ago, the tribes did not use writing. They joined around campfires. There they told about the past. In their tradition, winter was the time to share in this way. Some of their legends are now written for all of us to read.

Drawn by Cassandra Bacon, Hillsdale College student.

Henry Schoolcraft

Picture from Archives of Michigan 02374

The Ojibway tell a legend about a man who did magic. He also played tricks on people. In the 1820s **Henry Schoolcraft** heard this story. Mr. and Mrs. Schoolcraft lived in the Upper Peninsula. Henry's wife, Jane, was an Ojibway. She helped him gather stories from her tribe. The Schoolcrafts felt a need to write these stories. They did not want the legends to be forgotten over time.

Henry Wadsworth Longfellow

Later, a famous writer read these stories. He was **Henry Wadsworth Longfellow**. He was not from Michigan. He was not a Native American either. Longfellow changed one legend to sound like a long poem. He also changed the name of the hero to **Hiawatha** (HI eh WA tha). We are not sure why he did that. He called what he wrote *The Song of Hiawatha*.

YEAR 1855

Many people like his poem. In it, Hiawatha's grandmother sends him to find an evil warrior. Hiawatha goes off in his canoe. When the two men meet, there is a big fight. This warrior is strong and protected by a coat made of seashells. At first, Hiawatha can not hurt him. Then a woodpecker speaks to him.

The bird tells him where to aim his arrows. In the end, Hiawatha wins. Indian legends often have an animal with magical powers. This talking bird is an example.

There was a real man named Hiawatha. He lived in the 1500s. He was not from Michigan. The real Hiawatha was a leader of the Mohawk tribe. He taught how to plant crops and heal the sick.

No one knows what the real Hiawatha looked like. This is what one artist thinks.

Guidelines to Live By

The tribes know people need rules to live by. Some legends include rules. One of these is *The Seven Grandfathers and the Little Boy*. The story starts long ago. At that time the Ojibway had many problems. Their people were often sick.

The legend tells of seven spirits. They are called the seven grandfathers. These spirits are to watch over the earth's people. A young boy is brought to the seven grandfathers. They want the boy to help the earth's people. Each spirit gives the boy a gift of **wisdom**. He is to go back to his tribe. Then he will share the things he learned.

Here are the gifts they gave to the boy:

1. To seek knowledge is to know *wisdom*.
2. To know *love* is to know peace.
3. To honor all creation is to have *respect*.
4. *Bravery* is to face the enemy with honor.
5. *Honesty* to face a tough problem is to be brave.
6. *Humility* is to know yourself as a sacred part of creation.
7. *Truth* is to know all of these things.

An otter by Charles Schafer.

An otter guides the boy back home. Because of this, the otter is still very special to the Ojibway. The trip is a long one. By the time the boy returned, he is an old man. Then he tells the wisdom given to him. After that, the tribes have less sickness and live better lives.

To learn more about legends, talk to a Native American. Find one who really knows about them. Perhaps your class may visit a Native American center. One of these is Nokomis Learning Center in Okemos. There is another one in Mount Pleasant. Its name is the Ziibiwing Center.

Food and Crops

The next time you bite into a warm buttery ear of corn, think about the tribes. They were the first to grow it. The corn the tribes grew had smaller ears than today's corn.

There would be no pumpkin pie without the tribes. They were the first to grow corn and pumpkins. They were also the first to grow squash and beans. Tobacco was also one of their crops. It was new to the people of Europe when they got here. *Europe is a group of countries. Look on a map. You will find them across the Atlantic Ocean.*

Inventions

Do you know what an **invention** is? *It is an idea for something no one else has thought of before.* Have you ever paddled a canoe? Did you go down a swift river? The tribes invented this type of boat. Michigan's first people spent years learning how to make them just right.

It is hard to walk in deep snow. Have you tried it? When there was deep snow, the Native Americans had a way to walk over it! Their invention is the **snowshoe**. It lets people walk on top of the snow.

Snowshoes, invented by the Indians, make walking on deep snow much easier. Picture by Frederic Remington.

a toboggan

Members of the tribes have shared their art with us. This is a small box made from porcupine quills.

Have you ever gone down a hill on a sled? Traveling on snow led to another invention. This was the **toboggan**. Today it is used to have fun. The Indians used it for work. The toboggan let them move their belongings over snow.

The tribes used the bow and arrow, but this had been invented and used in other parts of the world too.

Names

Do you remember that the tribes gave us the name for our state? Michigan comes from the words, 'mishi' and 'gama.' They mean great lake or big water.

Other Michigan names come from words used by the tribes. **Mackinac** (MACK in aw) is one. It comes from a word that means *great turtle*. The tribes felt the island looked like a big turtle in the water. Mackinac Island is between our two peninsulas. Look at the map on the next page.

Several Michigan cities have Native American names. Here are five:

Kalamazoo (kal ah mah zoo) - means boiling water

Menominee (meh NOM eh nee) - means rice gatherers

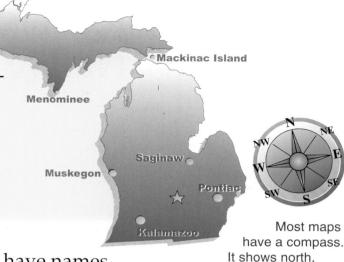

Muskegon (mus KEE gun) - means marsh
Pontiac (PON tee ak) - a chief's name
Saginaw (SAG en aw) - named after the Sauk tribe

Did you know 26 counties have names from the tribes? Muskegon and Washtenaw are just two of them. See the map on the next page.

The tribes helped to make our state what it is. They have passed on to us things that are a part of our lives now. They have shared their legends. They have shared their foods. They have shared their inventions and names. Native Americans are not people of the past. They live in all parts of Michigan today. Native Americans live in cities and on farms. They may be artists, business people, farmers or teachers.

Most maps have a compass. It shows north, south, east and west. The idea for a map compass comes from a real compass. A real compass has a dial that points north. The dial is attracted to a magnetic place on the earth.

Today, Native Americans look much like everyone else unless they are dressed for a special event. Courtesy Bill Mull.

75

Michigan Counties with Native American Names

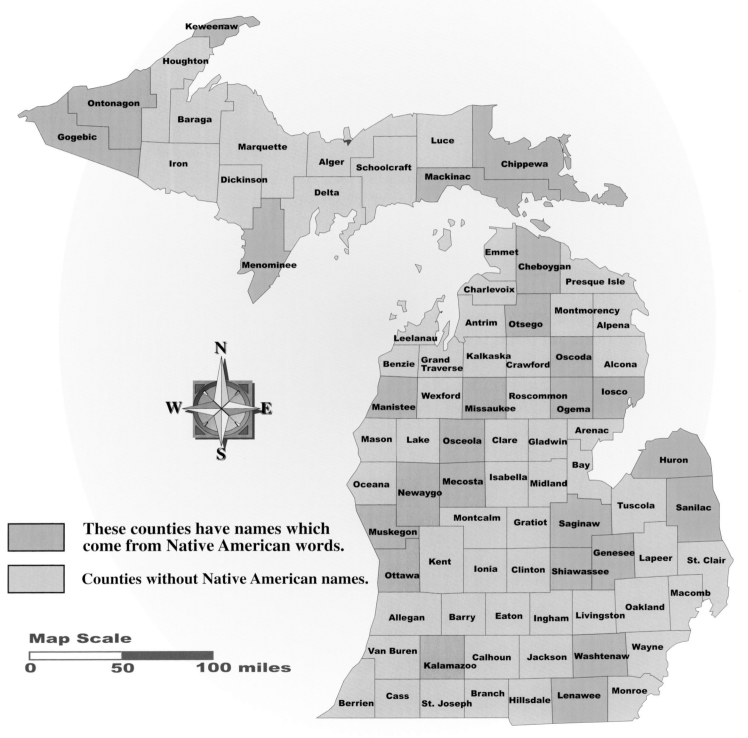

These counties have names which come from Native American words.

Counties without Native American names.

Map Scale

0   50   **100 miles**

Think About It. Write About It!

1. What did Henry and Jane Schoolcraft do to help save the legends told by the tribes?

2. What did you learn about the poem, *Song of Hiawatha*?

3. Name three Native American guidelines to live by.

4. Tell which Native American invention you believe is the best and why.

5. Do you think the name of your town is Native American? Explain your answer.

6. Find three nearby places that seem to have Native American names. (They can be cities, counties, rivers or lakes.) List them. Use the internet or your school library. Try to find what some of the names mean.

Brain Stretchers

     Explain what you have learned about the beliefs of the tribes by reading their legends. What ideas were important to the Native Americans? Why were they important to them?

Words In Action!

     How do the tribes from long ago still touch our lives today? Give four examples of things they have shared with us.

Visitors From Far Away

Chapter 3   Lesson 1

Ideas To Explore
opportunity cost

scarcity (skair seh tee)

People To Meet
French

traders

Places To Discover
France

Words to Welcome
bonjour (BOn jzure) French for
    good day or hello

opportunity (ah por tune uh tee)

Michigan
Social
Studies
GLCEs
3H3.0.1
3H3.0.3
3H3.0.5
3H3.0.6
3H3.0.10
3G1.0.1
3G4.0.2
3G5.0.1
3G5.0.2
3E1.0.1
3E1.0.3

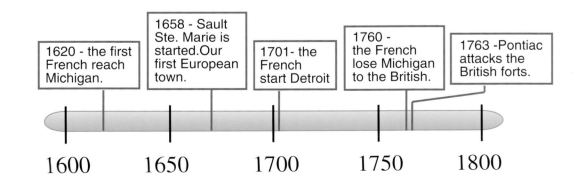

1620 - the first French reach Michigan.

1658 - Sault Ste. Marie is started. Our first European town.

1701- the French start Detroit

1760 - the French lose Michigan to the British.

1763 -Pontiac attacks the British forts.

1600   1650   1700   1750   1800

Visitors from Far Away

Think about this while you read.

How did life change for Michigan's tribes once they started trading furs with the French?

Story illustrated by Don Ellens.

Shhhh! Come to the shore of Lake Michigan. Two Ojibwa children wait near the beach. They are Giji and Nabek. They feel the breeze on their faces. Both listen. There is only the sound of the waves. They wait for the splash of canoe paddles. They hide behind the pine branches. They are excited and curious. Then they hear the paddles.

Giji says, "Look! The traders are coming. They are in two big canoes."

"I can see them, Giji. Look at them. Their skin is so light. They have hair on their faces. Ha! It looks like they have little bears on their cheeks!"

The canoes head to the beach. Ojibwa men and women are waiting there.

"**Bonjour** (BOn jzure)," shouts one of the traders.

Giji and Nabek did not understand. This is a **French** greeting. It means 'Good day!'

"Brother, listen. The **traders** talk so strangely. They speak some of our words, but they say them poorly!"

"Why not, Giji. I hear they come from far away. Their home is across a huge lake which is bigger than our own," Nabek said, as he pointed to Lake Michigan.

"Father said they come from a place called **France**."

A fur trader from France.

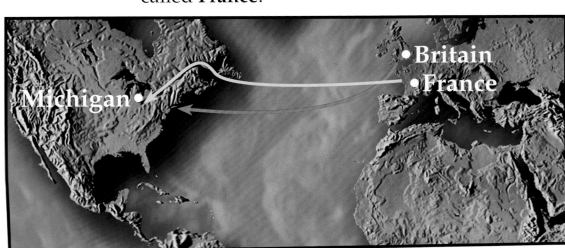

They Brought Exciting Things!
The traders are taking many things from their canoes.

"Look, Giji. Look what they have! They brought pretty beads. They have blankets with bright colors!"

"Oh, Nabek! Look at those shiny metal cooking pots. Mother would really like some of those. They are so much better for cooking than our clay ones."

"The metal pots are nice. Father also needs new animal traps and bullets," said Nabek.

"What do mother and father want from the traders, Nabek?"

"Father said he wants to trade for one of their long guns. He wants a nice rifle. He wants one like the traders use themselves. He will not settle for the cheap ones they bring to trade."

"Don't forget some of the black shooting powder," Giji reminded him.

How Did They Do?
"Father is handing them some of his furs. He caught many muskrat, beaver and fox last winter. The traders seem pleased."

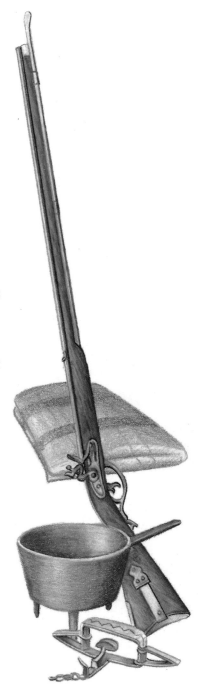

A hatchet. The tribes were not able to make iron tools like this. This is why they traded for them. Iron tools were scarce among the tribes.

Nabeck says, "Mother has her metal pots. She also has two blankets. I see she has sewing needles. Mother traded her maple sugar and wild rice. Father seems sad. I don't think father got the trader's nice gun."

Giji says, "But he has a new hatchet. Father also got bullets, shooting powder and a nice blanket. I see he has some new traps."

Now the traders are getting their canoes ready. It is time for them to leave. They are loading the furs. Giji and Nabek watch as they push away from the shore. The traders sing as they paddle away. Soon they are out of sight. Giji and Nabek hurry back to their village.

Why Did They Trade?

What did the French traders want from the Ojibwa? The French wanted furs. They wanted furs because they did not have many in France. France did not have many wild animals left. Furs were scarce in France. This brought the traders across the ocean.

What did the Ojibwa want from the traders? They wanted things which they could not make. The tribes could not make metal pots or metal traps. They could not make blankets with a lot of colors. They could not make pretty glass beads. The Ojibwa wanted things which were scarce here.

WHY DID THEY TRADE?

| Metal cooking pots scarce here | | Beaver fur scarce in France |

Each group wanted things which were scarce for them. They traded things which were not scarce. At that time, the tribes could get many furs. The French could make things from metal. They each had a lot of something that the other did not have. This means that **scarcity** brought them together. The lack of furs in France pushed them away from France. Since Michigan had beaver, it pulled the French here.

Scarcity still brings people together today. People far away buy iron or lumber from Michigan. They do this because it is scarce where they live.

The Choices We All Make

Their father said he tried to trade for the Frenchman's long gun or rifle. He offered the best furs for it. The trader said he would trade it if he got ALL the furs! Father could not do that. He had to think about the rest of the family. He had to do what would be good for everyone. They needed new traps and blankets. All the furs were too much to give for any gun.

The father made a tough choice. He gave up the nice rifle. Instead, he got the things his family must have. He had the **opportunity** to trade for the rifle. He made another choice. He traded for the blankets and new traps. He wanted the rifle, but it was his second choice. He gave up getting it.

People make choices when they buy or trade. When you buy one thing, you give up something else. There is not enough money to buy everything you want. You give up an

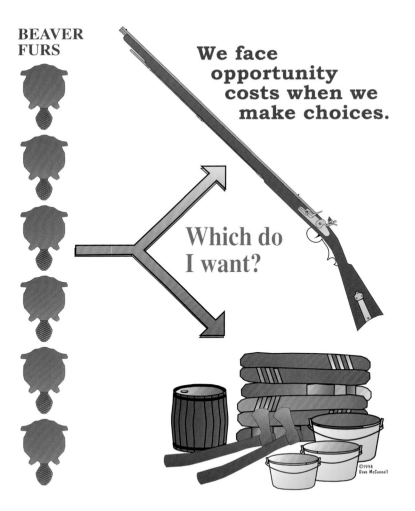

BEAVER FURS

We face opportunity costs when we make choices.

Which do I want?

©1998
Dave McConnell

opportunity to buy something else. The Ojibwa did not have enough furs to trade for every-thing. *There is a name for the second choice you gave up. It is called the* **opportunity cost.**

We Cannot Have Everything

If you have only enough money to buy a toy or a CD, you must choose one. *The one you do not choose is your opportunity cost.* If you buy the toy, there is a cost to your choice. You lose the opportunity to buy the CD.

People are always choosing one thing over another. Money is always limited. This is even true for rich people. They may choose the fancy car or the swimming pool. If they choose the car, what did they give up? They gave up the swim-ming pool. The pool was the opportunity cost.

Making wise choices is important. If you do not, your money will be gone and you will not have much to show for it.

HOW MANY FURS DOES IT COST?

Prices may change without notice!

BLANKET......................	3 BEAVER OR 4 DEER SKINS
GUNPOWDER	1 BEAVER FOR EACH POUND
BRASS KETTLE	1 POUND OF BEAVER FOR EACH POUND OF KETTLE
60 LEAD BULLETS.....	1 BEAVER OR 15 MUSKRATS
CLOTH	1 BEAVER FOR EACH YARD (3 FEET)
EARRINGS	1 SMALL BEAVER FOR EACH SET
HATCHET	5 BEAVER OR 10 FOX SKINS

Think About It. Write About It!

1. What country was home to the fur traders?

2. Name three things the Ojibwa got from the traders. How did these things make life easier for them?

3. What was scarce in France? Why did this bring fur traders here?

4. What was scarce for the Ojibwa? Why did they want to trade with the French?

Brain Stretchers

How do you think life will change for the tribes once they start trading furs with the French?

Tell how many beaver furs a French trader wanted for a blanket, two yards of cloth and two sets of earrings.

Think Like an Economist

Give an example when you bought something. Tell what you bought and what your second choice was. What was your opportunity cost?

Chapter 3 Lesson 2

Ideas To Explore
explore
specialization (spesh el iz a shun)

People To Meet
ancestors (an ces terz) relatives from long ago
Brule´ (broo-LAY)
Europeans (YOUR oh pea uns)
Iroquois (ear uh koy)
missionaries (mish un airies)
priests (preests)

Places To Discover
Britain (brit an)
Europe (your up)
New France
Ottawa River
St. Lawrence River (St. stands for Saint which
sounds like SAYnt. Lawrence sounds like LOR
ents)

Words to Welcome
silk
profits (prof its)
religious (ree lij us)
spices (spy sis)

Michigan
Social
Studies
GLCEs
3H3.0.1
3H3.0.3
3H3.0.6
3H3.0.10
3G1.0.1
3G4.0.2
3E1.0.1
3E1.0.3
3E2.0.1

Explorers From Far Away

Think about this while you read.

Why did the French want to explore the Great Lakes?

The French Came First

The French were the first **European**s to come here. *Europeans are people who live in Europe.* They can be from countries like **Britain** or France . There are other countries in Europe too. It was during this time that people from Europe moved west to **explore**. They were often exploring North America. *Someone who explores learns about a place which is new to him or her. He or she finds out about its land and people.*

Think Like a Historian- Why Did They Come?

1 You already know one reason the French came here. They came to trade. Furs were scarce in France. They traded with the tribes to get furs to take home.

The French found the land around Michigan had many animals with nice fur. The beaver was one good example. The French began to trade with the tribes for furs. Then they sold the furs in France. The **profits** they made attracted more fur traders. Soldiers came to protect the traders.

2 They had no idea North America was so large. There were no good maps in those days. They thought they could find a water route across it. They really wanted to sail to China. They thought it was not too far away. Maybe it was just west of the Great Lakes.

Why did they want to get to China? **Spices** and **silk** were also scarce in France. They did not have silk to make fine clothes. China had silk and spices. Those could be bought cheaply in China and sold in France. This is why the French wanted to find a shortcut to China.

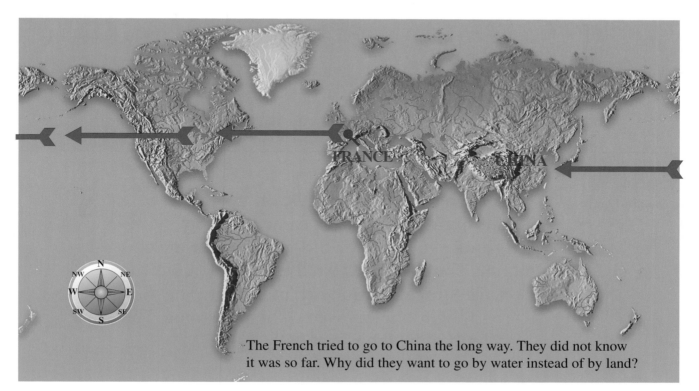

The French tried to go to China the long way. They did not know it was so far. Why did they want to go by water instead of by land?

To find a shortcut, the French explored. They traveled along the **St. Lawrence River** (SAYnt LOR ents). They used this big river like a highway. Their first forts and towns were started along it. They kept going west. Finally they found the Great Lakes. The French explored the rivers to find where the water went.

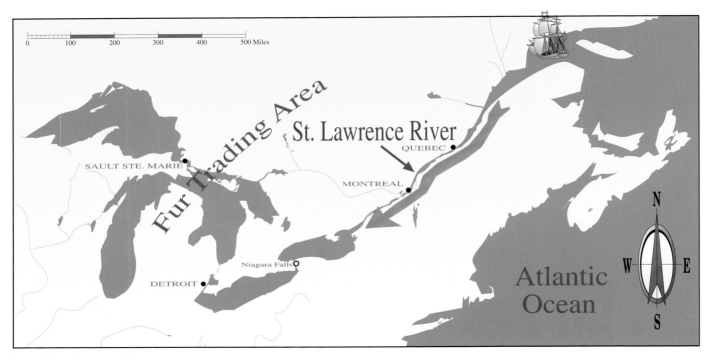

The French used the St. Lawrence River to head toward Michigan. The water was their highway.

Along with the traders, others came. **Missionaries** and **priests** came too. They were **religious** people. They did not come to make money. They wanted to tell the tribes about their God. The priests lived with the tribes. They learned their languages and their customs. They tried hard to be their friends.

3

These are the three reasons the French came here. They came to find a way to China. They came to trade furs. They came to tell the tribes about their God.

When did they arrive? The French reached Michigan a long time ago. They began to arrive in the 1600s. The first ones came about 1620.

Learning who came, why they came and when they came are good things to know. These are some questions historians ask about the past.

Whose Land Is It?

Soon the French claimed the land of Canada and the Great Lakes. They said it now belonged to France. They called it **New France.** Of course, they forgot the tribes were here first. The Europeans thought of themselves as better than the tribes. Europeans claimed every land which was new to them. Take the land and make it yours. This was their thinking at that time.

The First Frenchman Here- We think!

Who was the first person from France to reach Michigan? Who was the first to meet the tribes here? He was a young man named **Brulé** (broo-LAY). He lived far from here. His home was along the St. Lawrence River. Brulé had

YEAR 1620

a thrilling life. He joined Native Americans on long canoe trips. Young Brulé wanted to see where the rivers went. Maybe he could find China!

Brulé reached Michigan about 1620. He visited the Upper Peninsula. We do not know too much about what Brulé saw. This is because he could not read or write. He did not know how to draw good maps.

The shore of the Upper Peninsula along Pictured Rocks. Brulé may have gone by here.

Can you imagine what it was like for Brule´? Most of the time he was alone with the Native Americans. His trips may have lasted for months. Did he ever run out of food? Was he ever lost? Was he excited by what he saw?

Don't Go That Way!

Brulé had to watch the way he went. He could not canoe on Lake Ontario or Lake Erie. Why? The French had enemies in this area. The

Find out why the French went to the Upper Peninsula first.

Iroquois tribes lived along those lakes. The Iroquois hated the French. This was because the French helped the Huron tribe fight the Iroquois. The Iroquois never forgave them.

The French used the **Ottawa River** to go west. Can you find it on a map? This river took them to northern Lake Huron. This is why the French reached the Upper Peninsula first.

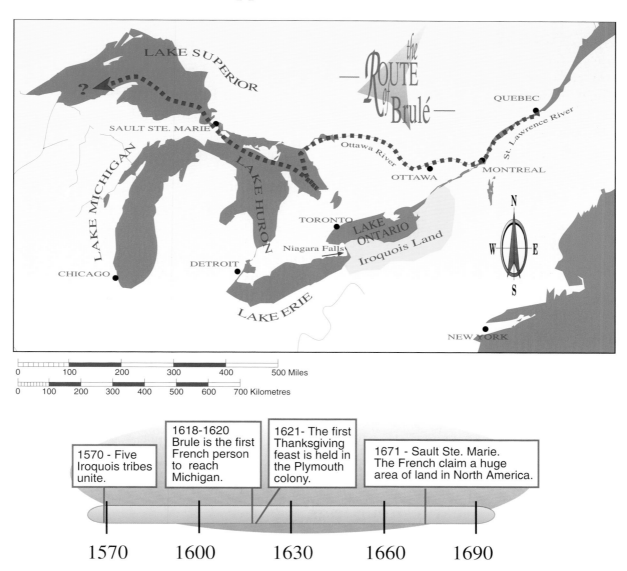

The Fur Trade - Each Person Has One Job

The French used this river for a long time. They brought things to trade in their canoes. They met the tribes at Mackinac Island. Once the trading was done, they put the furs in the canoes. They paddled back to Montreal in Canada.

One group of men always paddled the canoes. Another group did the trading with the tribes. There were clerks who counted the furs. The tribes caught the animals. They also got the furs ready to trade. People in France made the trade goods. They made the beads, cooking pots, the guns and the traps.

Each group had one job. This made the fur trade work smoothly. You can see people doing this at work today. *Each group learns to do one job. They become very good in doing this one thing. This is called* **specialization**. It helps businesses run smoothly. It cuts down on waste. It helps products cost less.

With specialization, we depend on each other. In the fur trade, the clerks would not be good as canoe paddlers. They would not have the muscles. The paddlers might not be good at counting the furs. They may not do well with math. It takes people with different skills to make a strong team.

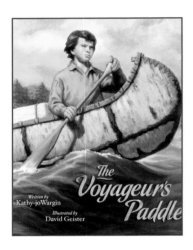

Try reading this book by Kathy-jo Wargin to learn more about the life of the fur traders.

Specialization

Each person does one job very well.

Think About It. Write About It!

1. The French came to Michigan for three reasons. Name these three reasons. Which reason did not make them any money?

2. About which year did the French first reach Michigan?

3. Which peninsula did the French visit first?

4. Scarcity is when there is not much of something. How did scarcity cause the French to come to Michigan?

5. Workers specialize when each person has one job to do. Write an example of specialization.

Use a Time Line Today

Long ago the Pilgrims had their first Thanksgiving. What was happening in Michigan about the same time?

1700
1800
1900

Brain Stretchers

What do you think your **ancestors** were doing when the French first reached Michigan?

Take a Stand!

The French claimed Michigan, but the tribes already lived here. Was it right for the French to do this? Give reasons that support your position.

Chapter 3 Lesson 3

Ideas To Explore
religion (ree lih jun)

People To Meet
Jacques Marquette (jHAK • mar KETT)

Places To Discover
Fox River of Wisconsin

Mississippi River (miss eh sip ee)

Pere Marquette River (peer • mar KETT)

Wisconsin River

Words to Welcome
Catholic (kath oh lik)

diary (die ah ree)

primary source (pri mary • sorse)

Michigan
Social
Studies
GLCEs
3H3.0.1
3H3.0.2
3H3.0.3
3H3.0.6
3H3.0.7
3H3.0.8
3H3.0.10
3G1.0.1
3G4.0.2

A book or diary written by a person who was there when an event happened is a primary source.

A Brave Priest

Think about this while you read.

How did Father Marquette affect Michigan's history?

Let's find out about one of the early French priests. This man came to Michigan a long time ago. He was one of the first French people to reach our land. If we could talk to him, he might have said this.

"Bonjour! My name is **Jacques Marquette** (jHAK mar KETT). I was born in 1637 to a good family. We lived in northern France. When I was 17, I decided to become a priest. I studied long and hard for this work. I had to read many books. I finished my training in 1666."

Father Marquette
Picture by George
Rasmussen.

"I belong to the **Catholic** church. In this church, priests are called 'Father.' This is done out of respect. Some people call me Father Marquette. When I finished my training, my great wish was to go to New France. This was our name for North America. Priests left France to go all over the world. We went to share our **religion** with other people. We told people about our God."

Think what Father Marquette faced. It might be like going to the moon today! His work would be exciting. It may also be dangerous. At last, he reached the Upper Peninsula. Here he learned to speak the languages of the tribes. He learned how to talk to the Odawa. He learned how to talk to the Huron and other tribes.

Michigan's First Two Towns

Marquette started two towns. He built a little church in each one. That was over 300 years ago. He did this in 1668 and 1671. The first was at Sault Ste. Marie. This town is across the river from Canada. St. Ignace was the second. They are both in the eastern Upper Peninsula. These are the two oldest towns in Michigan! Father Marquette played a part in our history!

Let Us Explore a Great River

In 1672 a fur trader visited the priest. He asked Marquette to come with him. He wanted to explore a great river. This was the **Mississippi**. Marquette could speak to the tribes on the way. No Europeans had explored this river. They would be the first ones.

It was May 17, 1673. The explorers loaded their supplies. Father Marquette said a prayer. They stepped into their canoes. Marquette probably wondered where his little boat would take him. The men dipped their paddles into the

Sault Ste. Marie
St. Ignace

water and started. They waved to their friends. The view of St. Ignace became smaller. They paddled along the north shore of Lake Michigan. Days later they reached Wisconsin and rested at a village of the Menominee tribe.

The Tribes Helped Them

The French men paddled up the **Fox River**. They stopped at another Indian village. They asked if anyone could help guide them. They wanted to find a way to the Mississippi.

On June 10, the Frenchmen and two guides left. An amazed crowd of Indians watched. They paddled through swamps and many small lakes. Marquette wrote:

"We greatly needed our two guides.... They helped us to carry our canoes to a second river. After this, the guides returned home. We were left alone in an unknown country...."

I was there!
Primary Source

Marquette wrote this down in his diary. The priests were very good about taking notes. Often they wrote down what took place each day. Marquette's **diary** is a **primary source**. *A primary source tells what actually happened. It was recorded by someone who was there.* Primary sources help historians know what happened. Primary sources are the best because the person was there. He or she wrote down what took place. She did it or saw it. He did it or saw it. People wrote about events in diaries, letters or books.

Alone In Dangerous Country

Now the men went down the **Wisconsin River**. Marquette wrote in his diary. The day was June 17, 1673. "We safely entered the Mississippi... with a joy I cannot express."

The French explorers kept going. The river carried them south. Days passed. They could tell the Mississippi did not go to the Pacific Ocean. It would need to go west to do that. It was not a way to China! The men had followed the river over 600 miles. They decided to turn back.

Picture drawn by Theresa Deeter.

Marquette Was Very Sick

The trip had been very hard. Now Marquette was sick. What should they do? It was decided. He stayed at an Indian village. The rest of the men headed back. Maybe he could rest and get better. It did not happen. In spite of that, he visited another tribe. His illness grew much worse.

Two French friends came to help him back to St. Ignace. The friends paddled hard and fast. Each hour Father Marquette was weaker. Sadly, he did not make it. One night he died along the shore of Lake Michigan. The year was 1675. His friends buried him near a river. Now this river is called the **Pere Marquette** in his honor. Marquette was a brave priest. Many priests worked hard to tell the tribes about their religion.

Picture drawn by Aaron Zenz.

Pere Marquette River

Think About It. Write About It!

1. Name Michigan's two oldest European towns. When were they started? Name the man who started them.

2. Did Marquette and the French explorers need help from the tribes on their trip to the Mississippi River? Explain your answer.

3. What primary source did Father Marquette leave behind? How does it help us know about history?

Brain Stretchers:

Make a map. Mark the route Marquette traveled from St. Ignace down the Mississippi River in 1673.

Make a time line. Add the dates when three old cities in the United States were started along with the dates when St. Ignace and Sault Ste. Marie were started. Label the cities.

1700

1800

1900

Think Like a Historian:

Write three questions you would like to ask Marquette if you could go back in time to talk with him.

How did Father Marquette affect Michigan's history?

Chapter 3 Lesson 4

Ideas To Explore

Controlling the fur trade

People To Meet

Antoine Cadillac (ahn TWAHN • KAD el ak)

Marie-Therese Cadillac (ma REE TER ees • KAD el ak)

Pontchartrain (pon shar train)

Alphonse de Tonty (al FONs • day TON tee)

Anne de Tonty

Places To Discover

Detroit (dee TROYt)

Montreal (mon tree all)

Paris (pair ess) a large city in France

Words to Welcome

brandy (bran dee) a strong drink with alcohol

colonies (KOL uh neez)

de troit (the French said- day twaw)

portage (por taj)

servant

settlements

Michigan
Social Studies
GLCEs
3H3.0.1,
3H3.0.3, 3H3.0.5
3H3.0.6, 3H3.0.7
3H3.0.8, 3H3.0.10
3G1.0.2, 3G4.0.2
3E1.0.1, 3E1.0.3

How Detroit Got Its Start

Think about this while you read.

**How did Cadillac affect the
history of Michigan?**

Today, **Detroit** is our largest city. About
800,000 people live there. It has highways going
north, south, east
and west. Each day
these highways are
full of cars. Detroit
has businesses of all
kinds, but it is a
center for making
cars and trucks.

Long ago it
was only a place by
a wide river. It was a
place where Native
Americans camped.
Let us learn how this great city got its start.

Downtown Detroit.

Detroit began in the mind of a Frenchman.
He began to think about it more than 300 years
ago. In a way it was born in far away France. It
may have happened this way. Imagine you are
there. Meet a boy who is a **servant** in a big
house. The man he works for has an important
job with the French government.

"Greetings! It is 1699 and I welcome you to France. My name is Andre (on dray). I am a servant boy in a big house. My master lives near **Paris**. He is an important man in the government who helps plan things for the king. My master mostly works with the French **colonies** (kol on ease). His name is **Pontchartrain** (pon shar train).

"Tonight he is having a special guest for dinner. It is my job to bring wood for the fireplace. The house is made of stone and can be cool much of the year. I keep the fire going and the room cozy warm.

"I just sit on the floor by the fireplace, unless I must go for more wood. No one pays attention to me so I can listen to the men talk. The guest is coming in now. His name is **Antoine Cadillac** (ahn TWAHN • KAD el ak) and he is from New France. You know that is a French colony in North America. Yes?

Cadillac by George Rasmussen

"This man Cadillac looks like someone of action. I'll bet he is good with a sword! I heard some other servants talk about Cadillac. They said he sometimes gets into trouble. He can make enemies of important people, but Pontchartrain likes him.

"After dinner the men are talking of some great plans. Cadillac has a large map spread on the table. He points and says this is the place! Here the lakes narrow into a river. He tells Pontchartrain a fort here will control all of the rest of the Great Lakes. We can stop our British enemies before they can move into the area! They will not be able to expand their fur trade.

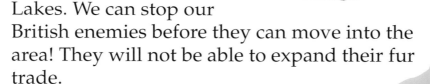

"Cadillac says, if he can bring settlers and women it will work. The tribes will come and trade with us, not the English! He wants many Indians to come to the fort. It will be at the narrow place on the river. [The French call a narrow place between two lakes a **de `troit**.]

"Pontchartrain says, this will probably upset the men now trading furs. They will need to move to the new fort. Cadillac told him not to worry. He will take care of that. Pontchartrain reminded him about the priests. They may not want to move to this new fort. Also, they may

not like the tribes trading with you. If you trade **brandy** to the tribes for furs, they will be very upset!

"Both men said this new fort was an important project. It would be the key to **controlling the fur trade** around the Great Lakes. Pontchartrain said he would convince the king. We must do this, he said.

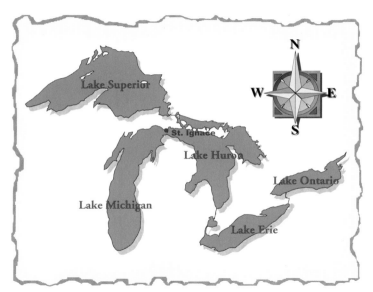

Cadillac's map of the Great Lakes.

"Oops, I have spent too much time talking. I must get more wood for the fireplace. I hope to see you again soon. Maybe I can go to New France someday."

Cadillac Heads Across the Ocean

Cadillac had already been to Michigan. He was once in charge of the fort at St. Ignace. While there, he traded in furs. He shipped those

furs back to his wife in Canada. **Marie-Therese** (ma REE TER ees) **Cadillac** was her name. She ran the business and sold the furs.

Cadillac liked the extra money from trading furs. However, there was a problem. Fur traders from Britain started to visit Michigan. The British had many **settlements** along the east coast of America. Now they sent traders west toward Michigan. He wanted to stop the British. He felt this would be good for France. It would also be good for him!

Cadillac's plan had some new ideas. He wanted many Indians to move to Detroit. He also wanted French families to come. He wanted them to start farms. Few French families lived in Michigan and there were hardly any farms.

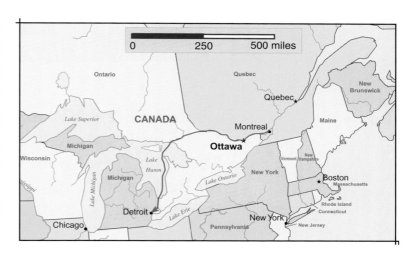

Detroit Is Born!

On June 4, 1701, Cadillac left **Montreal** (mon tree all) with 25 canoes. His second in command was **Alphonse de Tonty**. By July 23rd, the group reached the Detroit River. The trip took 49 days and they traveled about 600 miles! On the way they had to cross 30 **portages**. It was not an easy way to travel.

The next day they started building. The French were the first Europeans at Detroit. Now "Detroit" meant more than just French words for a narrow place between two lakes. Later, the French found out the British were almost ready to start a fort at Detroit. The British had made a treaty with the Iroquois. This would let the British travel to Detroit using Lake Ontario and Lake Erie.

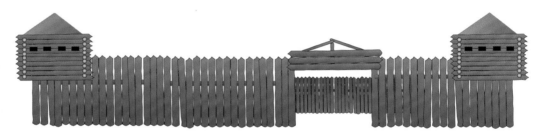

What Cadillac's fort at Detroit may have looked like.

The First French Women Here

Until now, no French women had come to Michigan. It was a rough land. It was a land of fur traders and explorers. Women were not thrilled about coming here.

The wives of Cadillac and de Tonty decided to move here. Marie Cadillac and **Anne de Tonty** would come with their children. This excited the tribes. They felt it meant the French were here to stay. The French would be able to protect them when needed.

The ladies traveled in canoes. They

A canoe

brought some of their children. Indians and soldiers did the paddling. Imagine what that trip must have been like! When the women arrived, the men were really excited. They shouted and shot their guns in the air! This was October, 1701.

Marie Cadillac was glad to see her husband at Detroit. Picture drawn by Aaron Zenz.

Success—But Problems Too

Indians did move to Detroit. The first winter there were 6,000! Cadillac started businesses that made the important things the town needed. They had a blacksmith and a tool maker. The Cadillac family built three houses. They also built two barns, a windmill and a bakery oven. Soon there was a church called Saint Anne's.

What did the tribes think about this new town? It was not like their villages. Did they ever think trading furs would cause the Europeans to build towns? How is life changing for the tribes?

Cadillac did upset other fur traders. Too many furs were going to Detroit. This was ruining their business. By 1711, those traders wanted Cadillac to leave. They knew how to do it. They got the king to give him a new job! Cadillac was made the governor of Louisiana. Our two states have a Cadillac connection! This is where the city of New Orleans is today.

Even though Cadillac left, Detroit kept going. Other French people came. Some of the early families still have relatives there today. Some streets still have French names. The streets are along the land of the old French farms. The farms were long and narrow. They started from the river. Do you know anyone with those last names? Maybe their family lived in Detroit long ago.

Detroit

This map is not to scale. Many streets are not shown.

Streets shown on map: Joseph Campau, Chene Street, Dubois Street, St. Aubin Street, Orleans Street, Riopelle Street, Rivard Street, St. Antoine Street, Beaubien Street

DETROIT RIVER

Let's Review

Animals with furs were a great natural resource here. Furs were scarce in France. This pulled the French to Michigan. The rivers and lakes were their highways. The French started Detroit because of its location. They wanted to use it to guard the Great Lakes. The French had been in Michigan for over 100 years. Still, not many French people had moved to Michigan. There were few towns here.

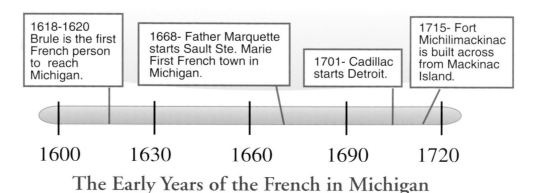

1618-1620 Brule is the first French person to reach Michigan.

1668- Father Marquette starts Sault Ste. Marie First French town in Michigan.

1701- Cadillac starts Detroit.

1715- Fort Michilimackinac is built across from Mackinac Island.

1600   1630   1660   1690   1720

The Early Years of the French in Michigan

Think About It. Write About It!

1. Who started what became Michigan's largest city?

2. Why did he want to start this city?

3. Who were the first two European women in Michigan?

4. Suppose you were a French fur trader. You worked at Mackinac Island. One day you heard about Cadillac's plans for Detroit. What might you think about it?

5. How did Cadillac affect Michigan history?

Make a Time Line Today

This time line will have three events and their dates. The events are:
1. When the French reached Michigan
2. When Father Marquette died
3. When Detroit was started

1700
1800
1900

Think Like a Geographer

Look at a map of North America. Which Great Lakes could the French control with a fort at Detroit? Could the French have chosen another place to control more of the Great Lakes? Please explain.

GEOGRAPHY

Think Like a Historian

Someone once wrote, "Detroit was started because an old king of France wore a beaver hat." Explain what this means.

Chapter 3 Lesson 5

Ideas To Explore
cause and effect
French and Indian War
pursuit of happiness (pur soot)

People To Meet
Chief Pontiac (PON tee ak)
Jean de Sable (jHAN day-SAW-bul)

Places To Discover

Appalachian Mountains (ah puh LAY shun)
Au Sable River (ah SAW bull)
Charlevoix (SHAR la voy)
Chicago (shi kah go)
Fort Michilimackinac (MISH ill eh MACK in aw)
Fort St. Joseph (SAYnt • joes if)
Haiti (hay tee)
Marquette (mar KET)
Niles (ni uls)
Traverse City (trav erss)

Michigan
Social Studies
GLCEs
3H3.0.1
3H3.0.2
3H3.0.3
3H3.0.6
3H3.0.8
3H3.0.10
3G4.0.2

Words to Welcome
baggatiway (bag gat i way)
proclamation (prok la may shun)
pursue (per SOO)
rebellion (ree bell yun)
settlers (set lers)
tomahawks (TOM ah hawks)

Trouble Between the British and French

Think about this while you read.
Why are the French not still in control here?
What happened?

In the 1700s the French built six more forts in Michigan. These forts protected their land. The forts protected them from the tribes. The tribes were not the greatest worry. The French were more worried about another enemy. This enemy had many soldiers and cannons. They were worried about the British!

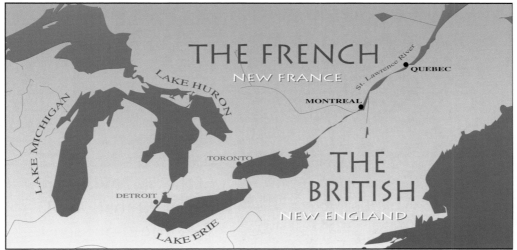

The British Want New France

The French had land in North America. Their colony was called New France. The British had land here too. Their colonies were along the Atlantic Ocean on the East Coast. These colonies

YEAR
1754

The French and
Indian War
1754-1763

•

A fight between
the French and
the British.

were hundreds of miles from Michigan. One of them was New York. These colonies had many towns and farms. They had more people than the French.

The French and British did not do things the same way. The British brought more of their people. The French did not need many people to trade furs. New France was a large land with few French people. The British and the French had been enemies for years. So in 1754, the British decided to push out the French. This became the **French and Indian War**. The French and many Indians fought together against the British.

Soldiers in the
French and
Indian War.

During this war there were several battles, but none were in Michigan. Near the end, the French lost control of the St. Lawrence River. At that point, they could not send supplies to their soldiers. Soon after, the war ended and the British won. If the French had won, you might speak French! Canada would still belong to France.

This war cost the British lots of money. They wanted people in America to help pay for it. The Americans did not want to help. This will cause bad feelings over the years.

What the French Left Behind

The French left some things behind for us. Our largest city, Detroit, has a French name. Other cities have French names too. **Traverse City** has a French name. **St. Joseph**, **Marquette** and **Charlevoix** (SHAR la voy) are French. Some of our rivers are named for the French. The Marquette and **Au Sable** are two rivers with French names.

A New Flag In Michigan

In 1760, British soldiers marched into Detroit in red uniforms. They beat drums. The British flag went up the flagpole. Now Michigan belonged to the British. Of course, they did not bother to ask the tribes who had lived here for so long.

When the French lost, it worried the tribes. The tribes needed many things they could not make. They depended on the fur trade to get them. The British did not see the tribes as friends. After all, the tribes had been fighting them. The British prices were high. The British

Pontiac may have looked like this. Art by George Rasmussen.

YEAR 1763

would not trade gunpowder. By now the tribes depended on it for hunting. The French always gave them gifts. The British would not give them gifts. The tribes were quite upset.

Chief Pontiac Takes Action

The Odawa **Chief Pontiac** (PON tee ak) thought about what to do. He lived across the river from Detroit. Pontiac had helped the French. Pontiac began to wonder. If the tribes beat the British, would the French trade with them again? Pontiac asked many tribes to come to a meeting near Detroit. It was April 27, 1763.

Chief Pontiac had a plan. He would ask to meet with the British in the fort. Pontiac would bring many warriors with him. Each man would wear a large blanket. Pontiac's warriors cut the barrels of their rifles short. The guns would be under the blankets when they walked into the fort! More Indians would be outside ready to run in and join the fight.

It was time. One morning Pontiac and 11 other chiefs with 60 warriors walked into the fort. Something was not right. The soldiers were not going about business as usual. They were armed and ready. Somehow the British learned of the plan!

Pontiac talked briefly and then asked to leave. The British let the Indians go. Maybe they hoped Pontiac had changed his mind. The 120 or so British inside the fort were in real danger. Pontiac had about 800 warriors outside!

Pontiac's warriors leave the fort at Detroit. Their idea for a surprise attack did not work. By Frederic Remington, Harpers Magazine April, 1897.

The Attack!

Two days later, yells and war cries came from the woods. Soldiers shouted, "Here they come!" Indians rushed up to the fort. They tried to chop a hole in the wall with their **tomahawks** (TOM ah hawks)! The British shot back. Many Indians died trying to get into the fort at Detroit.

That night the Indians crept up to the walls. They started fires against the wooden fort. British soldiers raced back and forth. They carried buckets of water to pour on the fires.

A tomahawk is like a hatchet. It was used to cut wood and in war as a weapon.

119

In 1763, Major Gladwin was in charge of the British fort at Detroit when Pontiac attacked.

From Archives of Michigan 13832

The battle for Detroit went on for weeks and weeks. Pontiac's warriors could not get in the fort. The British could not leave. The British became desperate. They did not have many bullets or much food left. They could not get any more supplies. Which side would give in first? Time was also against the Indians. It was now fall. They needed to go hunting and gather food for the winter. Warriors began to leave with their families.

Longest in Our History

It was now late October. Pontiac got a message from the French. It said France and Britain had made peace. The French would not come back. Pontiac decided to stop the attack. The fight lasted 153 days. This was the longest Native American battle in our country. It showed Pontiac's skill as a leader.

War Spread Far and Wide

The British still had worries. Many of their forts were attacked. The tribes worked together. Pontiac sent messages urging them to fight. The British lost five forts! Only Fort Detroit and two others held out. Then there was sad news for the British. The tribes had captured **Fort Michili-mackinac** (MISH ill eh MACK in aw)! That was the fort across from Mackinac Island.

What Happened at Michilimackinac?

One day many Native Americans came into the fort. They all wanted to trade. Some British were puzzled. The only thing the Indians wanted were tomahawks! One trader was Alexander Henry. He went to talk to the commander of the fort. Two tribes were going to play a kind of ball game. People were betting money on which tribe would win. Mr. Henry was worried. He thought there could be trouble. The commander of the fort did not listen to him. This is what Mr. Henry wrote in his diary.

This is a primary source. Mr. Henry was there when it happened.

"A Chipeway came to tell me that his nation was going to play at **bag gat i way** with another Indian nation for a large bet. He invited me to witness the sport. He said the commandant was to be there, and would bet on the side of the Chipeways. I went to the commandant and talked with him a little. I wondered if the Indians might possibly have something evil in mind. The commandant only smiled at my suspicions."

The Big Game

Many of the soldiers came out to watch the game. It was a great sight! The British commander made his bet on the Ojibwa side. It was a warm day, but the Indian women seemed to be cold. They sat wrapped in blankets near the gate.

121

Suddenly the ball went over the wall and into the fort. The players rushed in after it. As they ran, they grabbed weapons from under the women's blankets. Few of the soldiers had time to defend themselves. It was a quick victory for the tribes. Many soldiers were killed. Alexander Henry ran into a house and hid. He was really scared, but he survived.

Another Fort Taken

The tribes captured **Fort St. Joseph**. This happened in May, 1763. The fort was along the St. Joseph River. The fort was a small one. The city of **Niles** is there today. Most of the soldiers were killed. The commander was taken prisoner. The Indians marched him back to Detroit.

The Fighting Ends but the British Still Worry

It took awhile for all the tribes to make peace. Not until 1766 did everything calm down. This war is called Pontiac's **Rebellion**. Pontiac showed courage. He tried to help his people.

The British moved back into their forts. Still, they worried about more trouble with the Indians. The tribes were still angry. **Settlers** were tak-

Students dig at the site of old Fort St. Joseph. This work helps us understand what happened and how people lived long ago.

This rusted keyhole is an example of what they found. Photos courtesy Dr. Michael Nassaney at Western Michigan University.

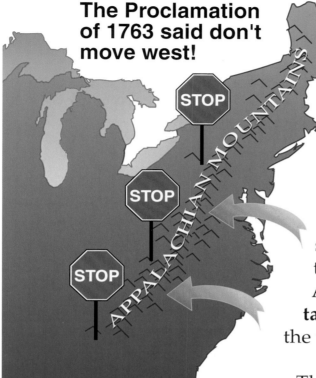

The Proclamation of 1763 said don't move west!

STOP

STOP

STOP

APPALACHIAN MOUNTAINS

ing their land. So, the British passed a law to stop settlers going west.

The law was called the **Proclamation of 1763** (prok la may shun). It said no settlers could go past the **Appalachian Mountains**. Would this keep the tribes happy?

This law let the tribes **pursue** (per SOO) their happiness. They could hunt where they wanted. They could live where they wanted.

Pursuit of happiness is a core democratic value. *It means let people do what they want. Let them be happy as long as it does not bother anyone else.*

Think Like a Historian

There are often two sides to each event. This makes history interesting. Now settlers could not move west. The tribes were happy, but the settlers were not. The settlers could not pursue their

happiness. They wanted to have more land. They wanted to start farms. They wanted to get away from the crowded towns in the East. The new law made the settlers mad at the British. It led to problems later.

First- the cause

Second- the effect

In history, one event can cause another. The first event is the cause. The second event is the effect. Historians call this **"cause and effect."**

Here is an example. The French lost the war with the British (the cause). The British took control of Michigan (the effect).

Pontiac led the tribes to attack the British (the cause). The British made the Proclamation of 1763 (the effect). Try to find more examples as you study Michigan.

The Black Trader

In the 1760s a fur trader came to Michigan. His name was **Jean de Sable** (jHAN day SAW bul). De Sable was a black man with a French background. He was born in **Haiti**, an island in the Atlantic Ocean.

Jean de Sable
by Aaron Zenz.

Jean de Sable was a friend of Chief Pontiac. He lived near Pontiac's camp. He traded with the tribes. When Pontiac left Michigan, so did de Sable. In 1779, de Sable settled along the shore of Lake Michigan. Over time his settlement became a huge city. Today we call it **Chicago**.

124

Think About It. Write About It!
Think like a historian when you answer.

1. The French no longer control Michigan. What happened?

2. Why did Chief Pontiac attack the fort at Detroit?

3. What happened at Fort Michilimackinac when the tribes played a game?

4. What did the Proclamation of 1763 say? How did it affect Michigan?

5. Why did the British come to Michigan?

6. Why did Jean de Sable come to Michigan?

Make a Time Line Today
    Make a time line for this lesson. Label each event and its date. Do research. Add one more event that took place somewhere else in the world.

Think Like a Historian
    How did things in far away Europe affect Michigan?

Words In Action!
    Explain the conflict between the pursuit of happiness for the tribes and for the settlers who wanted to move west.

1700

1800

1900

Becoming a State

Chapter 4 Lesson 1

Ideas To Explore
The War for Independence and the beginning of the United States

General Wayne

People To Meet
King George III (III means third)
Daniel Boone (BOON)
General Anthony Wayne (an thon ee   wayn)
President George Washington

Words to Welcome
independence (in dee pen dense)
liberty (lib er tee) - a core democratic value

Liberty was important to those who started our country. They put the word on our first coins.

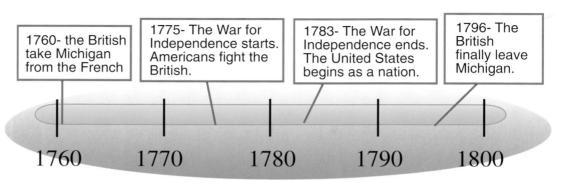

| 1760- the British take Michigan from the French | 1775- The War for Independence starts. Americans fight the British. | 1783- The War for Independence ends. The United States begins as a nation. | 1796- The British finally leave Michigan. |

1760   1770   1780   1790   1800

The British and the Americans

Becoming A State-
It Was Not Easy!

Think about this while you read.
How did the War for Independence change Michigan?

The U.S. Becomes a Nation

You have learned a lot about Michigan, but it was not yet a state. It is now 1770. Our country has not even been started. Before Michigan can be a state, the United States has to be a nation! This **key event** has to take place first.

Key Event

A key event may unlock the reason something happens later.

At this time, **George III** was king of Britain. The people here did not like a king telling them what to do. They did not like being told that they could not move west. They did not like paying taxes to the British. The people wanted to be free. They wanted to start their own country.

People did not want to pay taxes to Britain.

The British had 13 colonies in America. These were along the Atlantic Ocean. These colonies wanted to be free. In the spring of 1775 they started to fight for their freedom. This fight was called the War for **Independence**. *Independence means not to be ruled by someone else.* The

YEAR
1775

colonies also wanted **liberty**. Liberty is a core democratic value. *Liberty means to do what you wish as long as it does not hurt anyone. It is the freedom to do anything that is not against the law.*

The 13 states which were once the British colonies. The shapes of some have changed since the 1700s.

The British Use Michigan

Michigan was not one of the 13 colonies. Most of the fighting was far from Michigan. Still, British soldiers were here and they used Michigan as a base. The British sent their soldiers from Detroit and had the tribes help them. These men attacked the colonies.

Sometimes American settlers were kidnapped by the tribes. A few of these were brought to Detroit. **Daniel Boone** (BOON) was one of them. He was a famous pioneer and explorer. The Native Americans caught him and were proud of it.

Daniel Boone and his dog.

The Fort at Mackinac is Moved

The Americans made plans to march to Michigan. This worried the British here. The British felt Fort Michilimackinac was too easy to attack. They decided to move the fort. It would be safer on Mackinac Island. They built the new fort on a hill. It had a good view of the harbor. The British could see anyone coming from far away. The new fort was finished in 1781. If you visit the island, you can still see it today!

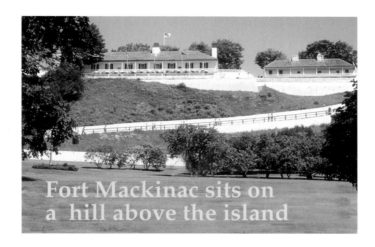

Fort Mackinac sits on a hill above the island

The Americans never marched to Michigan. Detroit was not attacked. The fort at Mackinac was safe.

The War Ends- The United States Begins

Finally the fighting ended. Peace at last! The War for Independence ended in 1783. The colonies were free from Britain! Each colony became a state in the new United States of

YEAR 1783

America. It started with 13 states. George Washington became the first President. The new country had much land that was not in the 13 states. Michigan was a part of that land. It was mostly forest. It was a place where Native Americans lived. There were only a few towns.

General Anthony Wayne lived from 1745 to 1796.

from Archives of Michigan 13862

YEAR 1796

But the British Stay in Michigan

Wait! After the war, the British did not leave Michigan. They stayed in their forts. They traded for furs with the tribes. They even gave them guns so they could fight American settlers. Maybe the British felt they could weaken our new nation. This was not fair! Michigan did not belong to the British now!

The Americans were fed up. **President George Washington** took action. He sent an army west. The general in charge was **Anthony Wayne**.

In 1794, there was a huge battle in Ohio. General Wayne fought the British and Native Americans there. He won the battle. In 1796, the British left Michigan. The tribes made peace with the Americans, at least for now.

Now there were American soldiers in the fort at Detroit. They also stayed at Mackinac

Island. They kept watch because the British were not far away. Canada still belonged to them. The enemy was just across the river!

General Wayne Leaves His Name Behind

General Wayne remained at Detroit for about four years. Then he left to go back home. Sadly, he died on the trip. People were proud of General Wayne. They were proud of what his soldiers had done. They named Wayne County after the general. Today this county has more people than any other in Michigan.

1796 Michigan was now a part of the new United States

Who Has Been In Charge?

The tribes lived here by themselves for thousands of years. They were here much longer than anyone else. The French were a big part of our past for 140 years (1620 to 1760). The British were in charge for about 36 years (1760 to 1796). How long has Michigan been a part of the

United States? It has been since 1796. You do the math. Tell how many years that has been.

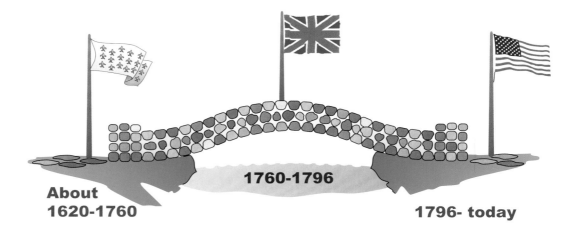

About
1620-1760

1760-1796

1796- today

The British were a bridge between the days of the French and the time of the Americans. The British left behind many ideas we use today. We speak their language. We use many of their laws. We follow many of their customs.

When the United States took over, big changes started. For a long time, Michigan was a land of Native Americans. There were few settlers and towns. There were almost no roads. Soon all of this will change. Michigan will start to grow in a hurry. Many new people will move here. They will make Michigan their home. Trees will be cut down and cabins built. Some people will say this is progress. Other people will not.

Think About It. Write About It

1. Name a key event that had to take place before Michigan could become a state?

2. Americans fought a War for Independence. Give one reason why they did this.

3. Whose soldiers were in Michigan during the War for Independence?

4. Why did the British move their fort to Mackinac Island?

5. Which general finally forced the British to leave Michigan? When did that happen?

Make Chart Today

Make a chart. Compare how long France, Britain and the United States have been in charge of Michigan. Label each part of your graph.

Be a Geographer

Make a simple map of Michigan. Draw Wayne county on the map. Put Detroit on your map. Label each of them.

GEOGRAPHY

Think Like a Historian!

Focus on the War for Independence. What happened? When did it happen? Why did it happen? Who was there?

Chapter 4 Lesson 2

Ideas to Explore
The War of 1812. The British and tribes try to take Michigan one last time, but they fail. Now Michigan is safely and firmly a part of the United States.
Control of the Great Lakes was a key to winning the War of 1812.

Oliver Hazard Perry

People To Meet
Oliver Hazard Perry (ol eh ver • haz ard • pear ee)
Tecumseh (Ta KUM see)
William Hull

Places To Discover
Monroe
River Raisin (RAY zin)

Michigan
Social
Studies
GLCEs
3H3.0.1
3H3.0.3
3H3.0.6
3H3.0.7
3H3.0.8
3H3.0.9
3H3.0.10
3P3.1.3

Words to Welcome
territory (tair uh tor ee) - A territory is land that is a part of the United States, but not yet a state.

Three Strikes Against the British

Think about this while you read.

How did the War of 1812 change life for the Native Americans around Michigan?

The fight with the British was not over. Our country has fought with Britain twice. The first time was the War for Independence. General Wayne fought them a second time a few years later. Now there would be more trouble.

What was Michigan like in those days? It was a land of thick woods and Native American villages. Fur trading was the main business. Some people here still spoke French. Detroit was the only place much like a city. There were hardly any roads here. Most people and supplies came by ship.

Governor
William Hull

YEAR 1805

Michigan was still not a state. The people here had no say in government. The President of the United States chose the person to be in charge. He named **William Hull** the first governor of our **territory** in 1805. Mr. Hull had a surprise when he reached Detroit. The town had burned to the ground!

135

We Have Had Enough! The War of 1812

The British were a thorn in the side of our young country. They stopped our ships on the oceans for no reason. They wanted Native Americans to attack our settlers. Finally, the United States became so angry it declared war! This war is called the **War of 1812**. However, our country was not ready and the war did not go well for our side. The British made a sneak attack on Fort Mackinac and they captured it! Was starting the war a mistake?

British soldiers at the fort on Mackinac Island. Picture drawn by George Rasumssen.

Governor Hull became General Hull. He was put in charge of the American soldiers here. Now he and his soldiers crossed the Detroit River. They planned to attack the British fort on the other side. General Hull had almost ten times more soldiers than the British. It should be easy to win!

Then General Hull began to worry. He worried about the Indians. Many of them fought on the British side. Hull was afraid their warriors would attack Detroit. He feared what they might do. Lots of people lived outside the fort. They had no protection. The general went back to Detroit.

The Breakfast Surprise!

The next thing people in Detroit knew, British cannon balls were falling on their homes! One family was just starting to eat breakfast. A cannon ball fell through the roof. It smashed through the table and went into the basement. It did not hurt them, but they left fast! A man climbed out of bed. He got up to see what was the matter. In that instant, a cannon ball went right through his bed!

YEAR 1812

Picture drawn by George Rasmussen.

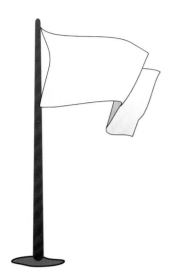

General Hull raised a white flag. He surrendered to the British. Their soldiers marched into Detroit.

YEAR 1812

Next, the British soldiers and Native Americans crossed the river. They marched on the fort. General Hull had his cannon ready to fire. His men were tense, but prepared. They would put up a good fight. Then General Hull surprised everyone. He told his men to give up. He wanted them to surrender. He did not ask anyone. People said, "What?" The men and women could not believe it. The British soldiers just walked in. They took Detroit and no shots were fired.

People have often wondered, did General Hull do the right thing? His action did save lives. On the other hand, Detroit was captured by another nation. This has happened to only a few American cities.

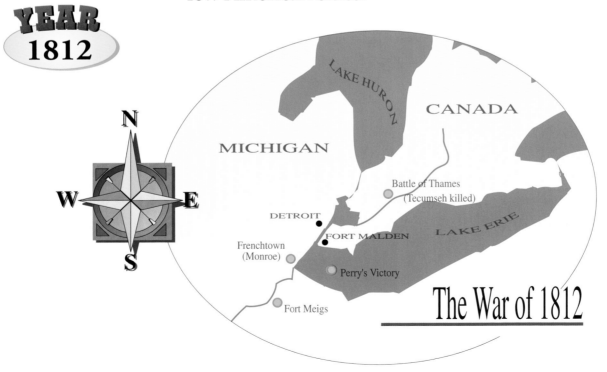

The War of 1812

The Biggest Battle

Other Americans did not give up so easily. They came from the south to take back Detroit. The British did not wait for them. They attacked first. It was the battle at the **River Raisin** near **Monroe**. Over two thousand men were in the fight. This was the biggest battle ever fought in Michigan. Sadly, the British won.

Oliver Hazard Perry was a young commander during the war of 1812.

Lake Erie Is Important. Who will Control it?

At the start of the war, the British controlled **Lake Erie**. Their ships stopped any others. The British ships brought supplies to their army. The Americans were going to do something about this. **Oliver Hazard Perry** built some ships to fight the British. Finally, the British ships and Perry's ships went to battle. The fight was fierce. Cannons boomed. Bullets and cannon balls whizzed through the air.

The Americans were not doing well. Most of the sailors on Perry's ship had been killed or hurt. The British thought they had won, but Perry would not quit. There was one American ship with almost no damage. Perry risked his life to reach it. He got into a rowboat and left his ship. Perry took over his undamaged warship.

Oliver Hazard Perry left his ship in the middle of the battle to reach another one.

Then he sailed near the British ships and fired his guns. Believe it or not, Perry finally won. News of his success spread across the nation.

YEAR
1813

Perry's win gave the Americans control of Lake Erie! The British were in trouble. They could not get supplies. They could not bring more soldiers to help. Remember, there were few roads in those days. Most travel was by boats on rivers or lakes.

What Did the Tribes Think?

The British had the help of many Native Americans. One of them was **Tecumseh**. He hoped the British would keep settlers away. The tribes did not want American settlers here. They did not want towns started. They did not want roads built. It was their land!

Tecumseh was a strong and proud leader. He is wearing part of a British uniform. Picture drawn by George Rasmussen.

I WAS THERE

Tecumseh Speaks!

One time Tecumseh heard of a new **treaty** between another tribe and the United States. That tribe got money for the land. He was very upset. In his own language he said, *"Sell a country! Why not sell the air, the clouds, and the* *great sea, as well as the earth? Did not the Great Spirit make them all for the use of his children?"* He felt the land belonged to all tribes, not just the one making the treaty. The Americans feared Tecumseh and his warriors.

The British Leave

Once the American ships controlled Lake Erie, the British left their fort near Detroit. Tecumseh heard about this and gave an angry speech. He told the British they were afraid. He said they were like animals running away with their tails between their legs. When he finished talking, all his warriors jumped up. They shook their tomahawks!

Even though Tecumseh was upset, he went with the British. They headed east. They were marching across Canada. Before long, the Americans caught them. There was a battle. Then an American soldier shot Tecumseh and he fell dead. The British lost this fight. All of this took place in September, 1813.

The British and the United States made peace in 1814. The British never touched Michigan again. With the British gone, more settlers wanted to move here. The British were still in Canada, so we kept soldiers in our forts–just in case!

An American soldier from the War of 1812. Picture drawn by Aaron Zenz.

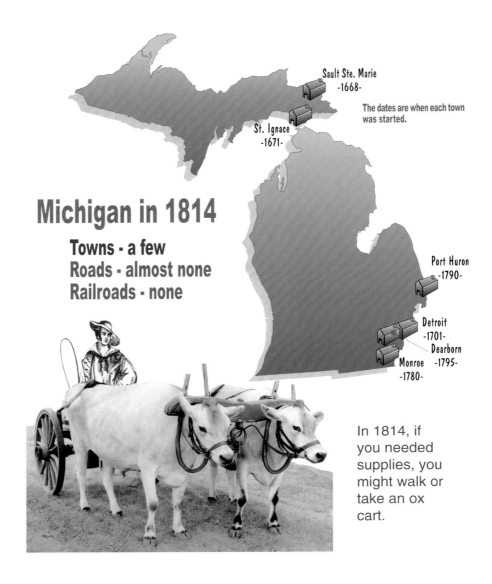

Michigan in 1814

Towns - a few
Roads - almost none
Railroads - none

Sault Ste. Marie
-1668-

The dates are when each town was started.

St. Ignace
-1671-

Port Huron
-1790-

Detroit
-1701-
Dearborn
-1795-

Monroe
-1780-

In 1814, if you needed supplies, you might walk or take an ox cart.

YEAR 1814

What was Michigan like in 1814? It was hard to travel. Most goods came by ship. The government said between 5,000 and 7,000 people lived here, but that did not count the Native Americans. There were still many of them living here. Fur trading was important. There were some farms. Most of the land was covered by trees.

Think About It. Write About It

1. What country did we fight in the War of 1812?

2. Name two Michigan forts captured in the War of 1812.

3. Why was Perry's victory important?

4. Why did Tecumseh and other Native Americans help the British in that war?

5. Where did the largest battle take place in Michigan?

Brain Stretchers

How did the War of 1812 change life for the Native Americans around Michigan?

Think Like a Historian

Choose Perry or Tecumseh. Tell how the person you chose affected the history of Michigan.

Write about cause and effect and the War of 1812. What were some causes? How did the war affect Michigan?

First- the cause

Second- the effect

Take a Stand!

The army put General Hull on trial after the war. This was because he surrendered Detroit. Take a stand. Did he do the right thing or the wrong thing? Support your position with a core democratic value. You may wish to include common good or patriotism.

Chapter 4 Lesson 3

Ideas To Explore
credit (kred it) - Money loaned to buy a product.
entrepreneur (on tray pren ur) - A person who takes
     the risks to run a business.
profit - The money left after a business pays its
     expenses.

People To Meet
Josette LaFramboise (la fom bwaws)
Madeline LaFramboise
Benjamin Pierce

Places To Discover
Ada (A da)
Lowell (low el)

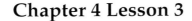

Words to Welcome
boozhoo (booz hoo) - the way the Ojibwa say
hello or welcome
capital resources
export (ex port)
flint and steel - old tools to start a fire
human resources
import (em port)
interest
tinder - something like dry grass that is easy to
     burn

Michigan
Social
Studies
GLCEs
3H3.0.3
3H3.0.7
3E1.0.1
3E1.0.3
3E1.0.4
3E3.0.1

The Fur Trade Goes On and On

Think about this while you read.
What was it like to live in Michigan and be in business as a fur trader long ago?

The French started the fur trade in Michigan. That was in the 1600s. People like Brulé were there at the beginning. Two hundred years later, some French were still trading here. The fur trade was still a big business. Wars did not really stop it. Changes in government did not stop it. You will learn that not all the fur traders were men.

Women from Long Ago

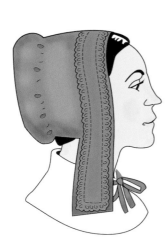

Sometimes we do not talk very much about women from the past. We do not want to leave them out. It is often hard to find out about them. There may not be records of what they did. Women were often quiet heroes. This was usually true long ago. The women fed their familes. They raised the children. They helped the men and the men did things that were noticed and recorded.

A Woman Fur Trader

Now, learn about the life of a woman. She lived in Michigan's past. Her name was **Madeline LaFramboise** (mad uh lin • la fom bwaws). This name means raspberry in English. Madeline was a

Native American. She married a French fur trader. Both of them worked hard to trade furs. One day her husband was murdered. This took place on the way back to their trading post! Her story is told by her daughter, **Josette** (Joe zet) **LaFramboise**.

Madeline and Josette may have looked like this. As far as we know, there are no pictures of them. Picture drawn by Eastman Johnson.

Visit the Trading Post

"Good day! Bonjour! (BOn jzure). **Boozhoo** (booz hoo). I speak English, French and Ojibwa just like my mother. I am Josette. I was born in 1795. My parents were fur traders. On a very sad day my father was killed. That was last year. It was the fall of 1806.

"Now mother runs the trading post. I help take care of my little brother. His name is Joseph and he is two years old. The trading post is on the Grand River.

BEAVER

Grand River Trading Post

We winter there. Each summer we fill our canoes with furs. We paddle all the way to Mackinac Island. On the island the furs are sold and we buy more things to trade.

"Those furs will be exported to France. *An export is something that is sent to another country and sold.* The things we trade to the tribes are imported. *An import is something that comes from another country and is bought.* We buy beads and metal pots from France. We trade those to the tribes for furs.

"Of course, mother was very sad when father was killed. She still had to keep working. We had to have food and money. Some Odawa friends were a big help. They were very sad about father too. Let us put the sadness behind us.

EXPORTS are products made here and sold in other countries.

IMPORTS are products made in other countries and sold here.

Everyday Life

"Are you hungry after your travels? Would you like some breakfast? Mother has made cornbread in the fireplace. We cook all our meals in the fireplace. You can have a real treat. There is a little smoked ham left. Next season we will try to bring another pig. It is not easy to get a pig this far into the wilderness. We must buy a baby pig because it has to travel in the canoe with us!

YEAR 1807

The ash barrel. Mixing water with the ashes makes lye. The lye is used to make soap.

The soap is ready!

The pioneers started a fire by hitting a piece of flint stone on a piece of steel to gets sparks.

"I hope you had enough breakfast to give you energy. It is time to go to work. Today we are making soap.

"Have you made soap before? I will tell you what to do. Take this pot of leftover grease. Put it on the fire so the grease melts. Next, pour the water from the ash barrel into it. Let it boil until lunch. I will ask mother if she has any scent for the soap. Then, we will pour it into the mold. After lunch it will be cool enough. Finally, we can cut the soap into bars. It will be ready for bath time on Saturday night. In the meantime, we will check our traps. Maybe we will find a rabbit for supper.

Using Credit or How to Pay Later

"Oh, look! Some Odawa have come to trade. I will call mother. She will know what to do. It is not time for them to bring furs. They get the best furs in the winter and bring them in the spring. Now they want supplies. Today they will get supplies on **credit**. *Credit means getting something now and promising to pay later.* They will need to pay a bit extra because they get credit. The extra amount is called **interest**.

"These Odawa want some flint and steel to start fires. If you did not know how to make soap, I bet you do not know how to use **flint and steel** either! You take a piece of flint. It is just like the one used on your rifle. You hit it on this little bit of steel to make lots of sparks. You do it so those sparks land on your **tinder**. *Tinder is dried grass, some wood* *shavings and maybe a bit of gunpowder.* The sparks start it to burn. Now you can light your campfire or fireplace.

"Mother keeps records of each person with credit. She writes it in a book. It is an important book. One we do not want to lose! She knows who must bring furs to pay off the credit. Today, Standing Fox got 4 flint and steel sets. Next spring he must bring two beaver furs to pay his credit.

"Mother decides the ones to trust. Some people like to forget about their credit. If they do not pay, she will not give them more the next time they ask. If a new person comes for credit, she will ask other Native Americans about them. She may ask other fur traders. If they have a bad credit history, she will say, no!

"There are many things for mother to think about. She is an early Michigan **entrepreneur**. There are risks to fur trading. She has to be smart. How much should she give for each fur? How much will she get for the furs in Mackinac? Will we make a **profit**? *A profit is the amount of money a business has left after paying the costs.*

"She must also decide how to use **human resources**. *Human resources are the workers in a business.* Can she find enough men to paddle the canoes to Mackinac? The canoe paddlers are human resources in the fur trade.

RISKS

"Mother deals with **capital resources** in her fur trading business. What are capital resources? *Capital resources are the tools, machines and equipment used in a business.* Can you think of a capital resource she uses? What about the canoes? She decides how many canoes we need each year. We may fill four or five canoes with furs. If we do not have enough canoes to move the furs, we would need to leave them behind. Doing that would be bad for the business. She must decide all of these things."

She Did Well

Madeline LaFramboise ran her business well. She made a good profit. She had money to send Josette away to school. Josette went to Montreal. That is hundreds of miles away. Going to school was important then. It is still important. Later, Madeline sold her trading post. It was between **Ada** and **Lowell**. She built a large home on Mackinac Island. She gave money and land to her church. She also helped the school on the island.

Madeline LaFramboise's home on Mackinac Island. This photo was probably taken after she died.

Josette came back to Mackinac Island. When she was 21 years old she fell in love. She married **Benjamin Pierce.** He was the commander of the fort on the island. It was a grand wedding. Her mother wore her Ojibwa dress that day.

Many years later, Benjamin's brother was in the news. He was famous. He became the President of the United States! Madeline and Josette have many connections with our history.

Think About It. Write About It!

1. Were Michigan furs imported or exported to France?

2. Explain what credit means.

3. Long ago there were no matches. What did people use to start fires at that time?

4. Tell some risks Madeline LaFramboise faced as a fur trader.

Be a Geographer

Make a simple map of Michigan. Label the Grand River. Label the fur trading post at Ada. Draw a route from Ada to Mackinac Island that Madeline LaFramboise may follow with her canoes of furs.

Think Like an Economist

Think about economics. Think about costs. Tell how Madeline LaFramboise can make a profit by trading furs.

Words In Action

Write a paragraph about daily life when the LaFramboise family lived here.

Use the Internet to find out what happened to Josette LaFramboise. Write a short report about her life.

Chapter 4 Lesson 4

Ideas To Explore
supply and demand - an economics idea
Venn diagram- a way to compare and contrast

People to Meet
William Nowlin (now lin) - a pioneer boy

Places To Discover
Erie Canal (ear ee • can al)
Farmington (farm ing ton)
gristmill (grist mill) grist means to grind. It is a
mill to grind grain into flour.
Kansas - a state
Midwest - a region with Michigan and the other
states nearby
New York - a state or the large city in that state
Oklahoma - a state
Rochester (rah chest ur)
Troy
Utica (you teh ka)

Michigan
Social
Studies
GLCEs
3H3.0.2
3H3.0.3
3H3.0.5
3H3.0.6
3H3.0.7
3H3.0.10
3G2.0.2
3G4.0.2
3G5.0.2

Words to Welcome
acre (a ker) An acre is a square of land about
209 feet by 209 feet.
canal (kan al)
cultures
deed
land office
population (pop you lay shun)
steam engine (steem • en jen)
surveyors (sir vay ors)

Settlers, On The Way!

Think about this question while you read.
What were the biggest changes settlers made to Michigan?

Two pioneer farmers. They cut their wheat and hay by hand with the tools they are holding. Picture drawn by George Rasmussen.

People Needed Land

Making a living was different in the early 1800s. Most people farmed. To have a farm, a person needs land. Land was becoming scarce in the eastern states. It was expensive to buy land for a new farm. Young families moved west to find land they could afford.

Land was not scarce in Michigan.

Cheap Land In Michigan!

Land was cheap in Michigan. It attracted or pulled people toward Michigan. It cost a dollar or two an **acre** here. It was cheap because there was a lot of it and few people. The **supply** was bigger than the **demand**.

Pioneers lived in cabins like this one. They built them from trees they cut once they reached Michigan. Photo by the author.

Pioneers often cooked in their fireplaces.

Picture from the Archives of Michigan.

Most of the people coming here came from the eastern states. They left states like New York and Vermont (VT). To move to Michigan they traveled west. Michigan is sort of in the middle of the west. Soon, Michigan and the states around it were known as the **Midwest**. The Midwest is a region. The land of the Midwest is similar. It is mostly flat with only small hills. It is not dry like a desert. The Midwest does not have rough, rocky mountains like the mountain states.

The Midwest

Reaching Michigan was another matter. It was hard to travel. The roads were very bad, if there were any at all. None of the roads were paved. They were just dirt paths. When it rained it was a muddy mess! A horse and wagon might only go 10 or 12 miles on a good day.

New Ways to Travel

In the 1820s and 1830s there were new ways to travel. Now, some ships were powered by **steam engines**. These ships could travel even when the wind did not blow. Using steamships, it was much easier to travel on a schedule. Some steamships went across Lake Erie to Detroit.

Many **canals** were being built then. *Canals are man-made rivers.* Today, we do not hear much about canals. They were very useful in the 1800s. Remember, there were few good roads. With canals, people could travel to places that had no rivers or good roads. Horses pulled small boats along the canals. That is an odd way to make a boat move!

The **Erie Canal** was one of the most important canals. It was a very big project to build it. Hundreds of men used shovels and hand tools to dig out the dirt. It opened in the 1820s. Using that canal and some rivers, people could go from **New York City** to Detroit by boat. They did not need to use the bad roads.

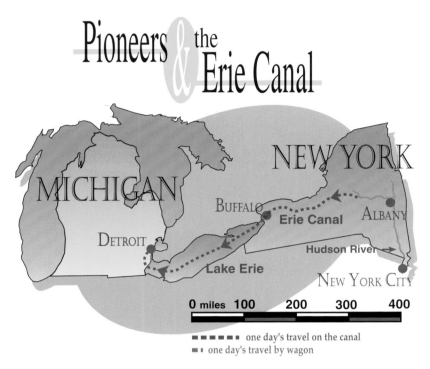

Pioneers & the Erie Canal

MICHIGAN

NEW YORK

DETROIT

BUFFALO Erie Canal ALBANY

Hudson River →

Lake Erie

NEW YORK CITY

0 miles 100   200   300   400

▪ ▪ ▪ ▪ ▪ one day's travel on the canal
▪ ▪ one day's travel by wagon

Many of the new settlers used the Erie Canal. They came from the state of **New York**. Almost all of them headed to Detroit. Why? It was the first Michigan city they could reach by boat. The area around Detroit began to grow quickly. Soon many new towns were started nearby.

Our **population** grew and grew. *The population is how many people live in a place.* In 1820 we only had 8,765 people. In 1840 we had 212,267! This did not count the Native Americans. Most of these new people came on the Erie Canal.

The new towns needed names. Often, settlers used the same name as the place they left. People left **Utica**, New York and started Utica, Michigan! They left **Farmington**, New

Sometimes settlers reused the names of their old towns. Both Michigan and New York have a Farmington and a Livonia. They both have a Rochester, a Troy and a Utica!

York and began a new Farmington here. You can find a Livonia and a **Troy** in both states too! There is a **Rochester** here and also in New York. Check a map. All of these towns are not far from Detroit. Detroit was the first place those settlers visited.

On the Way to Michigan! (1834)

Meet a real boy who came to Michigan! His family left New York state in 1834. This is a true story. Here is what he says....

"Let me introduce myself. I am **William Nowlin**. I was born in the state of New York. I was 11 years of age, when the word Michigan first grated upon my ear. Father talked continually of Michigan, but Mother was very much opposed to leaving her home.

"I am the oldest of five children. I was very much opposed to coming to Michigan too. I did all that a boy of my age could do to prevent it. The thought of Indians, bears and wolves terrified me.

"My mother's health was very poor. Many of her friends said she would not live to get to Michigan. She thought she could not survive the journey. She said that if she did, her and her family would be killed by the Indians, perish in the wilderness or starve to death.

"We did leave, however, early in the spring of 1834. Our friends were weeping for they thought we were going "out of the world."

"We traveled about fifty miles that brought us to Utica, New York. There we boarded a canal boat and moved slowly night and day to invade the forests of Michigan.

"When it was pleasant, we spent part of the time on the top of the long, low cabin. One day mother left my little brother, then four years old, in the care of my oldest sister, Rachel. Little brother decided to have a rock in an easy chair, rocked over, and took a cold bath in the canal.

"Mother and I were in the cabin when we heard the cry, "Overboard!" We rushed on deck and the first thing we saw was a man swimming with something ahead of him. It proved to be my brother held by the strong arm of an English gentleman. That Englishman was our ideal hero for many years. His bravery and skill were unparalleled by anything we had seen. He had saved our brother from a watery grave. That brother is now the John Smith Nowlin of Dearborn.

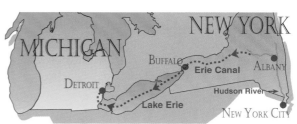

"When we arrived at Buffalo, the steamer *Michigan* was just ready for her second trip. We started the next morning.

"There was a great storm on the way across Lake Erie. People thought the ship was finished, but we arrived safely at Detroit. Mother did not die. No one was killed by Indians. Father bought some land near **Dearborn** and started a farm. It has been hard work, but we made it!"

All settlers like the Nowlins bought their land from the government. The government got the land from the tribes first. This is how that happened.....

Getting the Land

The United States government wanted the tribes to give up their land. The government made treaties with them to do this. The tribes were paid, but it was not that much. Some tribes kept the right to hunt and fish on the land. At least they would be able to feed themselves.

Often a tribe did not want to make a treaty. Still, they did not want trouble with the army, so they gave in. Between 1795 and 1842 the tribes gave up nearly all of Michigan.

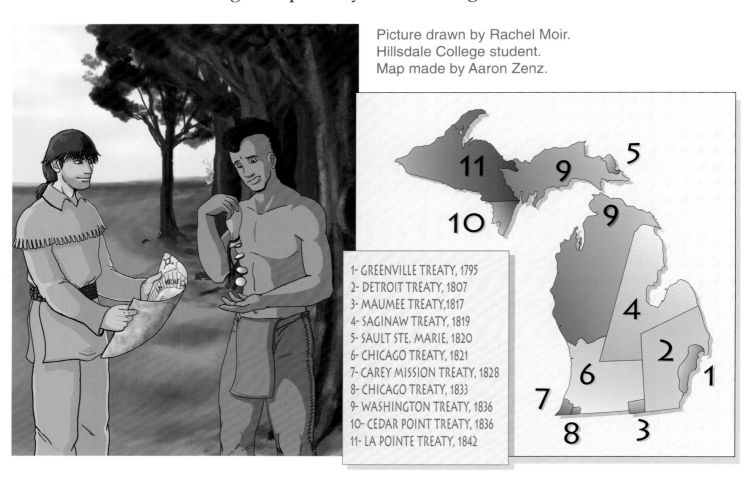

Picture drawn by Rachel Moir.
Hillsdale College student.
Map made by Aaron Zenz.

1- GREENVILLE TREATY, 1795
2- DETROIT TREATY, 1807
3- MAUMEE TREATY, 1817
4- SAGINAW TREATY, 1819
5- SAULT STE. MARIE, 1820
6- CHICAGO TREATY, 1821
7- CAREY MISSION TREATY, 1828
8- CHICAGO TREATY, 1833
9- WASHINGTON TREATY, 1836
10- CEDAR POINT TREATY, 1836
11- LA POINTE TREATY, 1842

Where Did They Go?

What happened to the tribes after the treaties? At first, life was much the same. There were few settlers. As more settlers came, they wanted the land. The settlers cut down trees. They built cabins. They planted crops. They started towns.

As farms and towns were built, the tribes had to move. At first, going a few miles was good enough. It was not long before people wanted the tribes far, far away. The U.S. government set up places for the tribes to live that most settlers would never want. These places were hundreds of miles away in the west.

By the 1840s, soldiers told most Native Americans they had to go. The southern part of Michigan was becoming crowded. New farmers wanted the land. Tribes like the Potawatomi had few places left to hunt. In spite of this, Michigan still has Native Americans today.

YEAR 1830-1840

Picture drawn by Jessica Bastian.
Hillsdale College student.

161

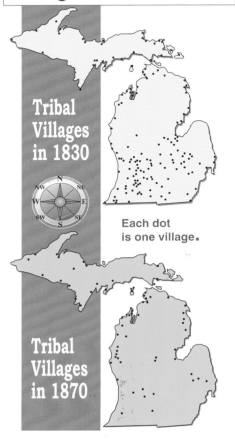

Changes Over 40 Years

Tribal Villages in 1830

Each dot is one village.

Tribal Villages in 1870

Look at the two maps. What do they tell you?

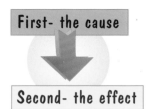

First- the cause

Second- the effect

The Michigan tribes often ended far from here. They were pushed west. Some were forced to **Kansas**. Others were forced to **Oklahoma**. Some went to other places. None of those places had many settlers then. They were in the middle of nowhere!

Mapping the Land

Settlers could not just build on any land they wanted. They needed to know exactly where each property was located. This was not simple with woods and trees everywhere. They needed to know where the land was on a map.

The government hired **surveyors** to look over the land. The surveyors traveled over the hills and through swamps. The surveyors used maps. They used compasses and chains to measure the land. The surveyors set up markers. It was hard work.

Buying the Land

Each settler looked for some good land where no one else lived. A source of clean water was important. This is why many towns were started along lakes or rivers.

Then the settler went to a **land office**. Using the surveyors' markers and maps, the settler described the land. The settler showed the land office the land he or she wished to buy. The price set for most land was $1.25 an acre. The money was paid and a **deed** given to the settler. *A deed is an official proof of ownership. It shows who owns each piece of land. It tells the borders of the land and where it can be found.*

The Tribes and the Settlers
• Compare Using the Land •

Tribes did this   **They both did this**   **Settlers did this**

shared the land
lived wherever
they wanted
hunted wherever
they wanted
moved wherever
they wanted

hunted
fished
put their homes
on it
planted crops

built roads
started farms
started towns
owned areas of land
cut down many trees

A Venn diagram

New Ways Are So Different

   This way of owning land was strange to the tribes. To them, land was there for everyone to use. The way the land was used was strange too. The Native Americans moved from place to place. They hunted and fished. Now farmers cut down the trees and planted crops. Fences were built. Roads and towns were built. It would be

Read more about what happened when the tribes were forced to leave. *Night of the Full Moon* by Gloria Whelan.

very hard for the two **cultures** to live together. What is a culture? *It is all the different ways a group lives. It includes their food, homes, jobs, beliefs, government and more.* The cultures of the tribes and the settlers were so different.

Too Many Trees- We Need Sunlight!

It is hard to realize how many trees were here then. They covered almost the whole state. Trees blocked the sunlight from the crops. The farmer's corn or wheat could not grow. If the trees stayed, the farmer could not. Thousands and thousands of trees were cut down.

A pioneer woman, with her little baby along for the ride, plows a field.

Starting a farm was very hard work.

Picture drawn by Jodi Olthouse. Hillsdale College student.

Next, farmers plowed the ground. There were no tractors. They used oxen or horses. The oxen pulled the plow. The farmer walked behind the plow to guide it. Land needs to be plowed before seeds are planted. There were many tree stumps and large rocks to move too. There was a great deal of hard work for each farm family. The women and men both worked hard. Sometimes they had trouble with bears or wolves.

Pioneer farmers had to make or grow almost all the things they needed. There might not be a store or town for miles. It was a treat when a new neighbor moved close by.

Gristmills, Rivers and New Towns

It is hard to bake without flour. Farmers took their corn and wheat to a **gristmill**. This mill ground the grain and made flour. Most gristmills were powered by water. They were often built along a river.

Flowing water turns the wheel. The wheel turns the grindstone inside the mill.

Water was important to a new town. It was used for power and drinking. New towns often started along a river. A gristmill might be the town's first building. Is your city on a river or lake? Maybe it once had a mill pond for a grist-mill.

Picture drawn by Emily Walsh. Hillsdale College student.

Here is the inside of the gristmill. The water power turns a round stone. That stone goes around against another round stone. The grain goes between the stones. This grinds the corn or wheat to make flour. This is a cutaway drawing. It shows what happens on the inside.

Think About It. Write About It!

1. Why did settlers want to come to Michigan? What pulled them here? What pushed them from where they were?

2. Why didn't more settlers come until the 1830s?

3. Look at a map. Where is the Erie Canal? Explain to a friend how to find it.

4. Look at the Venn Diagram. Compare the differences in the way the tribes and settlers used the land.

Think Like an Historian

What were the effects of the pioneers moving to Michigan? (The pioneers coming were the cause, so what were the effects?)

Brain Stretchers

Find out which treaty was made for the land that includes your town. Use the Internet to find out what was in this treaty.

Take a Stand!

Think about the treaties made with Michigan's tribes. Be a settler or a Native American. Decide if any core democratic values were forgotten in the process. Give reasons to support your position. Go to the end of this book for a list of the core democratic values.

Chapter 4 Lesson 5

Ideas To Explore
becoming a state
the Toledo War (toe lee doe)

People To Meet
Lewis Cass
Stevens T. Mason

Places To Discover
capitol building. Remember it has an "o" which is round like the dome of the building. (The capital city is spelled with an "al")
Marshall, MI
Northwest Territory (tair uh tor ee)

Words to Welcome
census (sen sus)
Congress (kon gres)
encouraged (in kur aged)
legislature (lej es lay tur)
national government
slaves (slayvs)
wolverine (wool ver een)

Michigan
Social
Studies
GLCEs
3H3.0.3
3H3.0.8
3H3.0.9
3H3.0.10

Becoming a State!

Think about this while you read.
What did a law called the Northwest Ordinance do for Michigan?

Just a Wilderness in the Northwest

Let's go back to the late 1700s. Michigan was still not a state. It was a land of trees, bears and wolves. Most of the people were Native Americans. Only a few settlers had arrived.

At that time there was a lot of extra land in the United States. **Congress** was dividing this land. It was making territories out of it. Remember, a territory is land that is a part of the United States, but not yet a state. Michigan was made a part of the **Northwest Territory**. That was done in 1787.

The Northwest Territory had much land. Later, it was divided into several states. Ohio and

Illinois came from that land. Indiana, Michigan and Wisconsin also came from that land. All of these states were once in the Northwest Territory.

NW

Why did they use the name Northwest Territory? At that time our nation was smaller. This land was in the northwest corner of the country.

An Important Law

Next, Congress formed the Northwest Territory. Then it wrote basic rules for the territory. This law told what to do to **become a state**. Here is what it said.

Step 1.

At first, a territory did not choose its leaders. Its people could not vote. The President of the United States picked four leaders. They were a governor and three judges.

Step 2.

To reach this step, there must be 5,000 free adult men. (Women, Indians and **slaves** did not count. That is the way it was at that time.) *Now they could vote for a group of lawmakers. This is called a* **legislature**. The governor approves all laws. The governor and judges are still named by the President.

Step 3.

The key is 60,000 people. Once 60,000 people lived there, things could move ahead. (Indians and slaves still did not count.) Then Congress votes to decide if the territory can become a state. If Congress says yes, it will be equal to all the other states.

Who Has the Power?

With this law, who has the power? It does not mention women. It says free adult men. Did you know women could not vote? That did not happen until over 130 years later. Slaves could not vote. The President said who was in charge. The President might not be in touch with events here. The wrong people might be put in charge. The people here wanted to become a state as soon as possible. They wanted to have their own say.

Some Key Points

Was this a bad law? No. It had good points. Here are some other things it said:

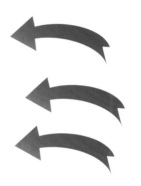

Key Points

1.   No new slaves could be brought here. (People who already had slaves could keep them.)
2.   Indians must be treated fairly. No land could be taken from them unless they agreed.
3.   Starting schools was **encouraged.** The lawmakers felt good schools were important.

The old school at Douglas, Michigan

They had three reasons in mind. Schools can help young people know about religion. They can help teach about what is right and wrong. They can give students useful knowledge.

Even with this law, the tribes did not get good deals for their land. Laws cannot make people do the right thing. It is what people have in their hearts that really counts.

Leaders for Our Territory

Our territory needed a leader. The President chose General Hull for the first governor. Remember, he had problems in the War of 1812 and left. Two others led our territory for a while. Then **Lewis Cass** was given the job. This was in 1813.

Lewis Cass

Picture from Archives of Michigan 02825

Governor Cass worked hard to help Michigan grow. He traveled and explored the land. He made treaties with the tribes. He told people why they should bring their families here. He wrote the state motto. He designed the state seal. Cass City and Cassopolis were named for him. A county and a river also have his name. Lewis Cass kept this job for 16 years.

YEAR 1813

Who Was Lewis Cass?

Lewis Cass was born in 1782. He did not live here then. His family was in New Hampshire. Like many others, he moved west. Moving west was the thing to do. That was where the excitement was. His father was given land in Ohio. This was a reward for fighting in the War for Independence in 1776.

He moved to Ohio with his father. Lewis helped his family cut down trees and start a farm. He grew and studied hard. Lewis wanted to be a lawyer. By 1803 he had set up his own law office. That same year Ohio became a state. Later, the young Cass won an election. He was voted into the Ohio legislature. Since Ohio was a state, it could vote for its leaders.

Next, Lewis Cass joined the army. He fought in the War of 1812. He was at Detroit with General Hull. Lewis Cass was in the newspapers when he won a battle against the British. Michigan was lucky to have him move from Ohio. In 1831 he was given a job with the **national government**. He left for Washington, D.C. Later, he served Michigan as a U.S. Senator. He even ran for President in the 1840s.

The places Lewis Cass lived.

YEAR 1831

173

Stevens T. Mason

Picture from
the Archives of
Michigan 03546

A Young New Leader

A fellow named John Mason came to
Michigan to work with Governor Cass.
Mr. Mason brought his son with him. His
son's name was **Stevens T. Mason**. He
often helped his father. When Cass was
away, John Mason was in charge.

John Mason was bored. He wanted
more excitement. He was going to Texas!
Lewis Cass and the Masons met with
President Jackson. Mr. Mason asked if his
son could take his job. President Jackson
liked the young man. He agreed. That
was how Stevens T. Mason got his start.
He became **secretary** for the Michigan
Territory. He was only 19 then. He was
not even old enough to vote!

Now there was a surprise. The young man
learned Lewis Cass was staying in Washington.
Cass was going to work for the national government. Stevens T. Mason would be alone in
Michigan. He would be in charge!

Would you
be scared?

The Boy Is In Charge?

Stevens T. Mason left for Detroit. There he
had a second surprise. He was met by a mob! A
crowd of 2,000 gathered in Detroit. Many people
were upset. How could the President let a young
person be in charge? They spoke out against

him. This could be like your mom or dad leaving your older brother or sister in charge. You might think he or she was too young. Would you be upset?

Stevens told everyone he would listen to the advice of older people. He was able to convince the crowd. Still, he was given the nickname "Boy Governor." In the next few years he would have lots to do.

Hey, We Are Ready!

Ohio became a state in 1803. Indiana became a state in 1816. Illinois became a state in 1818. Michigan was still just a territory. Boatloads of people came to Michigan once the Erie Canal opened. By 1834, we had over 60,000 people. That was enough to become a state! Stevens T. Mason asked the Congress in Washington, D.C., to vote on it. Let Michigan become a state. Congress said, "Not so fast."

What was the problem? Didn't Congress want to start new states? Here is the story. Michigan was arguing with Ohio. We were arguing over the land where Toledo is now. The boundary showed it was in Michigan. The state of Ohio did not agree.

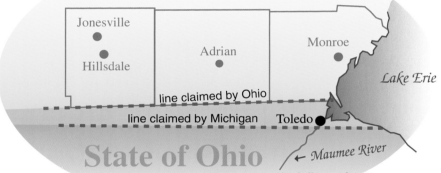

Territory of Michigan

Jonesville

Hillsdale

Adrian

Monroe

Lake Erie

line claimed by Ohio

line claimed by Michigan Toledo

State of Ohio ← Maumee River

Based on the S. Augustus Mitchell map of 1834

War With Ohio? You Must Be Kidding!

Neighbors may argue over where to put a fence. If they do, they may get upset. In the early 1830s, Michigan and Ohio were upset. Each state wanted a bit more land. They both wanted Toledo. People felt it would grow to be an important city.

Our soldiers marched to Toledo. They said, "We will keep Toledo for Michigan!" Some people expected a war to start. They expected to hear the boom of cannons. There were no battles. No one was killed.

Soldiers from Michigan march to Ohio.
Picture drawn by George Rasmussen.

There were some fist fights and shouting. The people from Ohio yelled, "You are nasty **wolverines**! You want to come and steal our land." This time of bad feelings with Ohio was known as the **Toledo War**.

Michigan men chased Ohio men away from the "Toledo Strip."

Wolverines are wild animals. They are known for their bad tempers and bad smell. They often stole food from cabins. The people from Ohio felt we were stealing their land.

Michigan's people may still be called wolverines, but now we are proud of this nickname.

A Trade!

Now President Jackson was upset. He said this is foolishness. It must stop! States should not fight each other. He said there should be a trade. Ohio will get Toledo and the land around it. Michigan will get the western

A wolverine. Picture drawn by George Rasmussen.

Before the Toledo War, the western part of the Upper Peninsula was not a part of Michigan!

Upper Peninsula. That land was not a part of Michigan.

Some Michiganians did not think the trade was a good idea. They thought the Upper Peninsula was too far away. They thought it was a frozen wasteland. What good was it? Well, they soon found out. It had many trees for lumber, much copper and iron too. It was a very good trade!

Congress voted. We did become a state. That was in 1837. Stevens T. Mason was the first state governor. That is the story of how Michigan became a state. It is also the story of how Toledo, Ohio, might have been Toledo, Michigan.

How Michigan Grew...

Each year more people moved here. The Erie Canal made it easier to reach Michigan. The cheap land pulled them to our state. The tribes gave up their land by treaties. As the number of settlers went up, the number of Native Americans fell. The people here were counted several times. The government took a **census** to do this. *A census is an official count of the people living in a place.*

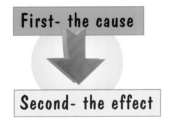

First- the cause

Second- the effect

What was the effect of the Toledo War?

1837

What is a census?

Year	People	(does not include Native Americans)
1773	1,550	more or less (most of these people lived in Detroit)
1810	5,000	more or less
1820	8,896	really slightly less- includes extra land
1830	31,639	really slightly less- includes extra land
1834	87,278	special census (1,422 lived in the U.P.)
1837	174,543	special census
1840	212,267	U.S census

Between 1830 and 1840 Michigan grew faster than any other state or territory!

Census information can be a primary source. It tells how many people lived here at different times.

Michigan's Capital

When we were a territory, the capital was Detroit. Detroit stayed the capital until 1847. Then some people felt it should be nearer the middle of the state. When people heard this, everyone wanted it to be their town! The people of **Marshall** even built a new house for the governor!

The legislature voted, but could not decide. No one voted for someone else's town. Finally, someone said, "Make it Lansing." Lansing? Where is that? There were only a few cabins in Lansing then.

LANSING

The first capitol building in Detroit.

The good thing about Lansing was its location. It was more in the middle of the state. The next time they voted everyone was shocked. Lansing won and the capital was moved in 1848. Today, Lansing is a large city. The capital is still there. The **capitol building** you see now was built in 1879.

Our capitol building in Lansing today.

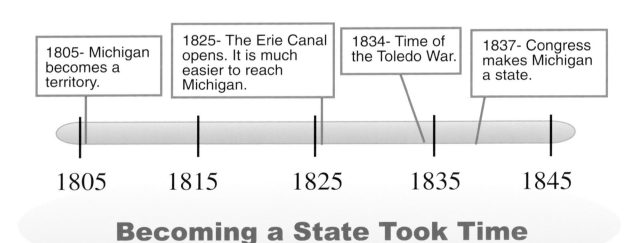

1805- Michigan becomes a territory.

1825- The Erie Canal opens. It is much easier to reach Michigan.

1834- Time of the Toledo War.

1837- Congress makes Michigan a state.

1805   1815   1825   1835   1845

Becoming a State Took Time

Here are some key events.

Think About It. Write About It!

1. How did Lewis Cass help Michigan?

2. Who was Stevens T. Mason? How did he help Michigan?

3. What argument kept Michigan from becoming a state for a while? When did we become a state?

4. How did the rest of the Upper Peninsula become a part of Michigan?

5. Write the steps the early settlers had to follow to become a state.

6. What was said about Michigan's growth from 1830 to 1840?

7. What reason was given to make Lansing our state capital?

Make a Chart Today

Make a chart. Show how the population of Michigan grew. Use the years 1830 to 1840.

Words In Action!

Write a paragraph. Focus on "cause and effect." How does the Toledo War connect with the Upper Peninsula?

Read points 1 and 2 from the Northwest Ordinance. They deal with slaves and Indians. Check the list of core democratic values at the back of the book. Write a paragraph about points 1 and 2. Include three core democratic values to support what you say.

Michigan Grows Up

Chapter 5 Lesson 1

Ideas To Explore

How natural resources helped the state grow.

Michigan's economy- (ee kon uh mee) It includes businesses, stores and factories. It includes what those places make and sell. It includes workers and what they earn. It includes consumers and what they buy. It is everything that is a part of producing and consuming products and services.

Modify the environment: people changing their surroundings to meet their wants and needs.

Foods to Feast On
apple butter
cider

People To Meet
farmers
pioneers - the settlers. The first people, after the Native Americans, to come to a place and make it their home.

Places To Discover
the Henry Ford- Dearborn, MI

Words to Welcome
barn raising- neighbors get together to build a new barn
churned- cream mixed rapidly so the butter comes to the top
hay- a grass- a food for farm animals.
natural resource- something found in nature that is used to meet people's needs. Soil, trees, metals or water are examples.
wool - the hairy coat from sheep.

Michigan
Social
Studies
GLCEs
3H3.0.3
3H3.0.5
3G4.0.2
3G5.0.1
3G5.0.2
3E1.0.1
3E1.0.3
4H3.0.1

Good Dirt Helped Michigan Grow as a State

Think about this question while you read.
How did the soil help Michigan grow?

Cheap Land Pulls People Here

When did this take place? The number of farms really began to increase in the 1830s. Each year more people moved to Michigan. They used new ways, like the Erie Canal, to get here. They left New York and other states in the East. They left because land was scarce there. Where it was scarce, it cost a lot to buy. Land in Michigan cost about $1.25 an acre. In those days, farms often had 40 to 80 acres.

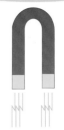

Like a magnet, cheap land pulled people to Michigan.

Building a cabin. How are these men modifying the environment?

Picture by Carly Gosine. Hillsdale College student.

YEAR 1830s

183

Almost all the people lived and worked on farms. Farming was how people fed their families. You cannot have a farm without land. Southern Michigan had good land. It was cheap too! It was not scarce here. Scarcity pushed **farmers** from New York and pulled them to Michigan. If you do not remember what scarcity means, find it in the glossary at the back of this book. Farmers needed good soil to grow crops. Dirt is also called soil. The soil helped people meet their need for food. The soil was a valuable **natural resource** for our state.

What Did They Grow and Raise?

Michigan farmers grew corn, oats and wheat. Often they planted potatoes too. Wheat was taken to a gristmill. There it was ground into flour. Families used the flour to make bread, cakes and cookies. Yummy! Often farms had apple trees. Apples were used to make **apple butter**. *Apple butter is a sweet like jam to spread on bread or toast.* Apples were also used to make pies and **cider**. Some people planted strawberries. The berries were made into jam. It is not possible to grow food without good soil.

Almost every farm had at least one cow. Maybe she was named Bessie. The cows gave milk. Butter and cheese were made from the milk. We cannot forget chickens. Farmers kept chickens for their eggs.

Farmers grew **hay**. They cut the hay and put it big stacks. It went into barns to feed the animals in the winter.

Most farms had some pigs or hogs too. The pigs provided meat. **Pioneers** wanted pigs around for another reason. In those times Michigan had many more snakes than today. Some areas had many rattlesnakes. Pigs would kill the snakes. Look carefully at a map. See if you can find a place named Hog Island. At some time it may have had lots of snakes. People put hogs on the islands to get rid of the snakes!

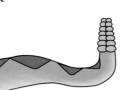

Sheep gave their **wool** to help make clothes and blankets. Everyone helped to shear the sheep. This means they cut off the wool. It was like giving them a haircut. The sheep did not mind. It made them cooler.

Hard Work On the Farms
Pioneer farming was not an easy life. This was long ago. It was in the 1830s, 1840s and

The Baker Family on their farm in Dansville, Michigan. Picture from Janice McConnell.

1850s. There were no tractors. There was no electricity. Horses provided the power. Maybe you have heard the word horsepower! That is where it started.

Farm families had many children. The young ones started to help as soon as they could. Girls fed the chickens and gathered eggs. They **churned** the **cream** to make butter. Maybe they helped to make cheese too. The boys helped plow the fields and plant the seeds. They cut the hay and stacked it in the barn. They helped put horseshoes on the horses. Everyone worked from the time the sun came up until it went down.

When it was time to build a new barn. Everyone helped. Neighbors came too. Building a barn was more work than one family could do alone. People depended on neighbors to help them. When the barn was done, everyone had a big meal. A **barn raising** was like a party, along with much work.

A girl churning cream to make butter.

Farming Becomes Big Business

By the 1830s, the fur trade was not very important. Farming replaced it as a big business. Farmers sold their crops. The food was shipped to markets near and far. At first the crops went by road and by ship. Later, they went by train. They went to big cities like Chicago and New York.

A barn raising.

Between 1830 and about 1900, farming was Michigan's largest business. More people worked in it than in any other business. Farming was an important part of our **economy**.

How Farms Changed Michigan

Farming changed the way Michigan looked. The farmers **modified the environment**. Many trees were cut down. Forests disappeared. Swamps were drained and turned into farm-land. Fences were built to keep in the animals. Roads were built to go to the farms. Towns were started to supply goods to the farmers. Many towns had gristmills to make flour. They had stores to sell cloth, nails, fence wire and horse-

To start farms, the trees had to go! Picture by Theresa Deeter.

shoes. Towns had farm markets to sell the ham, cheese and other foods.

Where You Can See a Pioneer Farm

You can still see what it was like to live on a farm. There are places that have farms like in days long ago. They are like living museums. You may see horses pulling wagons or plows. You may see the sheep getting their "haircuts." One of these old farms is at The Henry Ford in Dearborn.

Sheep being sheared. See all the wool on the ground? Later, the wool is made into yarn.

A woman taking care of the garden on a pioneer farm. Photo by the author.

Think About It and Write About It!

1. Name three animals raised on pioneer farms.

2. Think like a historian. *Who* were these pioneer farmers? *What* crops did they grow here? *When* did the number of farms in Michigan really begin to grow? *Where* did farmers find the best soil to start their new farms?

3. Is soil a natural resource? Explain your answer.

4. How did early pioneer farms change or modify Michigan's environment?

5. Name three things that are a part of Michigan's economy.

Think Like a Geographer

Use a map. Mark the movement of pioneer farmers to Michigan. Show how they came from states like New York. Mark the movement of farm crops from Michigan to big cities like New York and Chicago.

GEOGRAPHY

Words In Action!

How did good dirt help Michigan grow as a state?

Chapter 5 Lesson 2

Ideas To Explore ————————————————

Conservation (kon ser va shun): Not wasting
    natural resources. Leaving some to use later.
Negative consequences (kon see quin siss):
    These are the bad things that happen
    because of an event or decision.

People To Meet ——————————————————

lumberjacks (lum ber jaks)
Paul Bunyan
shanty boys (shan tee) This is another name for
    the loggers or lumberjacks. They lived in
    rough cabins called shanties.

Places To Discover ————————————————

Alpena (AL-PEE-na)
Bay City
Hartwick Pines State Park- A park that still has
    some of the really tall pine trees.
Maine - A state along the Atlantic Ocean.
Traverse City (trav erss)

Michigan
Social
Studies
GLCEs

3H3.0.3
3H3.0.5
3G4.0.2
3G5.0.1
3G5.0.2
3E1.0.1
3E1.0.3
4H3.0.1
4H3.0.3
4H3.0.8

Rivers to Float Down

Muskegon River,   Saginaw River

Words to Welcome

"big wheels" - large wheels used to move logs
log jam - when many logs pile up in a river and
    other logs cannot get past them.
sawmill - a place where big saws cut logs into
    boards.

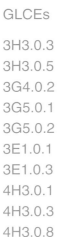

Trees Help Michigan Grow as a State

Think about these questions while you read. **What did Michigan gain from the way it used its trees? What did Michigan lose from the way it used its trees?**

Three shanty boys or lumberjacks cut down trees

Photo from Archives of Michigan 02236

Down Go the Tall Trees

"Timberrr!" shouts the man with the saw. The big tree slowly falls to the ground. It hits with a crash. Men scurry around. They cut off limbs and saw the trunk into logs. Smell that fresh sawdust!

The lumber days were exciting times in Michigan. There were some interesting people working the woods. They had nicknames like Cedar Root Charley and Slabwood Johnson. They were tough and they worked hard.

YEAR
1870s-
1890s

Once Wasted- Now Valuable

The first farmers got rid of trees just to plant crops. At that time there were lots of trees and few people here. There were many more trees than they could use. Many were cut and burned. They were wasted. The *supply of trees was much greater than the demand*. At that time, trees were not worth very much.

This big pine tree was about 150 feet tall. Photo from author's collection.

As our state grew, demand grew too. People built new homes in fast-growing cities. These were cities like Detroit and Grand Rapids. Lumber was also shipped from Michigan to cities like Chicago. Everyone needed more wood. Demand increased. The lumber now sold for more money.

Earlier, **Maine** had been a leading state for lumber. Now it's supply of trees was almost gone. Michigan had plenty of trees.

Where the Best Trees Were

The best tree for lumber was the White Pine- our state tree! Pines grow best in the northern part of the

Lower Peninsula and in the Upper Peninsula. About two-thirds of Michigan was covered by tall pine trees. Some of them reached over 100 feet toward the sky. The best trees could be 200 feet tall! They could be five to seven feet across. These tall trees had been growing for 300 years or more!

The Workers

The trees were cut with axes and hand saws. The saws were big and they needed two men. The men who did all the cutting and chopping were called **lumberjacks** or loggers. All the men lived in the lumber camp while they worked.

Once more, a natural resource brought jobs. People moved to Michigan from other countries. Some were from Sweden. Some were from

Finland. Some were born in Norway or Canada. The logging business needed human resources. It needed many workers.

Often a Winter Job

At first, loggers worked in the winter. It was easier to move the big logs over the ice and snow. The logs were put on sleds. Horses or oxen pulled the sleds. Still, it was too far to pull the logs all the way to the **sawmill**. The **shanty boys** often used rivers to carry the logs. How could they do that?

Rivers Move the Logs

Logs float; so rivers were perfect. The shanty boys dragged the logs to a river. The logs were stacked up along the bank. The stack grew each day until spring. After the ice melted, the rivers were full of water.

All at once, the logs were pushed into the river. Away they went! The men went along with them. Some men balanced on logs as they floated along. These daring men kept the logs from piling up into a **log jam**. If a log jam started, the whole river would fill for miles with logs. Rivers were an important way to move the logs.

Inside a sawmill. See the huge saw blade cut the logs into boards.

Photo from the Archives of Michigan.

In 1883 there was a huge log jam on the Grand River, right in the center of Grand Rapids, MI.

Photo from Archives of Michigan 07006

Towns Start Along the Rivers

Lumber camps started along the rivers. The first lumber region was on the **Saginaw River**. Once, there were 112 sawmills between Saginaw and **Bay City**! The other big lumber region was along the **Muskegon River**. Logging helped these regions grow and grow. Cities and towns grew too.

As the years passed, the loggers moved north. They went into the Upper Peninsula. New towns started in this area because of lumber. The towns began as people came to cut the trees. They also worked in sawmills. **Alpena** started because of lumber. Manistee did also. Menominee and **Traverse City** are two more examples.

The Life of a Lumberjack

The day began in the cold and dark. It was before the sun was up. The cook and the cook's helpers started first. Sometimes the cook was a woman. At other times a man did the cooking. It was a big job to make breakfast. Bread, biscuits, cookies, and pies were put into the oven. Doughnuts were fried. Pancakes were made. Gallons of coffee and tea were brewed. All of this cooking was done on a huge wood-burning stove.

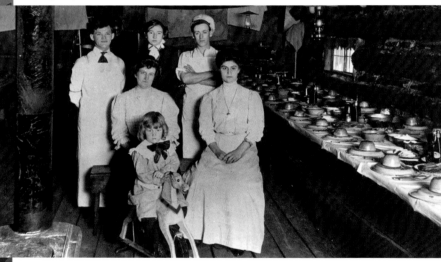

Photo from the Clarke Historical Library, Central Michigan University.

Soon the lumberjacks got up. They ate a huge breakfast. Talking was always forbidden while eating. It was an old loggers' custom.

They worked hard all day. Often they would not come back to the camp until dark. They worked six days each week. Their pay was about one dollar a day! Would you do all of that work for one dollar? Remember, this was a long time ago. It was a time when everything cost less.

Paul Bunyan and Tall Tales

During their day off, the shanty boys told stories. These were often stories they had made up and they called them "tall tales." One of their favorite tall tales was about **Paul Bunyan**. Some of the stories were hard to believe, but that just made them better. They might say Paul Bunyan stood 12 feet, 11 inches without his socks! They did call them *tall* tales!

Did you know Paul Bunyan had a pet ox? He called the ox Babe. Babe was huge and she was colored blue! Paul found Babe frozen in the ice of Lake Superior. Babe had turned blue from the cold!

Paul Bunyan was a make-believe lumberjack. He was supposed to be a huge man. He did many things that were hard to believe! Picture drawn by Theresa Deeter.

The Trees Fall Faster with New Technology

Everyone thought Michigan's trees would last forever! Over the years, the loggers used new ways to cut the trees faster. They built better equipment to move the logs.

Compare the size of the man and the size of the "big wheels."

A wagon maker from Manistee invented **big wheels**. These were really BIG wheels! They might be ten feet high! Now it was easier for horses or oxen to pull the logs. They moved them in the winter and in the summer.

Someone else thought of using small trains. The little trains took the logs to the sawmills. New saws were made for the sawmills. The logs were cut into boards faster than ever. More trees were cut than ever before. The trees did NOT last forever. Instead, most were cut in about 70 years.

How Much Was Cut?

This was a big business until about 1900. How much wood came from Michigan? In those years a huge number of trees were cut. There was more than enough wood cut to build a floor over the entire state! About ten million families lived in the United States then. It was said our state cut enough wood to build a house for each family in the country!

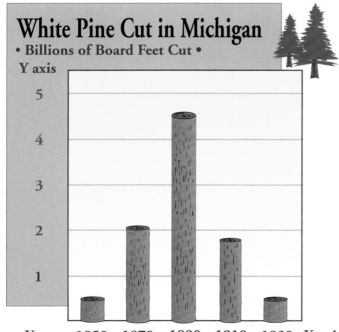

White Pine Cut in Michigan
• Billions of Board Feet Cut •
Y axis
5
4
3
2
1
Years • 1850 1870 1890 1910 1930 X axis

This shows the land after the loggers were done. The wind and rain washed away all the soil. The land was no longer good for anything. Photo from Archives of Michigan 08493.

First- the cause

Second- the effect

Think about cause and effect in the picture on the left.

Oops- They Forgot to Plant More!

Today we do not see many very tall trees in our state. The loggers did not think about planting more. There was very little **conservation**. *They did not think about saving any for tomorrow. That is what conservation means.* There was much waste by the loggers. The work was done with little thought for the future. They cut all the trees for quick money.

After the trees were gone, much of the land was ruined for any other use. The birds and animals had no place to live. The rain washed the soil away. Farmers could not grow much food on it. In the 1930s, the government began to plant new trees.

It took nature a long time to grow a state full of trees! It will take a long time for the giant trees to grow back. We will all have to help them grow. This means everyone should be careful in the woods. We should not cut down young trees. We should not leave campfires burning. Forest fires can kill many of the trees!

The Last Giants

There are only a few places with tall white pines left. One is at **Hartwick Pines**. This is a state park near Grayling. Most people will never see a 200-foot pine tree unless they visit the park. This is one of the **negative consequences** of logging. More trees have been planted, but they are not very big yet.

There is still logging. It is not as big a business as it was once, but it is still an important business. Now, most trees cut in Michigan are made into paper. Today, loggers do plant new trees to replace the ones they cut down.

A factory where paper is made in Escanaba.

Loading logs in Newberry.
Photos by the author.

Think About It and Write About It!

1. At one time, people burned trees just to get rid of them. What change caused the trees to become valuable?

2. What kind of tree was used the most during our lumber days?

3. Why were the rivers important to early lumbering?

4. Did the trees last as long as people first thought they would? What things changed?

5. What was a negative consequence of using our lumber resources?

Words In Action

Explain how loggers modified Michigan's environment?

Take A Stand!

You are living in the 1800s. Write a letter to a lawmaker in Lansing. Take a stand. Should Michigan have a law making loggers plant one tree for each one they cut down? Give reasons to support your stand. Use any facts or data from this chapter that supports your stand.

Brain Stretcher

Do some research. How are people in Michigan working to protect our forests today?

Chapter 5 Lesson 3

Ideas To Explore

How did nature provide our minerals?

incentive - An incentive is a reward for doing something. Your dad may give you an incentive to do your homework on time.

lock- This is a way to raise and lower ships. Locks and canals are often used together.

People To Meet

Douglass Houghton (HO tun)

William Burt

Places To Discover

Finland

Keweenaw Peninsula (KEY wa naw)

Norway (nor way)

Soo Locks

Sweden (swee din)

Words to Welcome

coal

limestone- a mostly white soft stone from very old sea shells.

minerals- natural resources from under the ground. Copper, gold, iron ore, limestone and salt are minerals.

ore (or) - a rock with some metal in it.

stock- a paper showing part ownership in a company.

ton- 2,000 pounds

Michigan
Social
Studies
GLCEs

3H3.0.2
3H3.0.3
3H3.0.5
3H3.0.10
3G4.0.2
3G5.0.1
3E1.0.1
3E1.0.2
3E1.0.3
3E1.0.4
4H3.0.1
4H3.0.3

Underground Resources Help Michigan Grow as a State

Think About this question while you read.
How did resources like copper, iron and limestone help our state grow?

You have just learned about soil and trees. Now look at some resources from under the ground. After Michigan became a state, other businesses started to grow. They were built around natural resources too.

What Is Under Our Feet?

Few people think about what is under where they walk. There are some valuable **minerals** under Michigan. We have copper, iron and salt. The iron is used to make steel. Oil and natural gas are there too. The oil is made into gasoline for our cars. **Limestone** also comes from under the ground. It is used to make cement. All of these things are gifts from nature.

Why do we have salt and limestone? They came from oceans. How is that possible? A very long time ago oceans covered much of the Lower Peninsula. When the oceans dried up, they left minerals behind. Salt and limestone are two examples. The limestone came from all the sea shells left behind. All oceans have salt in them.

A piece of salt as it comes from under the ground.

Salt

Most of the Lower Peninsula has thick layers of salt underground. In some places salt was mined. Detroit even has a salt mine. The tunnels of that mine are still under the city! Some salt was cleaned and used for table salt. You might have eaten a little bit of Michigan on your dinner! We also use some to melt ice on our roads.

Limestone

There are places in Michigan with much limestone. It can be in thick layers. We have some big limestone pits. One is near Alpena. The white limestone was once the shells of sea creatures. Over much time, the shells changed into limestone. Ships move the limestone to where it is needed. Limestone is used to make cement. Sometimes limestone is cut into blocks to build buildings. It is also ground up and spread on farmer's fields to help the crops grow.

Much limestone comes from around Rogers City. It is taken to market on ships. Picture drawn by George Rasmussen.

Coal and Oil From Really Old Plants

Many plants grew along the shore of the ancient sea. They died and fell to the ground. Great amounts piled up and decomposed. The plants became a dark muck. Over a very long time, this plant muck became coal. Some Michigan coal was once mined near Jackson and Lansing. The same thing happened to plants growing in the old sea. Those plants became oil.

A piece of coal.

Resources scarce in one place, bring jobs to places that can supply them.

Jobs and Natural Resources Go Together

Natural resources are used to make things people need and want. The resources help provide jobs. Where people live and work often depends on the natural resources nearby.

A Useful Metal– Copper

Copper is a very useful metal. It is not quite like any other. When it is clean and shiny, it has its own color. You see copper when you look at a penny. It conducts electricity and heat very well. In the 1800s it was used to make pots and pans. It went into brass buttons and cannons. Today it is found in wire, computers, televisions and electric motors. The demand for copper is always great.

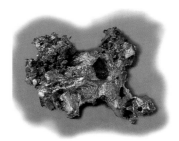

The Tribes Were the First Miners

Long before written history, some tribes used copper. They were the first miners here. They dug the copper on Isle Royale. Isle Royale is a large island. It is far north in Lake Superior. They also dug it on the **Keweenaw Peninsula**. This is a part of the Upper Peninsula. You can find it easily on a map. It goes way out into Lake Superior. You can still see their small pits in the ground.

The copper was used for spear points and arrowheads. Sometimes it was traded to other tribes. Pieces of Michigan copper are found buried at old Indian villages far from our state. After a long time, the tribes stopped mining copper. We do not know why they stopped. Maybe the copper near the surface was gone. Maybe they changed their beliefs about copper.

Search and Discover

In the 1830s, the state government wanted to learn about the land. The state was new. The government wondered what could be useful. It wanted to find the valuable things nature provided. The state government hired **Douglass Houghton** to find them. He traveled across Michigan looking for minerals like copper. He wrote reports about what he found and where it was.

Douglass Houghton

Picture from Archives of Michigan 02837

The state government felt finding natural resources would benefit everyone. Doing this would be for the common good. Working on projects like this is one of the services state government can do. We could not do it by ourselves.

The Great Copper Rush

Many people were interested in Mr. Houghton's reports. The reports said there was copper on the Keweenaw Peninsula.

People were excited. They wanted to get rich quick! They grabbed shovels and wheelbarrows. They got their hats and coats. They got on ships and sailed onto the Great Lakes. It was a Michigan copper rush! That was in 1843.

Copper was scarce in other places.

People thought the copper was just lying on the ground. They did not know anything about mining. They believed they could pick up big pieces. They felt they could make a lot of money. It was not that easy. These miners were swatting black flies in the summer. In the winter it was cold, cold, cold. Everything was frozen. All supplies had to come by ship. No roads reached that part of our state then.

The building in the back is the top of a copper mine. It goes down over 5,000 feet!

Dig Down, Down, Down

Most of the copper is far underground. It was too much work for one person. Even a dozen could not do it. Hundreds of hard workers were needed for each mine!

207

A mining stock. People who buy stocks take risks.

Some miners (human resources) from about 1895. Do you see what they use for light while they work?

The miners needed cash to buy equipment. They started companies. They sold **stock** in the companies to raise money. Each person who bought the stock owned a part of the company.

They thought like entrepreneurs. They were willing to take big risks to mine copper. They might make money or they might not. If they did not find copper, they could lose all their money.

The miners needed capital resources. This is equipment used in the mine. They needed shovels and carts to move the metal. They needed hammers to break the rock. They needed machines to pull the metal up from the deep mines. They needed machines to carry the workers up and down. They also needed human resources. These were the men and boys working in the mines.

Over time, some mines went down almost two miles! Those were very deep holes! Digging and working such a mine was expensive. Once they got it up to the top, the copper had to go by ship to Detroit. That was a long trip and the ships sailed over five hundred miles.

Nature's "Roadblock" Brings the Soo Locks

The trip was not easy. There was a big problem. At Sault Ste. Marie there were swift rapids. This is where Lake Superior and Lake

Huron meet. Lake Superior is about 20 feet higher than Lake Huron. A huge amount of water pours out of Lake Superior. Big ships were wrecked if they tried to go between the two lakes! The cargo had to be taken off the ships in one lake and loaded onto ships in the other lake. The unloading and reloading was hard work. It was expensive work. It was slow work. That copper was heavy!

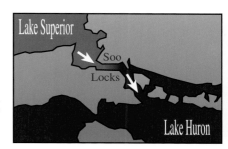

A way was needed to help ships go between the two big lakes. There were some people who thought like entrepreneurs. They had a big idea. Entrepreneurs often have big, new ideas. Some big, new ideas work and some do not. They thought about building a canal between the lakes.

Remember, a canal is a man-made river. They would have **locks** in the canal. These locks would raise and lower the ships.

This river connects Lake Superior and Lake Huron. The water is too fast for big ships. The Soo Locks go around the rapids.

Photo from the Library of Congress.

An Incentive to Build the Locks

Our nation's government wanted the canal and locks too. Well, some people did. Others felt Michigan was just a wilderness. Still, the nation's government offered an **incentive** to do this job. *An*

209

An Incentive

incentive is a reward or bonus for doing a certain action. Your mom says she will give you $5.00 if you are not late for the school bus this month. The $5.00 is an incentive. The government felt the canal and locks would benefit everyone. Building it would also be for the common good. This is another service government can do for us.

Land for the Locks

The government offered land as an incentive. The entrepreneurs would get a large amount of land (750,000 acres). They would only get it if the job was done by a certain time. The government offered land because they had plenty of it. The government did not offer money. In those days it did not have much money.

In 1855 the canal was finished. It goes around the rapids at Sault Ste. Marie. This big project took two years. About 1,600 men built the canal and locks. Locks raise and lower ships between the two big lakes. We call them the **Soo Locks**. Gravity helps the locks work. To raise a ship, water comes in from Lake Superior. The ship rises. Then it can sail out onto Lake Superior.

The Soo Locks are an example of changing the environment. People did it to meet their needs. The locks were a great help to mining in Michigan. One natural resource helped move another. Ships used the water in the Great Lakes.

Ships filled with copper and iron sailed from lake to lake. This helped the mining business. At one time, more copper was mined here than at any other place in the world!

This ship is being lowered in a lock. The doors to the lock close. The water flows out and the ship goes down. Photo by the author.

Towns Start Because of the Mines

Before the mines, there were few towns in that part of the state. When the mines started, many people moved there. They found work in the mines. One mine had over 2,000 workers. Others worked on ships moving the copper and iron. Some worked in stores selling supplies. Some were teachers and some were preachers.

New towns began. People even came from other countries for jobs. Soon the Upper Peninsula had miners from **Norway**, **Sweden** and **Finland**. Often these new workers felt the U.P. was like their old homes. They both had pine trees and cool weather. A few left and went back home, but

most stayed. They brought their customs to Michigan. They helped build our state.

Now It Is Too Expensive

As the years went by, the mines went deeper and deeper. It was very expensive to run such deep mines. Later, copper was found in other states and other countries. The copper in those places was not so deep. It did not cost so much to mine it.

There once were copper mines at Central. This was in the Keweenaw Peninsula. The first mine began in 1854. It had good profits. Before long, about 1,250 people worked and lived there. The mines and the town had 130 buildings. Over the years, 52 million pounds of copper came from the mines at Central. Then, in 1898 the mines closed. The copper was too hard to reach. Almost everyone left to find work someplace else. Today Central is a "ghost town." A church and about a dozen buildings are all that are left behind.

What is left of one mine building at another "ghost town" - Victoria, Michigan.

More Michigan copper mines closed. The last one was in 1995. The copper is still there, but far, far underground. It is too expensive to get it out. Other places have human resources that cost less. They do not have to pay their workers as much. They do not have many laws to protect the environment. Those mines do not have the extra costs of protecting the environment.

Iron- Another Useful Metal

Iron was found in Michigan soon after copper mining began. Iron is a key resource used in industry. It is used to make steel. It is used for tall buildings, cars and nails. Here is how iron was discovered in Michigan.

Iron is a very useful metal. It is used to make everything from cars to frying pans.

William Burt traveled to the Upper Peninsula. He was a surveyor. In 1844, he and his crew were working near Negaunee. Mr. Burt was trying to make good maps. For his work he used a compass. He needed to know which way was north and which was south.

My Compass Is Crazy!

One day, his compass needle did not point north at all! What could be wrong? Mr. Burt called out, "Boys, look around and see what you can find." Some men went east and some went west. They all came back with pieces of iron. Iron can be magnetic. It attracted the compass needle.

YEAR 1844

This surprised everyone. No one in Michigan had any idea the state had this mineral. Finding iron ore was a very nice surprise!

Where Were the Iron Mines?

Iron mines started near Marquette. Others

were near Iron Mountain. Ironwood and Iron River had mines too. These new towns began because of the iron mines. Families moved to those places. What do you think it was like to start a new town? What was it like to move somewhere that was a wilderness the year before?

They Needed Machines and Equipment

Iron mines also needed capital resources. Some mines had water in them. It just kept coming in all the time. One mine had 3,000 gallons of water coming in every minute. That would fill a swimming pool in about ten minutes! A huge pump was built for that mine. It was an expensive capital resource! Ships brought supplies to the Upper Peninsula. The parts of that pump are one example of what they carried.

The iron ore dock at Marquette. Picture from Archives of Michigan 06320.

Big docks were built to load **ore** into ships. One is at Marquette. Another is at Escanaba. Later, railroads were built to carry people and iron ore. All of this happened because iron ore was scarce in other places.

Working in a Mine

Would you like to have a job in a mine? If you think you are not old enough, you are wrong. You could work in a mine in those times. There were no laws to keep children from working then. Often boys worked in the mines with the men. It was hard work. It was dangerous work. Workers of all ages were often hurt and sometimes died.

Inside an iron mine. Photo from Archives of Michigan 02049.

What was it like in a mine? This is what Charles Wright said in 1877.

YEAR 1877

"We were standing near the edge. We looked down. We saw the small lamps of the busy miners. It was dim from the weak light. They looked like evil spirits all the more so because of the clanging of the drills and hammers. We heard the explosions from the blasts. We heard the rumbling of the ore cars moving up and down the shafts. All these sounds echoed and re-echoed from the rocky walls."

I WAS THERE

How Much Iron Came from Michigan?

Today, Michigan has only two iron mines. They still produce much iron ore. These are called open pit mines because iron ore is near the surface. They are not underground. Trucks go down and haul up the ore. Both mines are near Marquette. They still supply an important part of all the iron mined in the United States.

One of the open pit iron mines near Marquette. Workers do not need to be underground in an open pit mine.

Today, iron ore is shipped as little marbles like these. The huge ore boats are filled with them.

Over the years, workers have mined a lot of iron ore. How much did they mine? It was more than one billion **tons**! All of this came from our Upper Peninsula. That is a big pile of natural resource! It went into products used all over the United States. It went into cars, bridges, buildings and even thumbtacks!

Moving the Iron

Ships still carry the iron ore. Marquette and Escanaba have big, tall docks to load the ships. The ships move the iron ore to ports in many places. Some of the ore may even go across the ocean.

Think About It. Write About It!

1. Why are copper and iron useful natural resources?

2. Tell where copper and iron are found in Michigan.

3. Tell how the discovery of copper and iron helped the Upper Peninsula to grow?

4. Tell why there are no more copper mines in Michigan.

5. How was the copper and iron ore moved to where it was needed?

Think Like a Geographer

Make a simple map that shows where three of Michigan's minerals are found.

Think Like an Entrepreneur

Tell why you want to start a copper mine. Tell two capital resources you need to start your mine. Tell what kind of human resources you will need.

GEOGRAPHY

Make a Time Line Today

Find three events from this lesson. Put them on a time line. Label each event. Put a year with each event.

What was the incentive used to help build the Soo Locks? Name an incentive you could give to have someone do something for you.

1700

1800

1900

Chapter 5 Lesson 4

Ideas To Explore

migrate - to move a long way to start a new home

railroads - the tracks used by trains

Words to Welcome

migrating - moving to start a home in a new place

plank road - a road covered with wooden boards

port - a city on a lake or ocean where ships dock

stagecoach - a coach pulled by horses to carry passengers on a route from town to town.

steam engine - A steam engine burns fuel to heat water. The water turns to steam and powers an engine. On a ship, the engine turns paddles or a propeller that will push the ship through the water.

toll road - a private road. People who want to use a toll road pay a toll or fee. In the old days, each wagon and horse rider paid to use the road.

Michigan
Social
Studies
GLCES
3H3.0.1
3H3.0.3
3H3.0.5
3H3.0.10
3G4.0.2
3C1.0.1
3E1.0.1
3E1.0.3
3E1.0.4
4H3.0.1
4H3.0.2

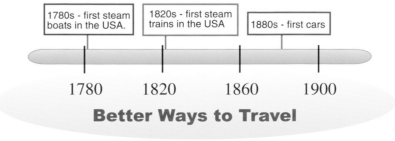

1780s - first steam boats in the USA.

1820s - first steam trains in the USA

1880s - first cars

1780   1820   1860   1900

Better Ways to Travel

Moving People and Products

Think about this question while you read.
   **Why was transportation needed to
          help Michigan grow?**

Go Back In Time

What was your city or town like a long time ago? Suppose you could use a time machine. It will take you back in time. Go ahead and get in. Let's start it. You can look out the window and watch the changes.

You will see buildings start to disappear. Your school has been replaced by an older one. The mall changed back into a wheat field. The airport is gone. Paved streets turned into dirt roads. The homes look different and there are not so many of them. All the power lines are gone! There are no cars. People are using wagons and buggies pulled by horses. The dial on the time machine keeps spinning. You no longer see any railroad tracks. There are no factories.

Everything Is So Different

You no longer know the street where you live! There are no street lights. At night you see some small lights in homes. Some are oil-burning lamps and some are candles. Most people go to bed about the time it is dark. You see a gristmill powered by a waterwheel. By now most of the

roads are gone, even the ones between towns. Much of the land is covered by trees. The years keep going backwards. Many towns have disappeared, too. This is Michigan in 1830. Go ahead and step out of the time machine. Stretch your legs and enjoy yourself!

Walk or Hitch a Ride

You are standing along a trail. You do not have a horse. All you can do is walk. You will find out it is much harder to go places. You cannot even find anyone with a bicycle. Maybe someone will give you a ride on their wagon.

Great! You see one coming now. You are in luck! This wagon is really full. It has a mom, a dad and six children. It has boxes, wooden chests and furniture. You ask if you can have a ride. The dad says something, but you do not understand his language. It is German, but you do not know that. He motions for you to get on the wagon.

Photo from the Library of Congress.

New People Move to Michigan

They give you a ride. You find out the family is moving to Ann Arbor. They are **migrating**. *When families **migrate**, they move a long way to start new homes.* Why did people like this family want to come here? Remember, we had cheap land. Our country also had its core democratic values. People like the freedom to do what they want. They like to go to the church they want. They like to have a government that is fair to them. In other parts of the world they did not have those rights. People also want good jobs.

Each year there were more jobs in Michigan. We had these jobs for several reasons. Michigan had natural resources. Those resources were scarce in other places. Before Michigan could use its resources, it had to be able to move them.

Come to one of Michigan's **port** cities in the 1800s. *A port is a place where ships dock. It is a town where people and products move on and off ships.* Look at all the ships! People are hurrying this way and that. Workers are rolling big barrels onto ships. Some ships are stacked high with boards from the sawmills.

People boarding passenger ships at Port Huron. The time is about 1890-1900. Photo from Library of Congress. Color added by Robert Morrison.

From Sail to Steam Engines

At first, most of the ships used sails. The wind moved them from place to place. Of course, the wind does not always blow when it is needed. Sometimes it blows too hard. Sailors wanted power that they controlled. **Steam engines** were the answer. *A steam engine burns fuel to heat water. The water turns to steam and powers an engine. The engine turns paddles or a propeller which pushes the ship through the water.*

Soon more ships used steam engines and fewer used sails. Now visit a port city. See smoke puffing up from the steamships. Hear the steam whistles blow!

Can you see the steam whistle on this ship? This ship is moved by big paddles along its sides.

We Needed Better Transportation

Since the 1600s we have had ships on the Great Lakes. In the 1830s and 1840s ships brought people to Detroit once they left the Erie Canal. Still, ships cannot go over land! Our roads were few and not very good. Some cities had brick streets. All the

roads between towns were just dirt. When it rained, they were just mud. Wagons got stuck and people stood in the mud to push. The mud squished up to their knees. Oh, that was a mess!

Who Built Early Roads?

The national government decided to build a few roads. They did this to promote the common good. Most Michigan settlers came to Detroit first, so that is where the roads started. The early roads helped them head west. One of the first roads went to Chicago. They called it the Chicago Road. It connected Detroit and Chicago. Later, a few roads went north. Some reached Pontiac and Flint. Some went to Saginaw and Bay City.

A few entrepreneurs saw the need for roads. They could build roads too. They would charge to use their roads. Those were called **toll roads**. *Each wagon driver and horse rider paid a fee or toll to use the road.* The money went to the people who built the road. The owners of the road hoped to make a profit. Remember, a profit is the money a business has left after all the expenses are paid. The reason the toll roads were

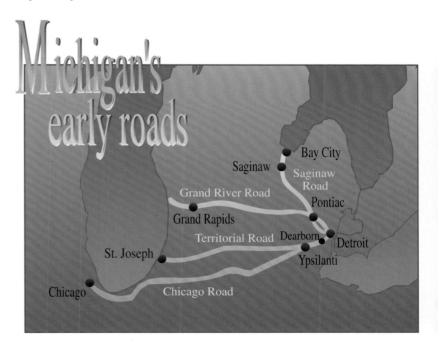

Michigan's early roads

Bay City
Saginaw
Saginaw Road
Grand River Road
Pontiac
Grand Rapids
Territorial Road   Dearborn   Detroit
St. Joseph   Ypsilanti
Chicago   Chicago Road

built was to make a profit. Making profits is the goal of all businesses. It does not always happen, but it is the goal. The search for profits decides what is built or produced. Entrepreneurs will not go into a business unless they think they can make a profit.

A plank road.
Picture drawn
by Aaron Zenz.

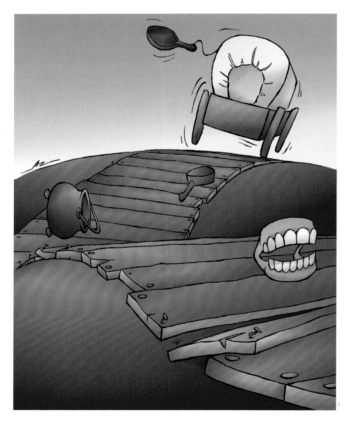

Less Mud On This Road

Some owners of toll roads tried a new idea. *They laid wooden boards or planks on the ground. A road built like this is a **plank road**.* Plank roads were nice for a few months. Then the boards began to bend and warp. These roads could be very bumpy. Someone said they could shake out a person's false teeth! The plank roads were not much of a help.

Stagecoaches were not just "out West." Michigan had them too. Stagecoach lines reached many cities. Most of the stagecoach lines started in the 1830s and 1840s. Riding in a stagecoach was still bumpy. By the 1860s trains were replacing the stagecoaches.

A Train is Coming- I think?

Michigan had its first **railroad** in 1836. It went from Toledo to Adrian. That is not very far. On the first day, the "train" started toward Adrian. But it was not quite what you might expect. It was pulled by horses! This railroad did not get its engine until the next year.

The first train in Michigan- after it got its steam engine!

Picture from the Archives of Michigan 00226

The first railroads may have looked funny. Still, they were exciting for the times. The trip from Detroit to Ypsilanti took two and a half hours instead of two and a half days! Before trains, it was quite expensive to move supplies. Now, prices began to fall. Products cost less. The cost of a barrel of salt fell from $15 to $9. (The railroad charged one dollar to move the salt from Toledo to Adrian.) Cheaper supplies meant more people would think about moving to Michigan.

Trains helped lower prices.

Trains, Trains Everywhere

Early railroads were very important. Every city and town wanted to be on one. Towns without railroads felt left out. Businesses could not get supplies. They could not ship products. People could not reach the town easily. Cities on railroads grew. Those without railroads did not grow and some even disappeared.

A map of the railroads in Michigan about 1900.

In 1836, Michigan had about 30 miles of railroads. By the year 1900, Michigan had over 10,000 miles of railroads! People could reach almost any town by train. That was good, since there were still very few roads. People often went to work by train. They used trains to go to larger cities to shop. Some cities had 50 or more trains stop each day!

By 1900, Michigan had a few good roads, many ships and many trains. Our economy could not grow without good transportation. Transportation brought people and products to Michigan. Transportation took Michigan products to markets in other places.

Think About It. Write About It!

1. Give one reason a family would migrate to Michigan in the 1800s.

2. What is a port city? Name one near your home-town. Do some research. What is shipped from this port?

3. Why would an entrepreneur build a plank road?

4. Why did early cities want railroads?

Think Like a Geographer

Make a simple map of Michigan. Mark and label a port city near where you live.

GEOGRAPHY

Think Like an Entrepreneur

What is a profit? Imagine you have a new business. Why do you want to have a profit in your business?

Words In Action

Why was good transportation needed to help Michigan grow?

Chapter 5 Lesson 5

Ideas To Explore

Civil War (1861-1865) When the United States broke into two parts that fought each other.

slavery- owning people and making them work without pay

Underground Railroad- a secret group who helped escaped slaves reach freedom

Why are cities where they are? Cities were often started along rivers and lakes. They were often started near useful natural resources.

Michigan
Social
Studies
GLCEs

3H3.0.1
3H3.0.10
3G1.0.2
3G4.0.2
3G5.0.1
3G5.0.2
3C5.0.1
3E1.0.1
3E1.0.4
4H3.0.1
4H3.0.2
4H3.0.3
4H3.0.4
4H3.0.7
4H3.0.9

People to Meet

Elizabeth Chandler	George de Baptiste
Henry Ford	Laura Haviland
Dr. John Harvey Kellogg	Will Keith Kellogg
William Lambert	Abraham Lincoln
Charles Post	Sojourner Truth

Places to Discover
Battle Creek
Dowagiac - do WAW jak
Holland (a country in Europe)
Poland (a country in Europe)

Words to Welcome
ballot- a paper used by each voter to record his or her choices
photography- taking pictures with a camera
slaves- people owned by other people. They had to work without pay.

Putting Resources to Work- How Our Towns Grew

Think about this question while you read.
Why did our early cities and towns grow so much?

YEAR 1850s

We are going to go back in time to the 1850s. Remember to think like a historian. Ask what happened? Ask when did it happen? Ask how and why did it happen? Ask who was there? Those are questions historians ask. They want to find out answers to those questions.

A Public Issue Changes Michigan and Its People

Michigan was just about to really grow, but there was a problem. Our nation allowed people to have **slaves** at that time. *Slaves are people owned by other people.* The slaves were forced to work without pay. They were often beaten to make them work harder. Slaves were bought and sold as if they were cattle. Slave families were often split up. A child might be sold and sent far away.

A slave family. Picture drawn by George Rasmussen.

229

Above- Sojourner Truth from the Archives of Michigan 05254.

Most states in the South wanted **slavery**. States in the North did not. People in the northern states wanted to end slavery. People in the southern states spoke out to keep it. Neither group of states trusted the other. It is very sad that slavery was ever allowed in our country, but it was.

Michigan did not allow slavery. Many people in our state took a stand against it. They believed it was wrong. **Laura Haviland** and **Sojourner Truth** spoke out against it. **Elizabeth Chandler** was another who did not like it. She helped start a group against slavery.

Laura Haviland

People Help Escaped Slaves

Sometimes slaves escaped. They ran away and headed north. The escaped slaves wanted to go to Canada. Canada did not allow slavery. They were safe there. No one could catch them and take them back to the United States.

William Lambert

William Lambert and **George de Baptiste** were a part of the **Underground Railroad**. The Underground Railroad was not underground. It was not a railroad either! Underground was a way to say it was out of sight. It was called a railroad since it helped people move from place to place. It was a way of hiding and moving escaped slaves to Canada. Nathan and Pamela Thomas were in that group too. They all helped slaves who had escaped. They hid the escaped slaves in barns and basements. They helped them move at night to other hiding places.

Nathan Thomas said this about slavery. "Slavery cannot continue to exist under our government. If it is not put down by the **ballot**, it will go down in blood." He meant people should vote against slavery. (*Voters use ballots to record their vote.*) They need to stop slavery or there would be a war. War is a terrible thing. It is still terrible even when it tries to make things better.

Escaped slaves at Detroit looking toward Canada

A photo of part of the Gateway To Freedom Underground Railroad Memorial.

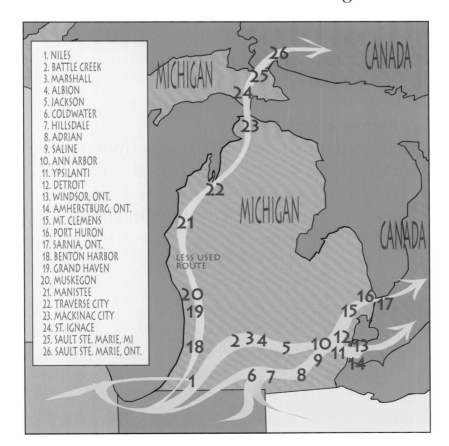

1. NILES
2. BATTLE CREEK
3. MARSHALL
4. ALBION
5. JACKSON
6. COLDWATER
7. HILLSDALE
8. ADRIAN
9. SALINE
10. ANN ARBOR
11. YPSILANTI
12. DETROIT
13. WINDSOR, ONT.
14. AMHERSTBURG, ONT.
15. MT. CLEMENS
16. PORT HURON
17. SARNIA, ONT.
18. BENTON HARBOR
19. GRAND HAVEN
20. MUSKEGON
21. MANISTEE
22. TRAVERSE CITY
23. MACKINAC CITY
24. ST. IGNACE
25. SAULT STE. MARIE, MI
26. SAULT STE. MARIE, ONT.

A map of part of the Underground Railroad. It was not underground. It was not a railroad!

A man named **Abraham Lincoln** made a speech. He wanted to become a U.S. Senator. He gave his thoughts about our nation. He said this in 1858. "A house (nation) divided against itself cannot stand (last). I believe this government cannot endure (keep going), half slave and half free. I do not expect the Union (the United States) to be dissolved (to break up).... I do not expect the house to fall... but I do expect it will cease (stop) to be divided. It will become all one thing or all the other." He means the United States should either get rid of slavery or the whole country will allow it. He did not think the country could last being half slave and half free. He was right.

1861 Brings a War

In 1861 a war did start. It was right here in the United States. Today we call this the **Civil War**. It has this name because it was a war between states. It was not a war with another country. It was a very sad event because the states were fighting among themselves. It was a fight over the right to have slaves.

The Southern states wanted to have slaves so they decided to leave the United States. Those states started a new country for a while. The Northern states did not think it was right for them to do that. The Civil War was also a fight to keep all the states in the U.S.

THE CIVIL WAR

This African American from Michigan fought for the Union side in the Civil War. Photo from the Archives of Michigan 03228.

The Slave States That Left the United States

This war lasted four years. In 1865 the states in the South surrendered. People in Michigan were happy. Many men and a few women from our state fought in that war. Now there would not be any more slaves in the United States. Now the soldiers came home. It felt so good to see their families once more. Everyone wanted peace and a chance to go back to work.

Picture drawn by Aaron Zenz.

Civil War Nurse 1861-1865

Michigan Makes Supplies for the War

In a way, the Civil War helped our state grow. Soldiers needed supplies. Many of those supplies were made with Michigan's natural resources. More copper and iron were mined. More trees were cut into boards. More crops were planted for food. More products were shipped on railroads. Michigan was lucky because no battles were fought here. When peace came, people wanted to buy things they could not get during the war. There was a demand for more products. More factories were built to make the products people wanted.

Many towns had mills powered by water.

Cities and Rivers- A Big Idea!

Most Michigan cities are on rivers. Think like a geographer. Why were cities started along rivers? Water to drink is not the main reason. It was for water power! Gristmills used water power. Factories used water power. **Battle Creek**, Kalamazoo

Grand Rapids is on the Grand River.

and Grand Rapids are all on rivers. Each had factories powered by water.

Making Products to Meet Needs

If you owned a factory in those times, what would you make? You would want to meet people's needs. So, what did they need?

People were moving to Michigan. Some came from far away. They may have come from **Holland** or **Poland**. The trip would mean crossing the ocean on a ship. They could not take everything for a new home on a ship. Families needed furniture. They needed stoves to heat their homes. Farmers needed plows and other farm tools. Michigan factories made all of these products.

Michigan Stoves

Visit a home in the 1880s. Come into the kitchen. Here is mother cooking on her wood burning stove. Her son has cut and split the wood and it is stacked up nearby. You can smell the beef roasting. The whole kitchen is warm and toasty from the hot stove. The kitchen always has a bit of the wood smoke smell. Mother's stove was a Round Oak made in **Dowagiac**, Michigan.

Come into the living room. In the middle of the room is another wood burning stove. Father sits in his chair close by. It is a good place to relax and read the newspaper.

These stoves were made with Michigan iron. The iron ore came by ship from the Upper Peninsula. Next, it went by train to the factories. All the cities that made stoves were connected by railroads. The stoves went by train to the customers. The Michigan stove business needed ships and trains.

Michigan Furniture

The new homes need furniture. Businesses began to make furniture in Grand Rapids. The wood came from nearby forests. The Grand River powered the first factories. Workers made beds, chairs, tables and sofas.

In 1863, C.C. Comstock had a new "Big Idea." He was an entrepreneur in the furniture business. He felt he could sell more furniture if customers could see it. **Photography** was a new invention. Mr. Comstock used it. He took photographs of his furniture. He mailed the pictures to stores around the country. His sales and profits increased! Without railroads he could not have sold furniture very far away.

The Widdicomb Furniture Company in Grand Rapids.

Photo from the Grand Rapids History and Special Collections Center, Archives, Grand Rapids Public Library.

The furniture business in Grand Rapids was good. It grew and grew. By 1900, there were over 6,000 furniture workers in the city. Grand Rapids furniture was exported to Europe. It was also shipped to South America.

Workers at the Irwin-Phoenix Furniture Company in Grand Rapids.

Photo from the Grand Rapids History and Special Collections Center, Archives, Grand Rapids Public Library.

Another Big Idea- Breakfast Cereal

Battle Creek is where another "Big Idea" got its start. In the 1890s, people came to Battle Creek from all over the country. They came because they were stressed and sick. Battle Creek had a well-known hospital run by **Dr. John Harvey Kellogg**. It was called the San. At the San, he helped these people get better. Dr. Kellogg told them how to eat better food and be healthy. He felt the right kind of food was important for good health.

Dr. John Harvey Kellogg

Dr. Kellogg made healthy foods for the patients. His brother, **Will Keith Kellogg**, helped

Charles Post

Will Kellogg

him. One of these was a kind of breakfast cereal. After the patients went home, they still wanted to buy it. The Kellogg brothers decided to sell their food products to the former patients.

On a cold winter day in 1891, **Charles Post** came to the San. He felt terrible. He was weak and sick. He was there for almost nine months and was still not any better! His wife took him home in a wheel chair. Mr. Post did like the breakfast cereal from the San. He worked to make something like it.

YEAR 1895

Charles Post Makes Breakfast Cereal

In 1895 he made a drink that was like coffee. In 1898 he started to sell a breakfast cereal called Grape-Nuts. Charles Post believed in advertising. He thought up all sorts of ideas for ads. His hard work on the ads paid off. His sales went up. Post sold about three million dollars of breakfast food in 1900. Making money seemed to help him feel better. Battle Creek was a good place for this business. Trains brought wheat, corn and molasses to his factory. The wheat and corn came from Michigan farms. Trains took the boxes of cereal to his customers.

Will Kellogg Makes Breakfast Cereal

The Kellogg bothers were upset. Mr. Post was making money with their idea! Still, Doctor Kellogg did not think it was right for a doctor to sell products. Will Kellogg felt they should advertise. They should tell people about their cereal. Finally in 1906, Will Kellogg started a cereal company by himself. It became the Kellogg company we know today. He worked hard and his company grew. Once, he shipped 21 train cars of cereal on a single day.

Cereal City U.S.A.

Battle Creek became the Cereal City. Breakfast cereal was a new big idea from Michigan. It changed what people all over the world ate for breakfast!

Michigan Is Growing Up

Each year Michigan had more businesses. They used our natural resources. They made products people wanted. Some of them made stoves, furniture and cereal. Workers in Kalamazoo made paper. Michigan wood went into the paper. Water from the Kalamazoo River was used to make the paper too. Orville Gibson started making guitars. His business was also in Kalamazoo. He used wood from Michigan's forests. Railroad cars were built in Detroit. One thousand people worked for the railroad in Jackson. They took care of train engines and rail-road cars. At one time, people moved to Michigan for the cheap land. Now people moved here for the factory jobs.

Moving from the Farm to the Factory

People began to leave the farms to work in

Many people left farms to work in factories.

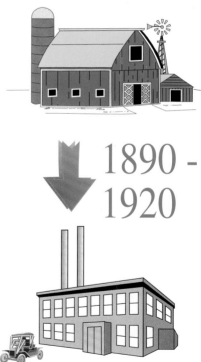

1890 - 1920

cities. By now, cities had electricity and telephones. Most farms did not have those things. One young man said he just could not sit and watch corn grow! Working on a farm could be lonely. There were often not many people to meet.

The young Henry Ford

A young fellow named **Henry Ford** is an example. He was born in 1863. That was in the middle of the great Civil War. Henry grew up on a farm near Detroit. He helped cut hay, feed pigs, pull weeds, milk cows and more. Someone asked him about the family farm. Henry said, "Considering the results, there is just too much work on the place."

Henry liked to spend his time finding out how machines worked. One time he saw a steam powered farm tractor! He asked all sort of questions about it. When Henry Ford was older, he left the farm. He moved to Detroit. He found a job fixing watches. Later, he fixed steam engines.

A steam powered farm tractor like one Henry Ford saw.

He took classes at a business college. He had a job at an electric power plant.

There were many jobs in Michigan's growing cities. Young people like Henry Ford left farms and moved to towns. You will learn more about Henry Ford in the next lesson.

Think About It. Write About It!

1. How did the Civil War help Michigan grow?

2. Why did people start moving from farms to cities in the 1890s and early 1900s?

3. What were three products made by early Michigan businesses? How did each one fill a need?

4. What were two natural resources used by our early businesses?

5. Why were railroads so important to our early businesses?

Think Like a Geographer

   Why were most Michigan cities started along rivers?

GEOGRAPHY

Think Like an Entrepreneur

   Name a big idea used by a Michigan entrepreneur in this lesson.

Make a Time Line Today

   Choose two dates from this lesson. Make a time line using those dates. Label the dates and events.

1700

1800

1900

Words In Action

   Why did our early cities and towns grow so much? Please give at least one example.

Chapter 5 Lesson 6

Ideas To Explore

moving assembly line - This idea helps people do more work in factories. The product moves along as the workers put it together.

People To Meet
Walter Chrysler
James Couzens
Billy Durant
Ransom Olds

Places To Discover
Lebanon (LEB a non) - country far to the east
Syria (SEAR ee ah) - country far to the east

Rivers to Float Down
River Rouge - a small river south of Detroit

Words to Welcome
horseless carriage - an old name for a car
Model T - a simple but popular car built by Henry Ford. It was made from 1908 to 1927.

Michigan

Social

Studies

GLCEs

3H3.0.1

3H3.0.3

3H3.0.8

3H3.0.10

3G4.0.1

3G4.0.2

3G5.0.2

3E1.0.4

3E1.0.5

3E2.0.1

4H3.0.2

4H3.0.3

4H3.0.5

4H3.0.6

4H3.0.9

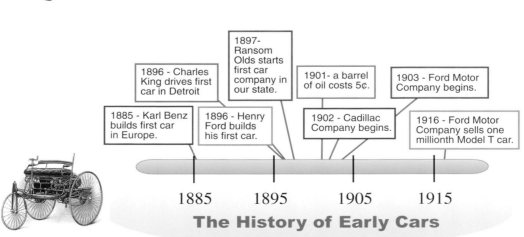

1896 - Charles King drives first car in Detroit

1897- Ransom Olds starts first car company in our state.

1901- a barrel of oil costs 5¢.

1903 - Ford Motor Company begins.

1885 - Karl Benz builds first car in Europe.

1896 - Henry Ford builds his first car.

1902 - Cadillac Company begins.

1916 - Ford Motor Company sells one millionth Model T car.

1885   1895   1905   1915

The History of Early Cars

The Car Business Zooms Along

Think about this question while you read.
**How did the car business change
Michigan and the world?**

Everyone Depends on Horses

Until about 1900, horse power came from horses. Horses pulled wagons and buggies. City streets were full of horses and wagons. Standing along a street you could hear the clip-clop of the horses' feet. Many homes in the cities had a barn in back for their horses. Maybe your job would have been to feed them. Blacksmiths did a big business making horseshoes. All of this was going to change.

What is a Horseless Carriage?

A few people had started to make cars. The first cars were called **horseless carriages**. Henry Ford dreamed of making cars. He did not invent the car. He did not even start the first car company in Michigan. A man named **Ransom Olds** did that.

An early Olds car.

Henry's wife was Clara. She urged him to make a car. Henry's nickname for Clara was "The

243

You may want to read this book by Hazel B. Aird to learn more about Henry Ford.

Believer." She felt he could do it. She urged him to try. One evening Henry made a motor and he wanted to try it out. He brought it into the kitchen. Clara helped him get it started. Boom, boom, pop, vroom! There were Clara and Henry running a smelly gas motor in their kitchen. It must have been something to see!

Henry Ford tried to start two companies to make cars. These did not work out. Henry Ford did not believe in giving up. He tried again. He found more investors to risk their money to help him. That money was the capital resource to start the company. It was needed to buy machines and supplies. Each investor owned a part of the new company- the Ford Motor Company. They would share the profits, if there were any.

Early Cars Were Expensive!

Early cars were not very practical. Most were open with no top or windshield. Oil from the engine leaked on people's clothes. The cars may need repairs at any time. Worst of all, they were very expensive to buy. A new car might cost as much as a very nice house, or more! Most folks felt cars were just toys for rich people. The demand for cars was low because the cost was so high.

This early car was very expensive. It cost about $5,000. In those times, many people only made a $1 or $2 a day!

Mr. Ford's Big Idea

The time is 1903. We are going to meet Henry Ford again. This young man is going to change Michigan probably more than anyone else in history! How did he do that?

Henry Ford

It is time to find out. He left his good job at the power company. Mr. Ford became an entrepreneur. Mr. Ford and a few others had $28,000. They started the Ford Motor Company. Soon it had 125 workers. At first it looked like they would run out of money. They had to pay workers. They had to buy parts. They had to rent buildings. Then people began to buy more of their cars. The business was good, but not great.

Let's visit Mr. Ford in the office of his early car factory. He is talking with Eugene Lewis. Mr. Lewis tells us what happened.

> "We were sitting on some stools in his office. Henry Ford was looking out the window. He suddenly turned, tapped me on the knee and said, "I AM going to make a motor car that will be light AND strong and CLEAN so that women will drive it. It will have enough power to do what is needed. It will be sold so anyone who can own a horse and buggy can afford to own a car."

Mr. Ford's Big Idea!

You just heard Henry Ford's big idea. He wanted to make a car *anyone could afford*. It would not be a car that was expensive. Some of the investors in his company did not agree. They felt an expensive car meant more profits. Henry said no, no, no. He said profits would come when everyone bought cars. The market for expensive cars was too small.

A New, Cheap Car

Henry Ford thought and worked on ideas for his low cost car. His men thought and worked on ideas too. Henry learned about ways to make steel stronger. He learned how to make engines more powerful. In 1908 they came out with a new car. They called it the **Model T**. The Model T was simple. It was built to last. It was easy to fix if it did have a problem.

2 Model T Ford cars. Picture drawn by George Rasmussen.

People liked the Model T. It worked well on dirt roads. That was a good thing. Most roads were dirt then. People could afford it and they bought it. Henry Ford always tried to lower the cost of the Model T. If it cost less to make, it could

sell for a lower price. Henry Ford was a successful entrepreneur. He used natural resources,
human resources and capital resources. He made
a product that met the needs of the people.

A Better Way to Make Cars

Here is how they made cars in those days.
Four or five workers had a space on the factory
floor. To start, they each picked up the parts they
needed. They laid the parts on the floor. Then they
began to put the parts together. When the car was
complete, they pushed it to the door. Then they
started another one. It took about 12.5 hours to
build a Model T.

YEAR
1913

In 1913 the people at the Ford company had a
new idea. It was a REALLY BIG IDEA, but it was
also a very simple idea. Have each worker stay in
one place and bring the parts to him. They would
do this by moving the car along as it was built.
They called the new idea a **moving assembly line**.

Photos can
be primary
sources, too.
Look at this
one closely.
What can you
see?

An assembly line

Picture from the
Ford Motor
Company

247

It saved time!

Did it help? Yes, it did. Now a Model T was built in just 1.5 hours. This allowed Ford to drop the price for the car. When he dropped the price, the demand went up. More people could afford a Model T. In 1912 Ford sold about 78,000 cars. Just two years later, they sold 248,000 cars. By this time the Ford Motor Company had 15,000 workers. That is a lot of human resources, but other car makers needed even more workers.

The moving assembly line was wonderful for the business. It was a great idea. Other car makers used 60,000 or 70,000 workers to make as many cars as Ford. This new idea changed the world! It was soon used in many countries. It was used in factories that made all kinds of products. It was used where shoes were made. It was used where furniture was made. This idea is still used in almost every factory today. Some workers did not like the assembly line. They had to do the same job over and over. Some said the line went too fast. It was really hard work.

A Big Idea Used Around the World

Workers on a moving assembly line. This was about 1920.

Picture from the Archives of Michigan 05352.

Many People Help Make Cars and Car Parts

Other companies made cars here too. **Billy Durant** started GM. General Motors was in Flint and Detroit. REO was run by Mr. Olds in Lansing. Chrysler was started by **Walter Chrysler**. In 1914, eight out of ten cars made in the United States were made here in Michigan!

Ransom Olds

Many Michigan businesses made parts for cars. Saginaw Steering Gear is one example. Car tires were made by the U.S. Rubber Company in Detroit. About 10,000 people worked there.

Billy Durant. Picture from the Archives of Michigan 05298.

Why Michigan?

Michigan had the natural resources needed to make cars. Iron and copper went into the cars. Wood went into cars too. Early cars used wood in the bodies. Michigan was close to the customers. Michigan was a good place to make cars, but cars were made in other states too. In the early 1900s there were hundreds of car companies.

Any state in the Midwest could use the same resources. Those resources could have gone by ship to other states. Chicago could have been the home of the biggest car makers. Here is the real

reason Michigan became number one. People from Michigan had the best "Big Ideas." People like Henry Ford helped make our state the leader.

We Needed Better Roads

As people bought more cars, they wanted better roads. At first, it took weeks to drive across the United States. To make that kind of trip in a car, you needed plenty of spare parts! State governments and our national government began to build better roads. More roads were paved. Better maps were printed and better road signs made. On early trips people might say, "Go to the red barn and turn left, when you reach the big oak tree, go right."

This road was not unusual for the early days. What would it be like to drive on this mess today?
Picture from the Archives of Michigan 08196.

Workers Came Here for the Jobs

Henry Ford made more cars each year. Each year he had more jobs in his factories. Since there were more jobs here, more people moved to Michigan to find work.

The Ford Company had many workers, but most did not stay long. It was hard work. In 1913 there were 15,000 workers, but only about 600 had been there for three years! The men in charge at Ford knew they had a problem. They spent a great deal of time training workers. Training new workers cost money. New workers were slower. New workers often made more mistakes.

The second in command at Ford was **James Couzens**. He thought about a way to keep the best workers. He had an idea and he told it to Mr. Ford. The plan was to double the pay for Ford workers. They decided they would do it.

In 1914 Henry Ford told the plan to the newspapers. The next morning 10,000 people were waiting outside. They all wanted jobs! Most Ford workers would be paid five dollars a day. This does not seem like much now. In 1914 everything cost much less. The five dollars a day meant Ford workers earned almost twice as much as other workers. What would your parents do if they could find a job that paid twice as much as they make now?

Whole World Wants to Work at Ford!

Newspapers told about the new wage. People all over the world read about it. Five dollars a day would be wonderful! People talked of moving here. People in Canada talked of moving to Michigan. People in Germany and Poland talked of moving to Michigan. People in the places we now call **Lebanon** and **Syria** talked of moving

James Couzens

Picture from the Archives of Michigan

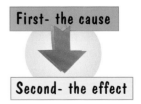

Key Event

First- the cause

Second- the effect

A 1923 Dodge
Brothers car

Special Thanks to
Robert and Mary
Palmer

The Ford River
Rouge factory

here too. They all wanted to have a job at Ford. The new Ford wage was pulling workers from everywhere. Later, Henry Ford said doubling the pay was the best cost cutting idea they ever had. The company got the best and hardest workers.

Good Times for Car Makers

These were some of the best years for our car companies. Ford sales went up. In 1925 they sold over two million Model T cars. Henry Ford built the world's largest factory. This was along the **Rouge River**. In one year it used 141 shiploads of supplies.

General Motors did very well too. General Motors is often called GM. It started the idea of a new model each year. Customers were excited to see the new cars each year. GM soon sold more cars than Ford. For about 19 years, Ford only sold the Model T.

Michigan was a leader in making cars. This happened because the people with the best big ideas were here. They worked hard to make sure those big ideas were successful. A state like Wisconsin had the same natural resources. It did not have the people with the right big ideas.

Think About It. Write About It!

1. Before 1900, how did most people go from place to place?

2. Henry Ford had a big idea about the right kind of car to make. What was his big idea? Name the car he made because of his big idea.

3. The people at the Ford company had another big idea that they used to cut the cost of making cars. What was this big idea? Why is it still important today?

4. What did the Ford company do which got people all over the world talking about moving to Michigan? How did this change our state?

Think Like a Historian

What do you think? Why did Michigan become a leader in making cars? Use facts from this lesson to support what you say.

Think about cause and effect. How have cars changed Michigan and the world?

Use a Time Line Today

Look at the time line from this lesson. Who built the first car in Europe? Who started the first car company in Michigan? In what year did Ford sell the one millionth Model T car?

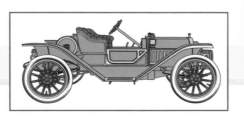

Chapter 5 Lesson 7

Ideas To Explore

Great Depression - This began is 1929. It was
a time when it was very hard to find a job.
Millions of people were out of work and out
of money.

union- a group of workers who want better
working conditions and pay.

People To Meet

Governor Frank Murphy
Walter Reuther

Places To Discover

Flint - a city in Michigan
Japan - a country across the Pacific Ocean
Korea - a country across the Pacific Ocean

Words to Welcome

bargaining - when a union talks with a company to
have better pay and working conditions.

National Guard - an army unit of the state

sit-down strike - a strike were workers do not
leave the factory

strike - when a group of workers decide to stop
working to get better pay and shorter hours

unite - when a group of people work together to
reach a goal.

United Auto Workers (U.A.W.) - a union of
workers who make cars and trucks

Michigan
Social
Studies
GLCEs
3H3.0.1
3H3.0.3
3H3.0.8
3G4.0.1
3C3.0.1
3E1.0.5
4H3.0.4
4H3.0.5
4H3.0.6
4H3.0.9

A Terrible Business Slowdown

Think about this question while you read.
How did the bad time called the Great Depression cause car workers to start unions?

In 1929, a terrible thing happened in the United States. The stock market crashed. This means the values of stocks fell quickly. People were rich one day and poor the next. Millions of people lost the money they had in the stock market.

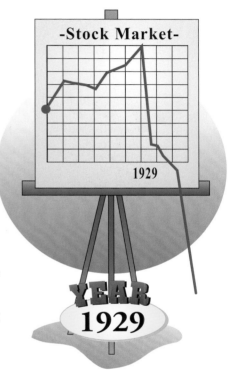

Banks had also put money in the stock market. Suddenly many banks went out of business. By 1932, nearly 200 banks in Michigan had closed. People with their savings in these banks lost it. People had saved money in case times got bad. Now times were bad, but their savings were also gone! Everyone was very worried. This time was called the **Great Depression.** It sounds depressing!

This really put the brakes on the economy. People just stopped buying things. In 1929, there were 4.5 million cars sold. By 1931, there were less than 2 million cars sold. Selling fewer cars meant fewer jobs in

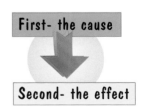

First- the cause

Second- the effect

People had no jobs.
People had no money.

Great
Depression

1930-1940

Michigan. Many people lost their jobs. Here is an example of what happened.

> Ford River Rouge factory workers 1929 - 98,337
> Ford River Rouge factory workers 1933 - 28,915

Work Harder and Faster or Else!

For those who had jobs, life was still not easy. Sales were way down. Companies had to cut costs. If they did not, they would go out of business. The companies pushed their workers to do more for less pay. There were long lines of people waiting for jobs. If a worker complained, he or she was replaced in a minute!

I WAS THERE

This is what one worker on a car assembly line said, "I was only 15 feet away from a drinking fountain. The line went by so fast I could never run over and get a quick drink!"

Another worker ground off the rough edges of car bodies. In 1928, he did eight bodies a day. He was paid $1.00 an hour for his work. By 1932, he did 32 car bodies a day. Now his pay was just 35 cents an hour! This was depressing!

Workers Need Help!

Workers felt crushed. They went home so tired each day. They needed their jobs to buy food. They could not quit. What could they do?

They began to think. If they stood together and talked to the companies, maybe they would listen. They would **unite** and work together as a group.

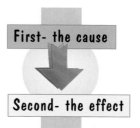

First- the cause

Second- the effect

This was called a **union**. *A union is a group of workers who want better working conditions and pay.* The union makes a deal with the company for all the workers. This is called **bargaining**. If a good deal cannot be made, the workers stop working. This is called a **strike**.

So, the workers said, "If you do not listen to us, all of us will stop working. You will not be able to make any cars." Workers did not want to strike. A strike meant no pay checks. They hoped the companies would listen without it. They talked about a strike to get the attention of the company.

Walter Reuther

Walter Reuther had a job at the Ford Motor Company. He joined the auto union. He and his two brothers became union leaders. His family always believed in trying to help people. They worked to help the **United Auto Workers** union get its start. This union was also called the **UAW**.

Walter Reuther. Picture drawn by Aaron Zenz.

Unions Not Always Popular

The car companies did not like the idea of a union. They did not want their workers to belong. The companies did not want unions to tell them

257

**Workers go
on strike!**

During the strike the workers did not go home. They slept where they could. Photos from the Library of Congress.

The 1937 sit-down strike at General Motors. Picture from the Archives of Michigan 16926.

how to run things. The companies did not like strikes. A strike meant no cars would be made. Still, working in the car factories got worse.

The Great Sit-Down Strike

By 1936, the car workers could not take it anymore. The workers were tired of low pay. They were tired of bad working conditions. They decided to have a strike. It took place in Flint. This was at General Motors. Suddenly, on December 30, all the workers stopped. They just sat down. They did not leave to go home. The company did not know what to think.

It was a **sit-down strike**. They blocked the doors so parts could not be taken out.

General Motors wanted the factories going again. They wanted to hire new workers. Fire the strikers! They told the police to get them out. Everyone was tense. What would happen next?

The Governor Comes

Governor **Frank Murphy** came to Flint. He worked to calm everyone. He sent 3,000 **National Guard** soldiers to Flint too. They arrived with all their guns. The governor did not want anyone starting a fight! He felt state government should keep the peace. It should protect people's rights.

National Guard soldiers at the Flint Strike

Governor Frank Murphy

Both photos from the Archives of Michigan

Victory For the Union

After 44 days, General Motors gave in. The United Auto Workers won the right to represent the workers. Wages were increased. The strikers were happy. The city of Flint was relieved.

That is how unions started in our state. There are several unions in Michigan today. In many ways unions have helped workers. Pay has gone up. Working hours are better. There is time to go to the water fountain. There is time for breaks.

There can be trade-offs though. Having unions also means products can cost more. Sometimes companies move their factories to places that do not have unions.

Michigan Specializes. We make Cars and Trucks

For almost 100 years, our state *specialized* in making cars and trucks. People in other states bought cars made here. We bought products they made. We depended on each other. When people specialize, they do depend on each other more.

What Happened Over the Years?

Our car companies are not doing as well today. Workers liked the idea of high pay. They also want good health care. Workers in other states and other countries often work for less pay. A car made in Michigan may cost more than a car made in **Japan** or **Korea**.

Sometimes the companies here make cars that use too much gas. When the price of gas goes up, people want smaller cars. Customers were buying more cars made in Japan or Korea. The customers felt those cars met their needs better.

Today, about 22 out of 100 cars made in this country are made in Michigan. In 1914 about 80 out of 100 cars were made in Michigan. That is a big difference! Can Michigan car companies grow again? It is hard to know. What will happen to our state if Michigan car companies close?

Trade-Offs

Specialize = Depend more on each other

Picture drawn by Aaron Zenz.

Think About It. Write About It!

1. Why was the Great Depression a bad time for workers?

2. What is a union and why did workers want to start one?

3. What did Walter Reuther do?

4. Which product has Michigan specialized in making for over 100 years?

Brain Stretchers

Think about cause and effect. How did the Great Depression lead to workers starting unions?

Think about the business of making cars in Michigan. Compare making cars in 1914 and making cars today. What has changed? Is the business better or worse? Make a graph to show the change.

Think Like an Entrepreneur

You are starting a new Michigan business. You will make a product. Decide what product you will make. Tell what need it meets. Tell what capital resources you need to make your product. Tell the human resources you must have. List the natural resources you will use to make this product.

Michigan Today and Tomorrow

Chapter 6 Lesson 1

Ideas To Explore

ethnic group (eth nik) - These are people who once lived together in another land. They have the same ancestors. In the past, they spoke the same language and had the same customs.

heritage (HAIR uh tij) - This is the history of a group of people. It includes foods and language. It includes the old ways of doing things. It includes the old customs and festivals.

Cities To Consider

Benton Harbor

Cassopolis (kass AH pul us)

People To Meet

ancestors (ann ces terz) - relatives from long ago

Places To Discover

Germany (jer man ee) - a country in Europe

Words to Welcome

Great Migration (my gray shun) - a time when people from the South came here to find better jobs

migrated (my grate id) - moved to a new place to start a home

Pow Wow - This is a special get-together or meeting of Native Americans. Pow Wows have dancing, singing and eating.

Michigan's People - Who Are We?

Think about this question while you read.
**Why did people from so many places
move to Michigan?**

It is exciting to learn about people. Michigan is home to people from many places.

Finding the home country of everyone is like a geography game. It will take you around the world. You may discover places that are new to you.

Having people from so many places is an advantage for Michigan. Why is this? We can learn so much from each other. We can learn about new foods. We can learn new games. We can find out new ways of doing things. We can share our holidays. We are ALL part of the Michigan family!

First, this was the land of the Native Americans. Today, Michigan has many groups of people. They came at many times and from many places. We call them **ethnic groups**.

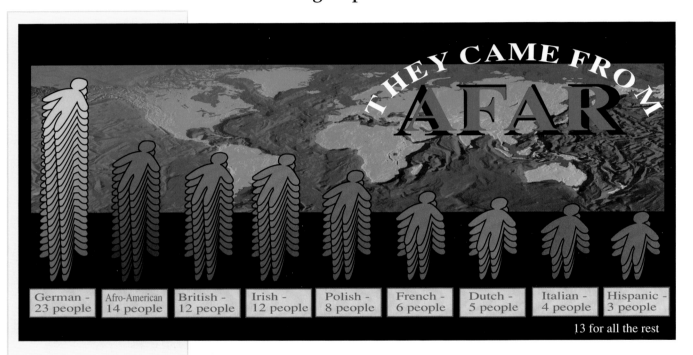

THEY CAME FROM AFAR

| German - 23 people | Afro-American 14 people | British - 12 people | Irish - 12 people | Polish - 8 people | French - 6 people | Dutch - 5 people | Italian - 4 people | Hispanic - 3 people |

13 for all the rest

This graph gives an average of what 100 people would say about their ancestors.

What About You?

Before your family came to Michigan, where did they live? Everyone moved here sometime. In which part of the world did your family first live? Did they move to the United States a long time ago? Maybe they just arrived.

The Native Americans- The First People

Who were the first people to live in Michigan? They were the Native Americans. They still live here. They did not disappear long ago. They were not all forced to move away. Today, they live and work much as everyone else. They may be teachers, computer programmers or home builders. If you sat next to a Native American at a ball game, you might not know it. They may look much like any other person.

A Native American girl

Native Americans do wear special clothes and headdresses for **Pow Wows**. They do this to help keep their history alive. They do the dances just as they did long ago. Some may beat on drums and others sing their old songs. Some learn to speak their native languages. They do this so their culture will not be forgotten.

Meet Some Native Americans

Meet Christine and Dakota. They live in Petoskey. They each enjoy doing Native American dances for Pow Wows. A Pow Wow is a special event. It is a time to renew the spirit of the tribe. It is a time to help keep their culture alive. A Pow Wow is a large meeting of many families. It has sacred ceremonies, dances, songs and food. In some ways it is like a family reunion.

At a Pow Wow each dance has a special meaning. Christine does a woman's dance. It is called the Southern Women's Traditional Dance. This dance represents the heartbeat of the Native American culture. The shawl Christine wears stands for the warmth women have for the young. It stands for the caring they give to the elders (the oldest adults).

Thank you Christine and Dakota!

265

Dakota does the grass dance. These dancers are the first at the meeting ground. They stamp down the long grass so it will be easier for the rest of the tribe. These dancers sway to imitate the long grass blowing in the wind.

All male dancers wear a headdress. These are made of things from animals and birds. Horsehair, porcupine quills and feathers may be used. There are different styles for each dance. The head-dress is worn to honor animals and birds.

The eagle is important to many Native Americans.

Native Americans have strong feelings for animals and birds. They have a tie with them. This tie goes back to the time of creation. The animals and birds are thought of as "brothers." They are honored whenever possible. This may be done through dances and art. Animal and bird designs are often seen in Native American art.

Shirley Brauker

Meet Shirley Brauker. She shares two cultures. Her mother is Odawa. Her father is German. Shirley lives in Coldwater with her husband. She has her own business there. It is called Moon Bear Pottery. Shirley is an artist who makes things from clay. She also teaches children. She tells them about Native American art and **heritage**.

Shirley Brauker and one of her creations.

Shirley thinks about her heritage as she works. Her pots have Native American designs. She often writes stories for each piece. The stories tell what the art means. She has won many awards for her work.

Where will you find Native Americans in Michigan? Where do they live? Each county has some, but Wayne County has the most. This is true for a number of groups since that county has the most people. Chippewa County is another with many Native Americans.

The French from the Fur Trading Days

The French began coming here in the 1600s. They started some of Michigan's first towns. They came to trade furs with the Native Americans. The need for furs pulled the French here. Over the years, jobs connected to natural resources brought many groups to Michigan.

The French also wanted spices and silk. These things were scarce in France. They did not find spices and silk here, but they knew China had them. They explored the Great Lakes looking for a way to reach China. They did not know it was so far away.

Later, more French **migrated,** or moved here. This was mostly during the logging days. Again,

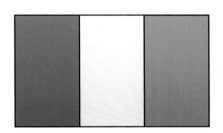

The flag used by France today

Mr. Cadillac is the person who started Detroit.

267

they came because of one of our great natural resources, the trees. They got jobs cutting down trees. They helped lumber towns like Bay City, Saginaw and Muskegon grow.

The flag Italy uses today

People from Italy

A few people from Italy came long ago. They came with the first French. Alphonse de Tonty was from Italy. He came to Detroit in 1701 with Cadillac. Later, Anne, his wife, joined him. Their daughter was the first European born in Detroit.

More Italians came here later. That was in the 1870s. They also moved here for jobs related to natural resources. They often went to the Upper Peninsula. They worked in the mines. They helped supply the human resources needed for the mines. They came to find a better life. In Italy there were few good jobs. The lack of good jobs in Italy pushed people away.

A miner from Italy

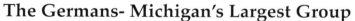

The Germans- Michigan's Largest Group

Many people here have **ancestors** from **Germany.** Germans are the largest ethnic group in Michigan. The first families came in the 1830s. They moved to Ann Arbor. They started the towns of Frankenmuth and Westphalia. They also moved to the land along the Saginaw River.

Why did the Germans leave home? They had two reasons. Both pushed them away. Their crops failed and they had political problems. In Michigan they often started farms. Later, they worked in factories. Walter Reuther was a famous labor leader. He had German ancestors.

Those With African Ancestors- 2nd Largest Group Here

Africa is a continent. It has many countries. It is a very large land. Africans do not all have the same customs or religion.

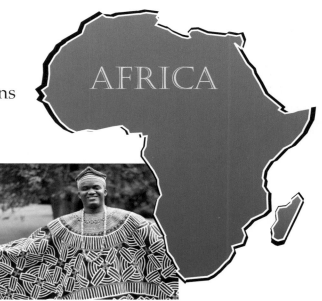

A few people with African ancestors came with the French. Remember Jean de Sable? His mother's family came from Africa. Most people from Africa did not come here until later.

A man from Cameroon in Africa

Seeking Freedom

Many people from Africa were taken by force. They were made slaves. Some of those slaves were shipped to the states in the south. Slaves had no freedom. They had no rights.

They ran away, even though doing so was dangerous. They might be beaten or killed if they were caught! The thought of freedom pulled them away. They could be free in Canada. They often used the Underground Railroad. This was a secret way of helping escaped slaves between 1830 and

Slaves did not have any rights. They were denied core democratic values.

1860. On their way, some stopped here and stayed. Some started farms. **Benton Harbor** and **Cassopolis** soon had many African Americans.

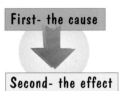

First- the cause

Second- the effect

The Great Migration

The South lost the Civil War in 1865. This ended slavery in our nation. Still, life was hard for African Americans in those states. Many worked on small farms and earned little money. They wanted a better life, but how? About 1914 they heard of jobs making cars in Michigan. They heard Henry Ford would pay five dollars a day! That was big money then. They left the farms in the southern states. They moved here to make cars and trucks. So many people moved north, it was called **The Great Migration**.

Leaders In Michigan

We have many African Americans who are leaders in our state. They may be teachers. Some own businesses. Others are lawyers. You may find them as lawmakers or judges. Several have become mayors.

Dennis Archer

It takes hard work to become a leader. Ask Dennis Archer. He knows. When he was a boy, he worked wherever he could. He washed dishes. He swept floors. Over the years, his jobs have really changed! He was a teacher and then a lawyer. He was also a justice on Michigan's State Supreme Court.

Rosa Parks (1913-2005) became famous for not giving up her seat on a bus. That was in Alabama. In 1957 she moved to Detroit.

Picture by George Rasmussen.

Dennis Archer also wanted to help his city- Detroit. He ran for the office of mayor. He won the election and was the mayor of Detroit from 1994 to 2001. He did well. *Newsweek* magazine honored him. It said he was one of the "25 Most Dynamic Mayors in America."

Today, Dennis Archer leads a large law firm in Detroit. For a time he was the president of the largest association of lawyers in our country. That was a great honor. People wonder if Mr. Archer may run for governor some day.

Dennis Archer

Think About It. Write About It!

1. Name the first two European groups to come to Michigan. What was something they were looking to find?

2. What is the largest ethnic group living in Michigan?

3. If a person *migrates*, what is he or she doing?

4. Which group often passed through Michigan on their way to Canada? Why were they going to Canada?

5. What was the Great Migration? About when did it start? What pulled those people to Michigan?

Words in Action

Tell what Native Americans may do today to keep their culture and heritage alive. Tell what you might see at one of these special events.

Chapter 6 Lesson 2

Cities To Consider ━━━━━━━━
Bronson
Frankenmuth (FRAY kin mooth)
Hamtramck (ham TRAM ik)
Hancock   Holland [the city]
Houghton (HO tun)
Iron Mountain   Iron River
Ishpeming (ISH pa ming)
Posen (POES in)
Southfield   Zeeland (ZEE lund)

People To Meet ━━━━━━━━
Arab Americans   Dutch
Hispanic (hiss pan ik)   Jewish (jew ish)

Places To Discover ━━━━━━━━
Finland
Holland (the country)
Iraq (I RACK)
Irish Hills
Jordan
Mexico (MEX eh co)
Saudi Arabia (SAW de • ah RAY bee ah)
Sweden (SWEE den)

Words to Welcome ━━━━━━━━
architect (ARK ih tekt)
Muslim (MUZ lem)
Nobel Prize (no BEL)
seaport (see port)

Michigan
Social
Studies
GLCES
3H3.0.3
3H3.0.10
3G1.0.2
3G4.0.2
3G4.0.3
3G5.0.2
3E1.0.1
4H3.0.2
4H3.0.3
4H3.0.9

More People Move to Michigan

Think about this question while you read.
What caused people to leave their home countries and move to Michigan?

Britain, Scotland, Cornwall and Wales

Europe

People from Britain- 3rd Largest Group Here

The British are also called the English. This group is the third largest group in Michigan.

There were many British in the first 13 states when our nation began. They left their mark on our country. Today, we speak their language. Our laws are based on British ideas. Most of the British started coming here about the time we became a state. That was in the 1830s. The Erie Canal helped make this possible.

The flag of Britain

The Irish- 4th largest Group Here

The year 1845 was a bad one in Ireland. That is when disease killed their potato crop. The Irish had very little to eat. The crop failure pushed them away. Many of them left their country.

Often the Irish made their new homes in Detroit. They helped that city grow. Many Irish also settled along U.S. 12. This area is now called "**The Irish Hills**."

Some Irish have been famous. One is Henry Ford. Henry's father was a poor Irish farmer. His name was William Ford. He came here in 1847. Henry became one of the richest people in the United States. Great things are possible here!

Ireland, Scotland, Wales, Britain, Holland, Poland, France, Italy

Frank Murphy also had Irish ancestors. He was one of our state governors in the 1930s. Later, he was on the United States Supreme Court.

The Polish- 5th Largest Group Here.

Poland is a country in Europe. Food was sometimes scarce there. At times, other countries attacked Poland. This made life difficult. Some Polish people wanted a safer place for their families. They came to the United States and to Michigan.

The country of Poland is a part of Europe.

Poland

EUROPE

The flag of Poland

A few Polish people have been here since the early times. The Godek family was here in 1762. They lived in Detroit. Most came much later.

In Michigan they often started farms. It was the work they knew best. They moved to small towns like **Bronson** and **Posen**. Bronson has a Polish festival each summer. Festivals like this are a way to keep their heritage alive. People get together and eat Polish food and do Polish dances.

Later, Polish people went to work in the car factories. They moved into towns like **Hamtramck** and helped it grow. They worked in the nearby Dodge factory.

The Dutch & Freedom of Religion

What if the government told churches what they could do and not do? That is what took place in the country of **Holland** long ago. This may sound strange to us now. Long ago, governments often controlled churches.

Some people in Holland did not like this. They could not change the government, so they left. Some of them reached Michigan in 1847. They started a new town. They named it Holland after their country. Grand Rapids also has many people with **Dutch** ancestors. So does **Zeeland**. *Dutch is another name for people from Holland.* The Dutch came here to find freedom of religion.

The people of Holland are known for growing tulips and for the windmills they once used.

Who are some people in Michigan with Dutch ancestors? Walter Chrysler is one. He started a car company in the 1920s. He created many jobs for our workers. The Meijer family came from Holland. They own the Meijer stores and built Meijer Gardens. Richard DeVos and Jay Van Andel are also famous. They started the Amway company.

Michigan Cities with Well-Known ETHNIC groups

275

The flag of Mexico

The Hispanic - A Group That Is Growing

This is a large group. It has people from many countries. **Mexico** is one of them. *Mexico is the country just south of the United States.* Most **Hispanic** people who live in Michigan came from Mexico.

At first, there were few Hispanic people here. As our state grew, it had more farms. Those farms needed helpers for the harvests. Farmers with fruit and vegetables needed many hands to pick the food. People from Mexico began to visit Michigan and help pick the crops. If you have ever tried it, you know picking crops is hard work.

By the 1920s, thousands of Hispanic workers helped with our harvests. Some brought their families and stayed. As the years passed, they found better jobs.

Some of the first Hispanic people in Michigan came here to help pick crops.

Photo from the Archives of Michigan.

Miguel "Mike" Navarro

In 1948, Miguel Navarro worked in the celery fields. He earned just 60 cents an hour. His wife, Isabel, worked beside him.

It took several years to find a good job. He wanted to start his own company. In 1977, Mr. Navarro bought a building. He made tortillas and taco chips. He sold these to Mexican restaurants. The business became very successful.

Miguel and Isabel are quick to encourage other Hispanics. He says, "Life, it's been a struggle, but there is no day that passes by that I don't thank the Lord. Thank him for the little bit that I have."

Tony and Carmen Benavides

The Benavides family left Mexico in 1952. They came to Lansing. The parents set goals for their children. They must be honest, work hard and have respect for others. They must have pride in themselves. They need to be a part of the community.

Tony was one of those children. He worked hard and studied hard. He harvested crops. He also worked in a grocery store to earn more money. He completed high school and college.

He was in charge of a community center for many years. He also served on the city council. He was elected the mayor of Lansing. That was in 2003. When he was mayor, he had a goal. His goal was to make Lansing a "Family Friendly City."

His wife Carmen also worked very hard. She went to college and became a teacher. Later, she was a school principal. Besides this, she was a mother with four children.

Tony and Carmen Benavides

Hispanic leaders urge young people to do well in school. They want them to achieve all they can in life!

People from Sweden - At Work In Forests and Mines

People from **Sweden** started to come to Michigan in the 1860s. They liked living in the Upper Peninsula. It was like their own country in many ways. It had many trees and lakes. It had much snow in the winter. They began to work in our mines and lumber camps.

The flag of Sweden

People from Sweden moved to Michigan in the 1800s.
They often settled in the Upper Peninsula.

Glenn Seaborg
at work in 1942.
Photos from
Lawrence Berkely
Laboratory.

William Milliken
when he was our
governor.
(to the right)

The scarcity of trees and copper in other places provided jobs here. The Swedish moved to towns like **Ishpeming**, **Iron River** and **Iron Mountain**. They helped these cities to grow. Many Swedes still live there.

People in Ishpeming are proud of Glenn Seaborg. He became famous. Glenn worked as a scientist and won a **Nobel Prize** in 1951. He got this prize for his work to help understand the atom.

Which Michigan governor served the most years? It was William Milliken. He was our governor for 14 years. His family also came from Sweden.

People from Finland

The people from **Finland** also came to the U.P. They began coming in the 1860s. The copper and iron mines gave them jobs. They also worked in the logging camps. Once again, work with natural resources pulled people to our state. They helped

cities like **Hancock** and **Houghton** grow. Learning was important to them. They started a college in Hancock.

People With Arab Ancestors

Michigan has a large group of Arabic people. It has more than most states. They live in cities near Detroit. Dearborn and **Southfield** are examples. They helped these cities grow. Many of them worked making cars and trucks.

This map shows where people with ancestors from Finland live.

Arabic people come from over 20 countries. **Saudi Arabia** is just one of them. People have moved here from **Jordan** and Lebanon. They have come from **Iraq** and Syria. Each year Detroit holds an Arab World Festival. People dance and eat. They listen to music. The festival preserves their culture. It is a time for them to remember their heritage.

The original lands of many Arabic people and the flags of some of their countries.

Many people living in the Arab world believe in the **Muslim religion**. However, quite a number of those living in Michigan are Christians.

Spencer Abraham is an **Arab American.** He grew up here. He has always been interested in government. He was elected as a U.S. Senator for Michigan. He was the only Arab American in the U. S. Senate at that time.

A mosque or Muslim place of worship in Dearborn, Michigan.

Casey Kasem's family came here from the small country of Lebanon. You may have heard of Mr. Kasem. He has worked in radio and television. For many years he had a radio program. It was about the top 40 songs. He also did voices for some characters on *Sesame Street*. Kasem wrote a short book, *Arab- Americans: Making a Difference*.

A Tough Trip- Moving Here Years Ago

It was not easy for many families to move to Michigan. Sometimes the father came first to earn money to bring the rest. That is what Darwin Toma did. He left Lebanon because there were few jobs there. He came to Dowagiac with his brother. He worked for six years and bought a small farm. He still did not have the money to pay for his wife and children to come. His brother decided to help. He sent money for tickets to the United States.

A trip to Michigan

What was it like to travel to Michigan from far away? Mrs. Toma rode camels and took a ship that sank along the way!

Mrs. Toma left in 1912. She and the children rode camels to the nearest **seaport**. They had a long ride on a ship to France. This was followed by a long train ride to another seaport. Was she afraid while she traveled? What was it like in a strange land? In France they boarded a big ship. It sailed to Britain and then headed to the United States.

One night everyone felt a big jolt. Soon the engines stopped. What was the matter? The ship hit an iceberg and was sinking! Mrs. Toma had to find her children and get into a lifeboat. They made it, but many people drowned in the cold Atlantic Ocean. Mr. Toma was so glad to see his family when they arrived in Dowagiac! You can read more about the Toma family in the book, *Grandma Survived the Titanic* by Joseph L. Thomas.

An iceberg sank her ship on the way to America and Michigan!

The Jewish

Ezekiel Solomon came to Michigan. That was in 1761. He was a fur trader at Mackinac Island. Chapman Abraham was another fur trader in Detroit. **Jewish** people came here from many countries over the years.

Jewish can mean different things. It can be a religion. It can be an ethnic group. Most Jewish people had ancestors from Israel long ago.

Other Jewish families reached Michigan beginning in the 1840s. The Emil Heineman family lived in Detroit. They gave clothes to help escaped slaves. Michigan had 151 Jewish families during the time of the Civil War. Out of those families, 181 men joined the army. They fought against slavery.

This is Albert Kahn in his office. Photo from the Archives of Michigan.

Albert Kahn was an **architect**. (ARK ih tekt) *Architects design buildings.* During his life he became famous. He is known for his car factory designs. He also designed other buildings. Most of his work was done in the 1920s and 1930s.

Some people of Jewish heritage have been politicians and judges. Charles Levin was a member of the state supreme court for many years. Carl Levin has been a U.S. Senator from Michigan for many years.

Mr. Yamasaki working with a model of the World Trade Center. Photo from the Library of Congress.

On the right is a Building he designed in East Lansing.

People from Japan

Some Japanese moved to Michigan after 1900. One of these was Minoru Yamasaki. (His name sounds like min or oo • yam ah sock ee.) Minoru was an architect. He worked in Detroit designing buildings. People liked his designs and he became famous. Yamasaki's best-known building was the World Trade Center. That was in New York City.

You could be at the mall. You see a Japanese family shopping. They may have moved to Michigan to manage a car parts company. Several Japanese companies are now in our state.

There Are More Groups

These are only a few of the groups who make our state great. There are many more you can study. The people who moved here did much to help Michigan grow. They started farms. They cut lumber. They mined natural resources. They built highways and worked in our factories. They have been teachers. They have been mayors, judges and lawmakers. They shared their cultures. They made Michigan a more interesting and better place to live.

This man from Scotland is playing a bagpipe.

You can see people playing bagpipes at Scotish festivals. One is held in Alma each year.

Think About It. Write About It!

1. How did people who moved from other countries help our cities grow?

2. Name a group who moved here to find freedom of religion.

3. Name one group where a push factor caused them to move to Michigan. Explain what pushed them from their homeland.

4. Name one group where a pull factor caused them to move to Michigan. Explain what pulled them here.

Words In Action!

Tell about some positive consequences of people migrating to Michigan.

Why do groups with ancestors from other countries have special festivals? Give an example.

Chapter 6 Lesson 3

Ideas To Explore

advertise - showing and telling customers about your products

interdependence - people depending on each other for products they each need

Places To Discover

Bangor

Colon

Mt. Clemens

Words to Welcome

brine - salt water that comes from under the ground

consumers - people who buy products. When you buy something, you are a consumer!

exported - a product that is shipped out of our country and sold

producers - the people and businesses that make products

trading partner - another country that we export products to or import products from

Michigan
Social
Studies
GLCES
3G4.0.1
3G4.0.3
3G5.0.2
3E1.0.1
3E1.0.3
3E2.0.1
3E3.0.1
4H3.0.1

284

Neat Stuff We Make Here

Think about this question while you read.
Why are products made where they are?

Many kinds of products are made in Michigan. People buy them. They use them to meet their needs and wants. Making and buying products is a part of our economy (ee kon uh me). What does economy mean? *The economy is all the activities that go into making and buying products and services. Filling needs and wants is what the economy is all about.*

The economy has two main parts. **Producers**, the makers, are one part. **Consumers**, the buyers, are the other.

In the economy, everyone makes choices. What should I buy? How much should I spend? How much should I save? What product should my company make? How many should we make? How much money should I charge for it?

People always decide the best way to use their resources. There are limits on every resource. There are limits on how many ice cream cones you can eat at one time. There are limits on the money to pay for them.

There are always limits.

There is never enough of everything for everyone!

What It Takes To Make A Product

It takes **3** kinds of resources to make any product.

1. natural resources

2. capital resources

3. human resources

Natural Resources

Materials from nature which are often used up to make the product

Oil to make plastic parts.

Iron ore to make the steel parts.

+

Capital Resources
or capital equipment

Acme Drop Forge Co.   Acme Drop Forge Co.

The machines and buildings used to make products.

+

Human Resources
- the workers -
or human capital

=

Products

Producers and Consumers
In Our Economy

Producers
make products

Consumers
buy and use products

YOU are a part of the economy too. Buying something or doing a job for someone makes you a part of it.

Everything on these two pages is a part of our economy. Businesses sell products to customers. Customers are also called consumers. They buy the products with their money.

How do businesses decide to make a new product? They look at the demand for it. Businesses want to make money. They want to earn a profit. If a new product will make them a profit, they will produce it. The desire to make what people will buy drives our economy.

The money businesses get from customers pays to make the product. It pays for the natural resources, capital resources and human resources used to make it. *The money left after these costs is* **profit** *for the business.*

Sharing Facts About Michigan Products

Your class wants to be e-mail pals with a class far away. Your teacher contacts a Florida school. Everyone in your class is excited. You want to tell your new Florida friends about Michigan!

You read to learn more about the things made and grown here. Soon you are very surprised. You had no idea so many things are made here- right in Michigan!

Cars and Trucks Are Big Business

What do many of our factory workers do? They make cars and trucks or parts for them! About 200,000 of our people do this kind of work. Three car companies have their headquarters in Michigan. They are Chrysler, Ford and General Motors.

Breakfast Cereal

Many of you start your day with breakfast cereal. It was probably made in Michigan. Kellogg's and Post cereals are made in Battle Creek. Battle Creek is the breakfast cereal capital for the country! Cereal made there is eaten around the world. The idea for many of these cereals started in Michigan. This changed the way millions of people begin their day!

Other Foods

Other yummy foods are made in Michigan. The Bob Evans company in Hillsdale makes sausage and other good things to eat. The Jiffy mixes you

A Japanese boy holding a box of cereal- Picture drawn by George Rasmussen

see in grocery stores are made in Chelsea. When you were a baby, you probably ate Gerber's baby food. That is made in Fremont. Vlassic pickles are made in Imlay City.

These products are made in Michigan. You may see them at the grocery store.

Helping People Feel Better

Some of you may take a vitamin at breakfast. Several kinds of medicine and vitamins are made in Kalamazoo. These are made by the Pfizer Company.

Dr. William Upjohn was a family doctor in the horse and buggy days. He began to make his own pills and medicines. The company Dr. Upjohn started has grown over the years. Today it has many scientists who spend their time looking for new medicines.

Kalamazoo also has a company called Stryker. Stryker helps people in many ways. If your granddad had to have a new knee, Stryker may have made it. They make replacement knees and hips and other medical products, like special hospital beds. One is called the "In Touch Bed." This bed can talk to doctors and patients! It helps the doctors know more about how to help patients.

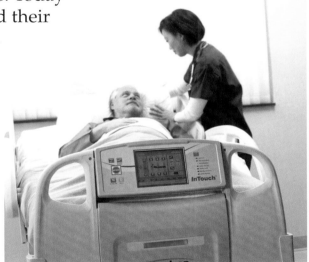

The *In Touch Bed* made by Stryker. Photo from Stryker.

A business can be started at a place because the person lives there. Dr. Upjohn's company was like that.

Other times, a business starts where the resources are. Mr. Dow started where he could get brine.

This is a well to bring up brine from under the ground. Brine is used to help make many products.

Why Are Businesses Started Where They Are?

When Dr. Upjohn started making pills, another man came to Michigan. He was Herbert Dow. Mr. Dow knew Michigan had much salt under it. A huge ocean left the salt. This ocean once covered the state.

The salt water can be pumped up using wells. This salty water is called **brine.** Herbert Dow knew a lot about science. He tested the brine. Besides salt, he found other chemicals. He wondered what he could make with them. He invented ways to take those chemicals out of the brine.

A Resource From Under the Ground

He began the Dow Chemical Company in Midland, Michigan. That was a good place for brine wells. This was in 1897. Soon his company was making many chemicals from brine. Today, Dow is the second largest chemical company in the country.

About 1940, some Dow scientists were making plastics. They made a clear, tough plastic wrap. Saran Wrap was born! For many years Saran Wrap was made in Midland. It is an interesting process. The plastic is melted and blown into big bubbles. The bubbles are rolled up and cut into strips. Those strips go into the boxes people buy.

Businesses often begin near the raw materials they use. Dow Chemical is one example. Michigan iron ore is made into steel for cars. Michigan corn goes into corn flakes. Wood was used to make furniture in Grand Rapids.

Furniture From West Michigan

Grand Rapids was a good place to make furniture. Cherry, maple and oak trees were nearby. Flowing water from the Grand River made the machines go. The Dutch workers were skilled in making things with wood.

At first, the furniture makers were small. They made beds and cabinets. They made chairs and tables. About 1870 they began to **advertise**. They took photographs of their furniture. They mailed the photos all over the country. Photos were new at that time. When people could see the furniture, they bought more. The factories became larger. Some used whole city blocks.

This is an ad for furniture from Grand Rapids. It is in a newspaper from 1915.

Ad from the Library of Congress

Railroads took the furniture to customers in many states. Grand Rapids became the furniture making capital. More was made there than anyplace else.

Facing Changes - What to Do?

In time, the furniture business changed. Furniture makers cut costs. It was cheaper to make it elsewhere. The Grand Rapids factories began to close. Some did not give up. They began to make a different kind of furniture. Now, they made furniture for offices and schools.

Now the Grand Rapids area is known for making office furniture. There are three big companies. Their names are Steelcase, Herman Miller and Haworth. They sell billions of dollars worth each year. About half of the office furniture made in this country comes from Michigan! It is even **exported**. That means it is shipped to other countries. Two of them are Canada and Mexico.

These pictures are from the Steelcase Company.

Products to Stand In and On!

You can ride in Michigan cars. You can eat Michigan food. You can sit on Michigan furniture.

You might be standing on another Michigan product. The sidewalk you walk on could be made

with Michigan cement. Yes, cement is made in Michigan! Alpena has one of the world's largest cement plants. You could be driving near Alpena and hear a big boom. The ground shakes. They are blasting limestone in a huge pit near the cement plant. It is dug from the ground near the plant. Ships take the cement to be used around the world.

The cement plant in Alpena, Michigan

Magic Is Big Business

When it is time for some fun, go to **Colon**, Michigan. Many magic supplies and tricks are made there. These products are exported to many countries and used by magicians. Can you figure out how they pull a rabbit out of the hat?

Think About Christmas!

Do you know someone who wants a model train for Christmas? Go to the factory and check them out. The Lionel Company, near **Mt. Clemens,** makes toy trains. The Kalamazoo Toy Train Company in **Bangor** also makes them.

Write your Christmas list. Then go and buy some lights and ornaments for the tree. There is no better place than a huge store in Frankenmuth. It is Bronner's and they sell all kinds of things for Christmas.

Many magic tricks are made in Colon, Michigan.

Who Is the Largest?

Michigan has many companies. They often sell products around the world. Some of our companies are huge. General Motors and Ford are two of the larger companies in the world.

Big Business!

Here is a list of some of the big companies in Michigan. They may also have factories and offices in other places.

TABLE: The Michigan Companies That Sell the Most

General Motors	$181 billion
Ford Motor	$154 billion
Dow Chemical	$53 billion
Whirlpool	$19 billion
Kellogg	$12 billion

These numbers are for a recent year. The numbers will change from year to year and the order may change too. *(Source: Value Line Investment Survey)*

It is hard to list all of the products made in our state. What is made in your hometown? Remember, Michigan has products you can wear, eat, ride and play with!

Selling to Other Countries- Exports

Michigan has some great products. Things made here are wanted all over the world. Many of Michigan's companies sell their products in other countries.

The Canadian flag

The flag of Mexico

The flag of Japan

TABLE: Where Michigan Products Go:

Canada	$26 billion
Mexico	$5 billion
China	$1.5 billion
Japan	$1.3 billion
Germany	$1.3 billion

There is a name for products sold to other countries. They are called exports. It is good we can export products. This brings money to Michigan. It makes jobs for Michigan people.

Buying From Other Countries- Imports

We cannot make everything here. Often we need to buy things from other countries. If it comes from another country, it is an import. Without imports, we would not have some things we use and eat. Bananas and chocolate are two examples. We also import coffee and tea. Often the fish you buy in the store is imported, too.

Lots of Imports From These Countries:

Canada (sends the most, about $49 billion worth)
Mexico
Japan and China

Look at the chart of exports and the one for imports. You can see Canada is our biggest **trading partner**.

Products are sent around the world in cargo ships like this. Photo from the author.

Why Do We Import Products?

Each place sells what it grows or makes the best. Farmers cannot grow bananas in Michigan. It is too cold for bananas here. Cherries and apples grow well in our state. It is too hot to grow apples in the jungles where bananas grow.

Each Place Specializes

Doing what you do best and using your strong points is **specialization**.

Specialization is doing what you do best.

Suppose Karri is the best pitcher but the worst catcher. If you play softball, Karri should pitch, not be the catcher.

Compare the farmers. People depend more on each other when they specialize. The banana farmer needs the apple farmer. Where else will he or she get apples? Depending on each other is called **interdependence.** This is another way to say each person needs the other.

As people specialize, there are more imports and exports. More products are shipped from one country to another. Bananas are shipped from the jungles to Michigan. Apples or cherries leave here and go there. Products cost less if you buy them from people who specialize.

Think About It. Write About It!

1. What are the two main parts of the economy?

2. Name the three types of resources used to make all products.

3. What do we call the money left over after a business has paid all its expenses?

4. Name a product that is imported to Michigan.

5. Making which product provides the most jobs in our state?

6. Name the country that is Michigan's biggest trading partner. It is the one from whom we import the most and to whom we export the most.

Brain Stretchers

Name a product made in or near your city. Name the company that makes it. Tell one natural resource used to make it.

Draw a picture to show how Michigan is a part of the world economy.

Make a Chart Today

Choose two of Michigan's trading partners. Make a chart to show the value of exports we sell to them in a year.

297

Chapter 6 Lesson 4

Ideas To Explore ————————————————————

climate - This is the pattern of weather in a region over a long time. Here are two climate questions. How much snow is there usually in December? How hot is it usually in June?

Words to Welcome————————————————————

maple syrup - a sweet dark liquid often used on pancakes and waffles. The real syrup comes from maple trees. Stores also sell syrup that is man-made.

sap - This is the clear liquid that moves from the roots to the branches of trees in the early spring. It is not sweet until it is boiled down. Syrup can be made from trees besides maple, but that is the best.

sugar beets - a big white beet that grows under the ground. It is the root of the plant. It has much sugar. Sugar sold in stores comes from sugar beets or sugar cane. Sugar cane does not grow in Michigan.

Places to Discover

fruit belt - This is the land along Lake Michigan that is very good for growing fruit. The lake helps keep the temperature just right.

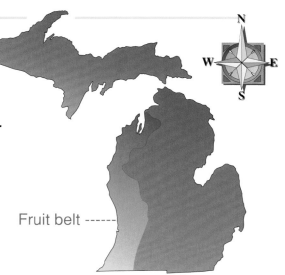

Fruit belt ------

Good Things to Eat From Michigan

Think about this question while you read.
**Why do Michigan farmers specialize
in some crops?**

Maybe we should call Michigan the yummy state! Many foods are grown here.

Why are foods grown where they are? Parts of Michigan have just the right conditions for some foods. The climate helps. The right kind of soil helps.

An apple orchard

The Fruit Belt

We have lots of cherries. Have you ever bought any at a roadside stand? Cherries come from around Traverse City. They are also grown in other towns near Lake Michigan. This area is called the **fruit belt**. The water of the lake helps to make the **climate** just right.

Michigan is the big producer of tart cherries. We grow more than any other state. If all our cherry crop went into one pie, it would be a monster. It would weigh more than 250 million pounds!

Other farms specialize in blueberries. The sandy soil along Lake Michigan is just right for them. Michigan grows more blueberries than any other state.

Michigan cherries-
above and blueberries
- below

299

Several kinds of dry beans are grown in Michigan.

Apples like a cold winter and warm summer. They grow well here. Only one state grows more apples than Michigan. Our farmers grow about one billion pounds of apples each year! Peaches are also grown in several parts of our state.

Beans, Beans, Beans

Ready for some hot chili? We will bring the beans! Michigan grows about 300 million pounds of beans each year! We are second among the states in growing dry beans that people eat. Dry beans are kinds other than green beans.

These beans are grown around Saginaw and Bay City. So many beans are grown here we cannot eat them all. What happens to the rest? They are exported to Europe on ships.

Sweet Stuff

Farmers in the thumb area grow an unusual crop. They grow **sugar beets**. These beets are not eaten. They are used to make sugar. Sugar from these beets is just like the sugar from sugar cane. The sugar you buy could be from Michigan sugar beets.

The Lower Peninsula's Thumb

A sugar beet harvestor and a sugar beet

The **maple syrup** on your pancakes may come from Michigan, too. Michigan is one of the leading makers of maple syrup! People collect the **sap** in February and March. Snow is often still on the ground.

Green Sprouts

Much celery is grown here. The farmers around Kalamazoo were pioneers in growing celery. Long ago, Michigan was the number one grower of celery. Now, more celery comes from California. Today, we are the third biggest celery grower.

Moo!

Do not forget Michigan cattle and cows. They give us beef and milk. The dairy business brings Michigan farmers the most money of all.

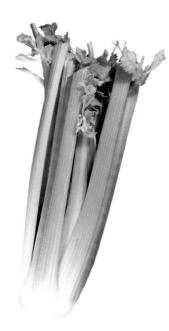

TABLE: Value of Michigan Food Products for a Recent Year in **millions of dollars.**

14	Celery
35	Tart Cherries
50	Blueberries
50	Cucumbers
75	Dry Beans
85	Apples
112	Sugar beets
166	Pork (pigs)
205	Beef
365	Soybeans
365	Corn
712	Milk

(There can be big changes year to year.)

A photo of Holstein cows from Michael and Susan Dietz

301

Keep your eyes open. Michigan potatoes can come in many shapes!

TABLE: How Much We Grow Each Year in **Millions of Pounds**

Apples	1,000
Beans (dry)	600
Beef	485
Celery	99
Cherries (tart)	250
Corn	13,000
Cucumbers	120
Grapes	43
Milk	5,945
Pork	503
Soybeans	4,700
Sugar Beets	6,400
Wheat	1,920

Let's Say Thanks!

Michigan farmers give us much good food to eat. It is hard work to grow all this food. Most farmers work long hours. The average farmer produces enough to feed about 125 people! Be grateful to the farmers for the work they do for us.

Thanks

Jonathan enjoys some Michigan watermelon.

Think About It. Write About It!

1. Name two foods Michigan grows more of than any other state.

2. Why do some Michigan farmers specialize in certain crops? How does this make us more interdependent?

3. Which farm product brings farmers the most money in our state?

4. Think about cause and effect. Choose a fruit shown on the table from page 302. What would be the effect on the crop of a bad frost in May?

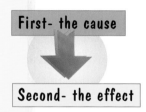

Think Like a Geographer

Draw a simple map of Michigan. Show where the fruit belt is found. Label it and name a food grown there. Show the "Thumb." Label it and name a crop grown there.

Think Like an Economist

Name one capital resource used by farmers. Name one natural resource used by farmers. How do farmers use these things to produce our food?

Think Like a Historian

How has farming in Michigan changed since the days of the pioneers? You may wish to compare the number of farmers, the crops, the equipment and other things you believe are important.

Make a Chart Today

Choose three foods grown in Michigan. Make a chart showing information about these foods. Label each part of your chart correctly.

Chapter 6 Lesson 5

Ideas To Explore

service jobs - Doctors, nurses and teachers do jobs
that are services. You cannot usually hold a
service in your hand like a product.

People To Meet

President Gerald Ford

tourists - These are the people from other places
who visit us while on vacation.

Places To Discover

Munising
Sleeping Bear Sand Dunes
Tahquamenon Falls
The Soo - Sault Ste. Marie

Words to Welcome

tourist attractions - These are places tourists like to
visit. See examples on the map on page 312.

The lighthouse
at Escanaba

Miner's Castle at
the Pictured Rocks

304

Tourists Are Big Business

Think about this question while you read.
Why do people come to Michigan for vacations?

Who are **tourists**? Why are they important to Michigan's economy? *Tourists are people from other places who visit while on their vacations.* They are important because they spend about $18 billion a year in Michigan! That is a lot of money.

Tourists spend money at motels. They buy meals in restaurants. They buy gas in gas stations. They get gifts from shops to take home. This brings money to the people who own these businesses.

About 150,000 people in our state have jobs because of tourists. Some people wait on tables. Others work in gas stations. Some make the beds in motels.

It Is a Service Business

Most tourist businesses offer services, not products like cars. You cannot hold a service in your hand. In Michigan, the number of **service jobs** is growing. Doctors, nurses and teachers are others who provide services.

Where Do They Visit?

Which are the places tourists visit? You can learn about them by region. Here are some of the most popular places.

THE DETROIT REGION–

Southeastern Michigan has many places to visit. They are all near Detroit.

Dearborn

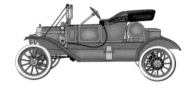

Honk! Honk! Watch out; here comes a Model T. You cannot stand in the middle of the street! Model Ts still drive down the streets at The Henry Ford. That is the name for Greenfield Village and the Henry Ford Museum. The Henry Ford is in Dearborn. Yes, you can ride in a Model T. You can also take a steam train to the next station at the Henry Ford. You can see what a factory was like 120 years ago.

Motown Museum

Detroit

Do you want to see where the Supremes and Stevie Wonder worked? Then visit the Motown Museum in Detroit. This is a great stop if you like the music once made there.

One of Detroit's newest museums is the Museum of African American History. Discover the accomplishments of African Americans in Michigan and the nation.

Museum of African American History

306

THE MID STATE REGION–

REGGIE REGION

Drive northwest from Detroit. A few miles beyond Flint is the small town of Frankenmuth.

Frankenmuth

Need to buy some things for your Christmas tree? Visit Bronners in Frankenmuth. If shopping makes you hungry, this town is well-known for good places to eat. It is a top tourist stop. In Frankenmuth many of the people have German ancestors.

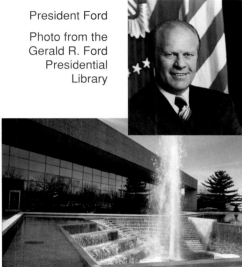

President Ford

Photo from the Gerald R. Ford Presidential Library

Grand Rapids

Have you ever wanted to visit the White House? You can do it. You do not even need to leave Michigan. Just go to Grand Rapids. Grand Rapids has two big museums downtown. One is in honor of past **President Gerald Ford**. This is his hometown. Inside the museum you can see a copy of the Oval Office from the White House. It is just like it was when Mr. Ford was President. That was from 1974 to 1977.

Gerald Ford Presidential Museum

The other museum is the Van Andel Museum Center. Here you can walk down an old street and visit the stores. You can learn all about how furniture was made. The museum even has a big carousel that kids can ride.

Van Andel Museum Center in Grand Rapids

Another great place is Meijer Gardens in Grand Rapids. The gardens have beautiful flowers. There is a giant statue of a horse and a butterfly house.

Holland

Where can you see fields and fields full of tulips? Go to Holland, Michigan, for its tulip festival. It is held each spring. There are acres of red, yellow, pink and orange tulips.

Kalamazoo

Do you like airplanes? Visit the Kalamazoo Aviation History Museum. Sometimes it is called the Air Zoo. It has all kinds of old planes to see. Some of them are really big.

Lansing

Where do thousands of students visit each year? Students like you go to the Michigan Historical Museum in Lansing. Inside you can see part of a copper mine. You can touch real "big wheels" like the lumberjacks used. It is almost like going back in time.

Muskegon

Ready for some thrills? Try out roller coasters and some great water rides. Go to Michigan's Adventure Park. It is near Muskegon.

Picture supplied by Michigan's Adventure Amusement Park.

There are over 50 rides at the park. With names like the Funnel of Fear tornado slide, it is no wonder over 800,000 people stop here each year!

THE NORTHERN REGION
Mackinac

Drive north on I-75 to the Mackinac Bridge. In the summer you will not be alone. Thousands of tourists travel north to see this part of Michigan. You will see campers and motor homes along the way.

Near the south end of the bridge is a fort. This is Fort Michilimackinac. It was captured by Chief Pontiac's warriors in 1763. They have people dressed as they did years ago. Some British soldiers are marching by now!

Drive north across the bridge. It is so tall you can see ships go under it. It is like driving in the sky! Look to the right. You can see Mackinac Island.

Mackinac Island really takes you back in time. You must use a boat to go to it. There are no cars on the island. Everyone must walk, ride a bicycle or use a horse. Horses pull carriages on the island. The carriages take people

No to cars
Yes to fudge!

where they need to go. It is just like it was over 100 years ago. Mackinac Island is a popular place to visit.

Pictured Rocks

Go to **Munising**. Take a boat ride in Lake Superior. It is the best way to see the Pictured Rocks. These high cliffs are streaked in many colors. I hope you have your camera. You will want to take pictures of the rocks!

Sleeping Bear Dunes by Nancy Hanatyk

Sleeping Bear Dunes

Did you like to play in a sandbox when you were little? Where is the world's biggest sand pile? It may be **Sleeping Bear Sand Dunes**. There is sand as far as you can see! It goes for about 35 miles. There is a legend about how the dunes were formed. Do you know the story?

The Soo

Sault Ste. Marie is also called "**the Soo**." On one side is Lake Superior. On the other side is Lake Huron. The Soo Locks are in between. Lake Superior is higher than Lake Huron. Water rushes between them. Without the locks, ships cannot sail between the lakes. You can stand at the locks and watch the ships go through.

Tahquamenon Falls

Pretty waterfalls always are a nice place to visit. **Tahquamenon Falls** are in the eastern part of the Upper Peninsula. Tourists visit them all year. Hear the water roar as it goes over the edge. These are Michigan's largest waterfalls.

Several tourist stops are natural resources. This is often true in the northern region. These are not resources that are mined or cut down. These are resources people enjoy seeing. They pull people to visit this part of Michigan. Many tourist businesses are located near pretty places.

It is important to make sure these places stay clean. It is important they are not damaged by pollution. We want people to enjoy visiting Michigan.

Do you have other places you like to visit in Michigan? You may want to tell your class about your favorite. There are many we did not mention.

See Michigan!

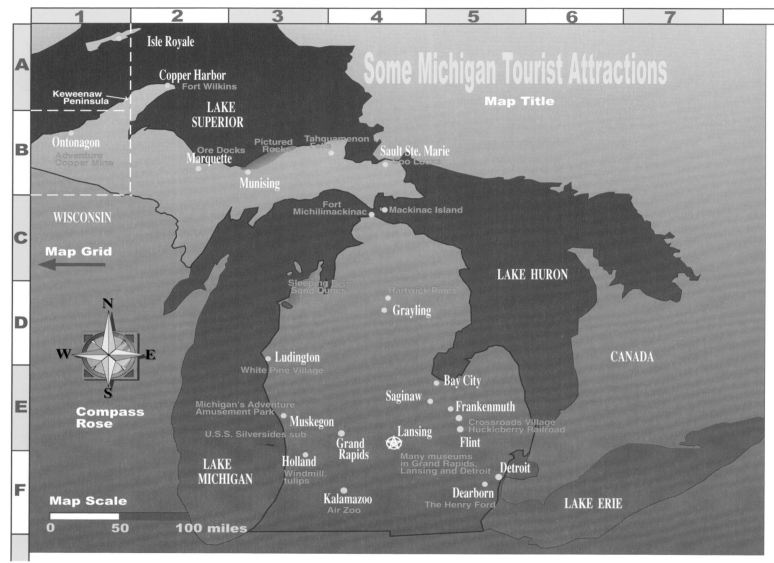

Using a Map

This map shows places tourists like to visit. It also has features that help people use the map. It has a map grid along two sides. You can use the grid to help others find places on the map. Look at the top left corner. The grid makes boxes on the map. Two are shown. The Adventure Copper Mine is in B-1. Where is the dot for Fort Wilkins?

The map also has a map scale. It helps tell the distance between places. This scale shows 50 and 100 miles. You can see it is more than 50 miles across Lake Michigan, but less than 100 miles. What is the map title? What does the compass rose tell you?

Think About It. Write About It!

1. Why are tourists an important part of Michigan's economy?

2. Name three places tourists like to visit in Michigan. Tell in which region each is found.

3. Some tourist attractions are also natural resources. Name one example.

4. Why is it important to the tourist business to keep our state clean and pretty?

Be a Geographer

Choose a tourist attraction from the map on page 312. Plan a trip from your home to this place. Give its location using the map grid. Tell which direction you will travel. Tell about how many miles you will drive there and back.

Promote a Place

Pick a tourist attraction. Plan a web site for this place. Tell what you would put on 4 screens for the web site. Why should they visit it? What do you think people should know about it? How will they find it? (Once you are done, see if they already have a web site. Visit it. See what they put on their web site.)

Chapter 6 Lesson 6

Ideas To Explore

high technology- This is the use of science in business and research. It may use many computers and complex machines.

Places To Discover

automation alley - A nickname for the cities around Detroit where many research and technology businesses are located. Automation is using machines to do more work faster and easier with fewer people.

Words to Welcome

life sciences - the areas of science related to living things and medicine

loan - A loan is borrowing money for some purpose. Loans must be paid back plus some extra money which is called interest.

research - Research is using science to find new ways to do things.

solar cells - devices that change the light energy from the sun into electricity

tax breaks - incentives from the government for people or businesses to do certain things

universities - These are places where people go to learn more once they finish high school. Universities usually have thousands of students. Students often do research at universities.

Michigan
Social
Studies
GLCES
3G4.0.1
3E1.0.2
3E1.0.5

Tomorrow's Jobs
What Will You Do?

Think about this question while you read.
How can you get ready for the kind of work you will do when you are an adult?

Michigan has been around for a long time. Many years ago the fur trade was our biggest business. Over the years, this business slowed down. Now it is gone. Later, we had copper mining. Now all the copper mines are closed. Once loggers worked hard cutting down our trees. How many loggers do you know today? These businesses are not what they once were. About 80 years ago most cars were made here. We still make cars, but that is changing too.

We all face changes. The products people need and want change. The businesses that can make products for the lowest costs change.

Today, workers in other countries work for less. The cost of human resources in Michigan is higher. This means most products can be made for less in another place. This is a big issue for Michigan. What can we do about it? For us to succeed, we must work smarter and work harder.

Businesses will always be important. We need them to give us jobs. We need them to hire workers.

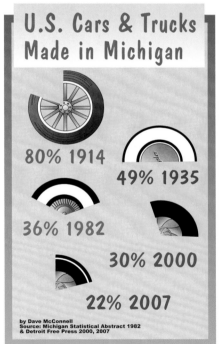

U.S. Cars & Trucks Made in Michigan

80% 1914

49% 1935

36% 1982

30% 2000

22% 2007

by Dave McConnell
Source: Michigan Statistical Abstract 1982
& Detroit Free Press 2000, 2007

The question is, which businesses will they be? It is important to have new businesses to replace ones that have faded away. If we do not do this, there may not be enough jobs. Long ago, people left their home countries to find work here. We do not want people to leave here to find work someplace else.

Many of tomorrow's jobs will be very complex. Workers will need all kinds of skills.

Our state wants new businesses. It likes ones that use **high technology** or high tech. The governor has talked about it. Workers in these businesses need education. They must know how to use computers. They need to know how to use complex machines.

Who knows what kind of technology we will see in the future!

There is a part of Michigan called **automation alley**. What does this mean? Automation is a way for machines to do most of the work by themselves. An alley is a small street. It does not actually mean a small street in this case. It is a nickname. They call it an alley because it is an area. It is a part of Michigan with many high tech companies. This area is near Detroit. It includes eight counties.

Here is a robot welding arm.
This is an example of automation.

Over 300,000 highly skilled people work in the "alley." A company there may make robots. It might design software for computers. It might make **solar cells**. *Solar cells take light from the sun and change it into electricity.*

Subhendu Guha is the president of United Solar Ovonic in Auburn Hills. He is holding some solar cell film. Photo from the company.

Research is important to high tech companies. *Research is using science to find new ways to do things.* High tech business is often found near **universities**. There they have men and women who know much about science. They also spend a lot of time doing research. The universities can help these new businesses. They can share knowledge. They help to find answers.

Universities also do research in the **life sciences**. What are life sciences? They are connected to health. People working in these areas may try to cure a disease like cancer. They may

A life sciences research worker

Doctors work in the life sciences.

make products to help people feel better and live longer. We already have some big life science businesses. Many people want to see us have more of these businesses here.

Starting a high tech business is not easy. It takes a great deal of money. The business needs computers and other equipment. Paying scientists cost a lot, too. There are risks in this kind of business. Sometimes things do not work out. The business may fail. If that happens, the investors lose all of their money.

Our government wants new businesses to start here, too. Businesses pay taxes. They pay wages to workers. The workers also pay taxes. This helps the government to pay its costs. Business is good for all of us.

**WANTED
New Businesses**

Since government wants new businesses, they may help start them. How do they do that? They may give them incentives. Remember, an incentive is a reward for doing a certain action. In this case, it is a reward for starting a business. It is to help a business start in Michigan. Incentives may be **tax breaks**. They may be **loans** of money. These things make is easier for new businesses to get started. They help new companies keep going until they are bigger and stronger.

What kinds of jobs will you have when you grow up? Maybe you will help make cars that can go places by themselves. Maybe you will help build windmills that make electricity.

Think About It. Write About It!

1. Often old businesses fade away. Why is it important to replace them with new ones?

2. Michigan faces a big issue with the cost of human resources. What is it?

3. Automation alley is an area in our state. It has this nickname because of its high tech businesses. Give an example of a business that could be in this part of our state.

4. Give an example of a product that a life sciences company could make.

5. Why are high tech businesses often near universities?

6. What is an incentive our state may give to a new high tech business?

7. Think of the incentive from question 6. How could it help a new business decide to start in Michigan?

Words In Action

Think about your future. What kind of job would you like to have when you grow up? What education will you need to do this job?

The Government of Michigan

Chapter 7 Lesson 1

Ideas To Explore

democracy - dem oc russ ee

voting - It is the way to decide whom the people want to represent them.

Why do we have government? We need government because we cannot do everything by ourselves.

Candidates run
for office

People to Meet

candidates - These are the people who want to hold an office, such as mayor. The voters will choose one of the candidates.

dictator - This is a person who takes over and does what he or she wants to do. A dictator does not ask others what they want.

mayor - the leader of city government

voters - These are the citizens over 18. They decide which person will hold a government office.

Michigan
Social
Studies
GLCES

3C1.0.1
3C3.0.2

Words To Welcome

consequences - What happens when something is done. If you hit someone, there will be negative consequences.

election - This is the time when the voters choose people to hold government offices.

rights - the freedoms given to us by the constitution

tax - money paid by people to run the government

Why Do We Have Government?

Here are two questions for you to think
about while you read.
**Which of our needs does government do for us?
How does it take care of them?**

Our government has many parts and does
many things. Let's start by finding out one reason
we have government.

A True Story

To do that, go back in time over 100 years.
Here is a true event. A man and his wife were going
down a country road. They rode in their horse-
drawn buggy. They reached a small bridge and
began to go across. Suddenly the bridge gave way!
The man, the lady, the horse and the buggy all
splashed into the river. They were left gurgling and
splashing in the water. They were not hurt, but their
trip was ruined.

Picture drawn
by Aaron Zenz.

The people were surprised, but not too surprised. They saw the bridge was not in good shape. Why was the bridge left in bad condition? Who was taking care of the bridge? This is the point of the story. No one was in charge of taking care of the bridge!

Many years earlier a farmer built the bridge. He spent his own money to do the job. When it was done, he took care of it. For years no one else helped him. Finally, he grew tired of doing the repairs and stopped.

At that time, Michigan state government did not build or repair roads! Each landowner along a road helped to take care of it. That is the way it used to be!

Services

One Reason - Services We Cannot Do Alone

This story shows one reason why we have government. It can do things for us that are hard for us to do alone. What if each person took care of the road in front of his or her home? It would be hard to have the good roads we have today. Travel would be very hard.

Today, our government builds roads and bridges. It runs our schools and courts. In the city, it brings us our water. It provides police. It hires fire fighters. It can also build parks, schools and other things that few people could do on their own. Doing these things helps the common good. Everyone can use them and benefit from them. Everyone has a better life because of these services.

Second Reason- Protecting Our Rights

Our government also helps protect our **rights**. It keeps the strong from ruling everyone else. It helps give us all justice. What are our rights? These are the freedoms we have. We have the right to free speech, the right to own property and many others.

Protecting our rights

Here is a true story. A long time ago a man named Erastus Hussey lived in Battle Creek. He was firmly against slavery. He helped escaped slaves on the Underground Railroad. Erastus also printed a newspaper called the *Liberty Press*. He used it to tell others why slavery was wrong. Mr. Hussey was using his right of free speech when he took a stand against slavery.

Someone did not like what Mr. Hussey printed in his newspaper. One night they set fire to his building. That was on June 9, 1849. If we did not have any government, things like this might happen often. The government tries to protect the rights of people like Mr. Hussey.

Third Reason - Making Our Laws

Laws are rules to live by. We have laws so people will be safe and can have a good life. Laws help keep people from doing things they should not do– like driving too fast.

Making laws

Laws protect us
from people
who do not behave!

Come on.
We can
do this!

Leadership

Most laws are just common sense. People should be nice to each other. They should not do things that hurt or bother others. Sadly, many people think only of themselves. There are those who cheat others. Some people pollute the air we all breathe or the water we all drink. Some bad people rob others. Laws remind us to behave and punish those who do not behave. What would it be like to live in a place that had no laws?

Our laws also help manage conflicts between people. Suppose your neighbor parks his car on your lawn. He says you have more room than he does. There are laws about this kind of thing. They remind us to think about the rights of others.

Fourth Reason- Leadership and Planning

People need leaders. They need someone to plan what projects must be done. We need people who know how to solve problems. Our president, governor and mayors work to give us leadership. They work to find ways to solve the problems we face. They try to get people to understand issues. They try to be good examples for us.

An Election Brings A Big Change

Imagine your town is going to have an **election**. It will choose a new **mayor**. Your class is going to study the election. *An election is when people decide which person will hold each office.* The people do this by **voting**. *Those who want these jobs are called* **candidates**. The people choose the candidate they think will be the best. The person with the most votes gets the job.

Two people want to become the mayor of your town. Each one has different ideas. Your class is reading newspapers to find out about their ideas. You are also listening to the radio and watching television to see what the candidates say.

Mr. Sam Same is one candidate. He tells people city government is doing a good job. He says he will keep doing things just the same.

Sally Saver is the second person who wants to be mayor. She has other ideas. She has heard people complain they pay too many **taxes**. Tax money is the way we pay for government. Sally thinks if there is less government, taxes can be lowered. She believes this is what most people want in your town.

Sally Saver thinks by doing what people want, they will vote for her. Sally hands out papers explaining her stand. She speaks to groups of voters to tell them what she will do once she is the mayor.

Everyone talks about taxes!

325

Who Can Vote?

Today is the election. The **voters** are ready to decide which person will be the new mayor. Who are the voters? Who can vote? Each voter must also be a citizen of the United States. They must be at least 18 years old.

The radio station gave the results that night. Sam Same had 1,500 votes and Sally Saver had 1,850. Sally Saver is the new mayor!

A Big Change- No Government At All!

Now Sally must decide what to do as mayor. She promised to cut taxes. Cutting taxes will save everyone money. She believes the more money people save, the more they will like her as mayor.

Mayor Sally Saver says, to save the most money, there will not be any city government! She will not be paid. She thinks this will make her a very popular mayor. City government has ended. What will the city be like the next day?

What Will You Miss the Most?

What service would you miss the most with no city government? This is the opportunity cost of the change. Do you remember what opportunity cost means? Check the glossary for a review. Do you think Mayor Sally Saver's plan will be a good one? Will there be **consequences** of no government? What are consequences? *Consequences are things that happen because of an event. The event is the cause and the consequences are the effects.* Will people in the

Opportunity Cost !

town face other costs because there is no city government?

What could be some problems if this were your town? What will happen if there is a fire and your town has no fire department? What will happen if there is a break-in and no police? What will happen if there is a big hole in your main street? Who will fix it? Can you think of some other issues that will cause problems?

Is it possible to have too little government? What do you think?

What About Too Much Government?

Can there be too much government? Can too much government create problems? Can you think of some issues too much government may cause? For one thing, government costs money. The more government, the more money it needs from taxes. The more people pay in taxes, the less they have left for themselves.

What would your streets be like if there was no city government?

If our government were too large, it might forget about what people want. It might spend its time finding ways to become even larger and more powerful. These are some reasons we do not want a huge government.

A really big government has problems, too.

In our government, the power comes from the people. We have a **democracy**. This means, in the end, the voters decide what happens. They have the final say.

Dictators have no rules.

Governments in some countries have a **dictator** in charge. *A dictator does whatever he or she wants. A dictator has no rules. He or she just takes over. A dictator does not need to be elected.* A dictator does not need to ask YOU what YOU want. There might not ever be any votes in a nation with a dictator.

They Are Interested in You!

The leaders of our government ARE interested in what you want. Still, they must balance the needs and wants of all the people. This means some people may not like what is done some of the time. If the leaders fail to do what most people want, they will be voted out of office.

Think About It. Talk About It!

1. Give four reasons why we have government.

2. Name two things you would miss the most if your town had no government.

3. How do government leaders get their jobs?

4. Who is allowed to vote?

5. Name two ways city government helps us.

6. How do we pay for government?

7. Who has the final say in our government?

Words in Action

What problems can happen if a town has no government?

What kind of problems can we have if there is too much government?

Brain Stretchers

What limits the amount of money government can spend?

Chapter 7 Lesson 2

Ideas To Explore
representative government

republic - The kind of government where people use their power by voting. It comes from old Latin words meaning "people matter."

People to Meet
city council - the people who govern a city

county commission - the group who govern a county

representatives - the people who take our places in government

Places To Discover

district - This is an area of land. All the people living there are represented by the same person.

state house of representatives - one part of the state law makers

state senate - the other part of the state law makers

Washington, D.C. - our nation's capital city

Words To Welcome
communication - keeping in touch by talking, using letters, e-mails, radio and television

income tax - a part of the money people earn that goes to pay for the government

property tax - a part of the value of homes, offices and farms that goes to pay for the government

sales tax - an extra amount added to the cost of most things bought in stores which helps pay for the government

surveys - asking what people think about issues

Michigan
Social
Studies
GLCES
3C2.0.1
3C3.0.2

Who Takes Your Place and Why?

Here are two big idea questions for you
to think about while you read.
What is representative government?
Why do we have it?

We make new laws to solve new problems.
Making new laws is important. Still, most people
are too busy to help make laws. They do not have
time to go to Lansing. We vote for others to do this
for us. These people represent us. Since they do this
for us, we call them **representatives**. Having others
take our place gives us "**representative govern-
men**t."

This kind of government is also called a
republic. Republic comes from old Latin words.
These words mean "people matter." Remember,
the power comes from the people. They use this
power when they vote. In the end, the people
control the government. To be a good voter, each
person needs to know about the candidates. They
need to know what they will do in office.

How Many Lawmakers Does Michigan Have?

Michigan has 148 lawmakers. This is a lot of
people! These lawmakers are divided into two
groups. One is the **state house of representatives**.
The other is the **state senate**. Each group does the
same kind of work. Ideas for new laws can start in
either one. After one group says okay to a new law,
the idea goes to the other one. Then that group talks
about the idea or bill and votes on it.

They Are Elected to Their Jobs

How do we choose the people who represent us? We vote for them. They are elected. Each lawmaker is elected from a **district** where he or she lives. Each district is a small part of our state. Each district has the same number of people.

There are districts for the house and others for the senate. Michigan has 110 house districts and 38 senate districts. We have many districts so those elected are close to the people. They live near them. They know what is happening. They understand the problems in their district.

We also elect other leaders. The president, the governor, mayors and state judges are all elected. In each election the person with the most votes gets the job.

We vote for some leaders every two years. For others the elections are four years apart. A few are voted on every six years. We vote for the president and governor every four years. We voted for the president in 2008. We will vote again in 2012. Add four more years to find the next election. The next vote for the governor is in 2010. We will vote again in 2014.

Keep In Touch

Communication is important in a republic. Those who take our place need to know our needs. The representatives try to do what people want.

The dark green area is one district. Many districts are much smaller. Each has the same number of people.

They work hard to find out. They often mail **surveys** to them. They often talk with them at meetings.

The Four Main Levels of Government

Our government has many parts. It is like a small box inside a bigger box in an even bigger box. Did you ever see a gift wrapped like that? The smallest box is our city government. The largest box is our nation's government. Here are the four main parts.

City Representatives

Each city has a **city council**. We vote for representatives to serve on the city council. You can visit those meetings. The mayor leads the meetings.

County Representatives

Each county has its government. It is called the **county commission.** We elect representatives to it also. The commission meets in the county courthouse. In most counties, a chairperson leads the meetings.

What does your county do for you? Counties provide some needed services. Taking care of roads is an important one. A county can have over 1,000 miles of roads. All of these roads

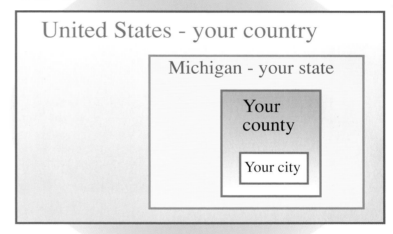

Our Governments

United States - your country

Michigan - your state

Your county

Your city

Each county has many miles of roads.

333

have potholes to be filled. The snow must be plowed each winter. This work has to be done to make sure the roads are safe for drivers. The sheriff is a part of county government. Some county governments run the 911 phone service. Counties also keep many important records. They record who owns all the property in the county.

Here is the Ingham County courthouse in Mason, Michigan.

State Representatives

Find out the names of your state representative and state senator. Remember, these people work in the state capitol. Each one has a web site where you can learn more about them.

[Check out http://house.michigan.gov. or http://senate.michigan.gov]

National Representatives

There are also men and women who represent us in our national government. This is in **Washington, D.C.** Michigan has 15 representatives in Congress and two in the Senate. There are no districts for the Senate. The two people for the Senate are voted on by the whole state.

Paying for the Cost of Government

Government is not free. It costs money to pay wages and build buildings and offices. It costs money to build roads and schools. Who pays for the cost of government? Everyone does! People provide this money with their taxes. Even students help pay when they buy something.

There are three main taxes in Michigan.
1. What people earn is taxed. This is called an *income tax*.

2. The homes people live in are taxed. This is called a *property tax*.

3. We also have a *sales tax*. When you buy things, you pay a sales tax. There is no sales tax on food at the grocery store.

When you buy most things at a store, you pay a state sales tax.
Picture drawn by Aaron Zenz.

335

Think About It and Talk About It!

1. Why do we need people to take our places in state government?

2. What is the Latin name for the kind of government we have in the United States?

3. Which two groups make our laws in Lansing?

4. How do we choose our representatives?

5. In the end, who controls government?

6. What does a person need to do to be a good voter?

7. Name three kinds of taxes used in Michigan.

Words In Action!
Name each of the four main levels of government. Name the leader of each level. Give an example of a service done by each level.

Internet Research
Find out who represents your district in the state house and the state senate. Find the web site for each of these people. Write a paragraph telling what you learned from their web sites.

Chapter 7 Lesson 3

Ideas To Explore

running for office - This is what people say when a candidate works to be elected to a government office. It can seem like a race to see who wins.

People to Meet

county clerk - the person who keeps the records for a county

county treasurer - the person who handles the money for county government

registrar of deeds - the person who keeps records of the sale of homes and property in a county

Places To Discover

counties - Michigan has 83 counties and each one is like a small state government.

courthouse - the building that is the home for county government and its courts

state house - one part of the state's lawmakers

state senate - one part of the state's lawmakers

Words To Welcome

deeds - papers that give the location and details for each home, building and farm in a county

federal government - another name for the national government in Washington, D.C.

marriage license - the paper from the county that allows people to be married

public services - things government does for us

reelection - being elected to an office more than once

veto - when the governor says no to a new law

Michigan
Social
Studies
GLCES

3C3.0.1

Lansing Or Local- Who Does What?

Think about this question while you read.
Which services come from the city and which come from the state ?

Local Government

Your town or city has its own government. This is called local government. It provides services for the people of your local area. Taking care of the streets is one example. Having a police force is another example.

Mayors are important leaders. They are even more important in large cities like Detroit. The mayor leads city government. Cities also have a city council. The mayor and the council work together. They usually meet once a month to talk about what they should do. Anyone can go to these meetings. You can go and hear what they are discussing. Most meetings have a time when anyone can speak.

Alex and Andrew visit Mayor Michael Sessions of Hillsdale. They are in the room where the city council meets. The mayor is explaining about city government.

The mayor and the men and women on the city council are elected. Often they serve for four years. At that time another election is held. They may run for **reelection** or they may decide not to run again. Mayors and members of the councils, put in a great deal of work to do their jobs. The pay is not that much. Most of these government leaders want to help their towns. They want to make them better places to live. This is why they take these jobs.

Vote for me. I want to help!

City Government Services

What does city government do? It is in charge of the police and firefighters. It repairs the streets. It takes care of city parks and, if you have one, the city swimming pool. It may also pick up the garbage. We call these services **public services**. *They have this name because they are done for the people.* To help you remember them, think of the sounds which go along with each of them.

Fire fighters provide a public service.

Your city takes care of other issues too. What are some city issues? Here are some examples. Should the city build a new park? Should skateboarding be allowed on the sidewalks? Should the city dig a new well for drinking water? These are all issues cities decide.

Learn more about what your city does. Visit a city council meeting! They are held at your city hall.

All government meetings are open to anyone who wants to go and listen. These meetings are often shown on the local cable TV channel.

What About Schools?

Schools are in cities, but they are not a part of city government. Schools have their own school boards. Members of each school board are elected. The school board hires the principals and teachers.

The Little Boxes on Our Maps - Our Counties

On some maps Michigan might look like a jig-saw puzzle. You can see many squares and other small shapes. Why? Those maps show our **counties.** Each box or shape is one of Michigan's 83 counties.

Each has its own name. Counties are named after different things. Iron County has iron mines. Chippewa County is named after an Indian tribe. Jackson County is named after a president. Do you know the name of the county where you live? Have someone help you find it on a map. Check to see what other counties touch yours.

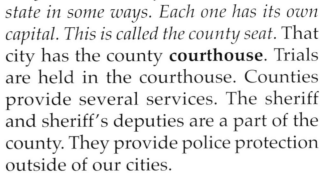

What is a county? It is an area of land. It is like a little state in some ways. Each one has its own capital. This is called the county seat. That city has the county **courthouse**. Trials are held in the courthouse. Counties provide several services. The sheriff and sheriff's deputies are a part of the county. They provide police protection outside of our cities.

The Clinton County courthouse in St. Johns, Michigan

Michigan's Counties

N
W   E
S

0   50   100 miles

Keweenaw

Houghton

Ontonagon

Baraga

Gogebic

Marquette

Iron

Alger

Dickinson

Schoolcraft

Luce

Delta

Mackinac

Chippewa

Menominee

Emmet

Cheboygan

Charlevoix

Presque Isle

Antrim

Otsego

Montmorency

Alpena

Leelanau

Benzie

Grand Traverse

Kalkaska

Crawford

Oscoda

Alcona

Manistee

Wexford

Missaukee

Roscommon

Ogemaw

Iosco

Mason

Lake

Osceola

Clare

Gladwin

Arenac

Huron

Oceana

Newaygo

Mecosta

Isabella

Midland

Bay

Tuscola

Sanilac

Montcalm

Gratiot

Saginaw

Muskegon

Genesee

Lapeer

St. Clair

Ottawa

Kent

Ionia

Clinton

Shiawassee

Oakland

Macomb

Allegan

Barry

Eaton

Ingham

Livingston

Van Buren

Kalamazoo

Calhoun

Jackson

Washtenaw

Wayne

Berrien

Cass

St. Joseph

Branch

Hillsdale

Lenawee

Monroe

Counties keep many records about their people and property.

Picture drawn by Theresa Deeter

The county keeps many records that can be helpful. Each has a **county clerk, county treasurer,** and a **registrar of deeds.** This last person keeps all the records of who owns property. These records are called **deeds.** The county clerk's office is the place to go for a **marriage license.**

The county may also decide to build drains. They do this to stop flooding when it rains too much. Each county takes care of miles of roads outside the cities. The people who work in the county courthouse are a part of county government.

Why Are There So Many Counties?

Having 83 counties makes it easier for people. They do not need to travel far to the courthouse. Driving a long way to go to court or find records would be a bother. Our needs are often different. If our counties were huge, it might be hard to help all the people.

State Government

Our state government is in Lansing. It deals with issues affecting the whole state. State government may decide how many days of school you have each year. It may decide if we need a new state symbol. It may decide how many state police to have on the highways.

Michigan's capitol building in Lansing
Photo by the author

The governor leads state government just as the mayor leads city government.

Making State Laws

Cities have the city councils to make laws. The state has the **house** and **senate**. It has two groups of lawmakers while the city has only one. The state lawmakers work in the capitol building. (The name of the building is spelled capitol with an "ol" at the end. The city is spelled capital with "al" at the end.)

The way state laws are made is more complex. Before an idea can become a law, it goes to both groups. An idea can start in the house or in the senate. It is voted on and if it passes, it goes to the other group. Then the other group talks about it and votes on it, too. If both groups say it is okay, it goes to the governor.

Governor Jennifer Granholm. She is the first woman to be Michigan's governor.

Photo by Gary Shrewsbury

Then the governor decides what he or she thinks. If the governor likes it, he or she signs it. If the governor really does not like the idea of this new law, he or she can **veto** it. *A veto is another way of saying no.*

YEAR 2002

The Nation's Government

Our country has its own government. It makes laws for the whole nation. The president leads the national government. He or she works in Washington, D.C. Sometimes the national government is called the

343

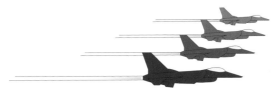

federal government. It provides our air force, army and navy. It makes our money. It also makes treaties with other countries.

The federal government provides the air force.

Who Does That Job?

With four main levels of government it may be hard to know what each one does. Let's look at an example about highways, roads and streets.

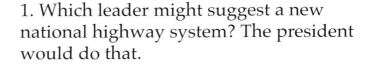

1. Which leader might suggest a new national highway system? The president would do that.

2. Which leader could work to change the speed limit on Michigan's highways? The governor would do that.

3. Which leader would make sure a bridge was fixed on a county road? A county commissioner would do that.

4. Which leader may suggest a place for a new stop sign on a city street? A city mayor would do that.

Being Close To The Situation

Government needs to be close to the people. It must understand their problems and needs. This is why we have so many levels of government. How can someone in Washington, D.C. know what your city needs? They are far away. They may never have even visited your city.

Examples- How State Government Works in These Areas

Doing Things We Cannot Do Alone

How does our state government help us? It provides services we could not do by ourselves. Building the Mackinac Bridge is one example. Taking care of our modern state highways is another. Providing state parks is a third. State government helps us all have better lives. It promotes the common good.

State government built the Mackinac Bridge for the common good of the people.

Protecting Our Rights

It also provides us with state police. These men and women protect us and help keep us safe. They help protect our rights. State government makes laws that explain our rights. It works to protect our rights using these laws. There are state courts and judges who work to protect our rights and freedoms.

A group of Michigan State Police officers

Photo from the Michigan State Police

Making Our Laws

Our state laws are made in Lansing at the capitol. The capitol is the building with the big white dome. No one can make a law alone. It takes people working together to make new laws. The goal of our new laws is to make Michigan a better place to live.

Leadership

Michigan's governor works hard to lead our state. He or she tries to help find answers to problems. The governor makes speeches. He or she visits groups to talk about the things our state should do. The governor tries to find ways to bring new jobs to Michigan.

Inside Michigan's capitol

The front of the house of representatives

Looking up into the capitol dome

The governor's office in the capitol

 All photos taken by the author.

Think About It. Talk About It!

1. Who is the person in charge of state government?

2. Who is the person in charge of city government?

3. Why do we have more than one level of government?

4. Give an example of a state law.

5. Give an example of a city law.

6. What can the governor do if he or she really does not like the idea for a new law?

Brain Stretchers

Get a copy of your city's budget. Work in small groups. Decide how to make a chart of the budget for your classroom.

If you need a bigger challenge, do the same for the state budget and compare it to your city budget.

The outside of the capitol dome

347

Chapter 7 Lesson 4

Ideas To Explore

constitution - The constitution is like a rule book for government. It tells what the government can do and what it cannot do. It lists the rights that people have.

Words To Welcome

amendment - This is an official change to the constitution. It must be voted on by the people.

supreme court - This is the highest court in Michigan. It chooses the cases that go before it. It may decide what a law means.

term limits - This is not letting the same person have the same government job several times in a row. It limits the number of times he or she can be elected.

Michigan
Social
Studies
GLCES

3C3.0.5

LANSING
Michigan's capital city

Grant points to our capital city.

348

The Rule Book for Government

Think about this question while you read.
Why should we have limits on our government?

When our nation began, one of the first things it did was to write a constitution. It explains how our government works. It talks about the big ideas. Since then, each state has also written a **constitution**. *Constitutions are like rule books for government. They tell what the government can do and what it cannot do. They list the rights that people have.* Everyone has rules to follow. We have rules for a reason, like no running in the hall. This is also true for government!

Constitutions put limits on our government. They keep government from becoming too big. They keep it from being too powerful. It cannot do just anything it might want to do. They keep it from taking over our lives. Suppose the governor says, "I will make all the laws myself. I will take over the courts and decide who is guilty. I do not need lawmakers anymore. Elect me and I will take care of everything." The state constitution says this is wrong.

The constitution is like a rule book for government.

Dictators like being in charge. They like power. They do whatever they want.

The constitution lists our rights. It contains core democratic values.

Why Do We Need Constitutions?

Why do we need rules for governments? People need rules. Sometimes they think about doing the wrong thing. This can also happen to governments. In some countries there are dictators. A dictator does whatever he or she wants. A dictator has no rules. A dictator does not need to be fair. The constitution has rules to keep government from being too powerful. It helps government be fair. It sets rules so the government has justice for everyone.

Limited Government

Big government begins to think more about itself than about the people. Big government does what it wants to do. It can act like a bully. It can push people around. It forgets to ask people what they want.

How does the state constitution limit government? Look at our Michigan constitution. It begins with over 24 rights we have as citizens. One of these is the right to free speech. Another is the right to worship as you please. It says the government cannot take these rights or freedoms away from you.

The state constitution divides government into three branches. This is so each branch can watch the others. It is so the power is divided.

The state constitution says the meetings of the house and senate will be open so people can see what is going on. It cannot meet in secret.

Michigan's constitution spells out what each branch can do and how it can do it. Government cannot do just anything it wants. It must follow these rules.

What if There is a Disagreement?

What happens if two students disagree about a school rule? They may visit the principal to sort it out. Sometimes people do not agree what the constitution means. This does happen. Then it is the job of the **supreme court** to decide. It is like visiting the principal. The supreme court decides who is right. Michigan has its own supreme court and so does the national government.

The Michigan State Supreme Court

Photo by
www.domagalskiphotography.com

Doing What It Says

The constitution is not worth much if people do not do what it says. It is up to the people to take a stand. They need to be sure government follows it. If no one cares what government does, it will soon do only what a few people in charge want.

Can We Change It? Yes, we can!

We can make changes to the constitution. These changes are called **amendments**. It is not easy to make amendments. The constitution is very important. It is hard to change it without a very good reason.

Here Is An Example

In 1992 Michigan voters passed an amendment. They added **term limits**. You may hear someone on the news talk about term limits. Term limits tell the number of times the same person can have the same job. For example, the same person can only be governor twice.

Why was this change made? Some people believe government leaders should not be elected too many times. They feel government is best when new people hold office. They think new people bring fresh ideas.

Others think new people do not know as much about what they are doing. They think it takes time for those elected to understand the best ways of doing their jobs. Maybe both sides have some truth in what they think.

Making a New Constitution

Sometimes many changes are needed all at once. When this happens, a large group meets to talk it over. Then they write a new constitution. Once it is written, the voters must approve it. Our state is very different from the pioneer days. It has had four constitutions. They were written in 1835, 1850, 1908, and 1963.

A new constitution can be made when times change. In 1835, the land was mostly forest and there were few roads. By 1850, many towns had started. The first railroads were being built. By 1908, people were beginning to buy cars and highways were needed. In 1963, many people were moving out of the big cities. They built homes in smaller towns nearby. Our freeways and shopping malls were being built. As Michigan changed, its constitution has changed, too.

Think About It and Talk About It!

1. What is a constitution?

2. Who decides if there is a disagreement over what the state constitution means?

3. How does the state constitution put limits on government?

4. Our state has had more than one constitution. How many have there been?

5. Why would the state constitution ever need changes?

Make a Time Line Today!
Make a time line of the four Michigan state constitutions.

Words In Action
Explain why we should limit the power of government.

1700
1800
1900

Chapter 7 Lesson 5

Ideas To Explore

enforcing laws and rules - This is what the people in the executive branch of our state government do. They make sure everyone follows the rules.

rule of law - following our laws and not doing whatever we want

separation of powers - dividing government into 3 main parts so no part can become too powerful

People to Meet

attorney general - the lawyer for the state

judge - the person in charge of courts and trials

secretary of state - the person in charge of drivers' licenses and elections

Words To Welcome

bill- the idea for a new law

budget

Department of Transportation - the part of state government that watches over the highways, airports and trains

executive branch - the part of state government headed by the governor

judicial branch - the part of government with our courts and judges

legislative branch - the lawmakers

Michigan
Social
Studies
GLCES

3C3.0.2

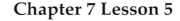

What Happens Under the Big Dome?

Think about this question while you read.
How is state government set up or organized?

Three Main Parts of State Government

The constitution divides state government into three parts. One reason it does this is to make sure government does not become too powerful. Each part watches the other parts. It is a way to limit government.

Here are the three parts of the state government. Each part is called a branch. These are like three big branches in a tree. One is for the lawmakers. One is for the governor and one is for the courts.

The Governor's Branch – the Executive Branch

The **executive branch** can also be called the governor's branch. The governor is in charge of this branch. It is a big branch. It has about 20 parts or departments. It helps carry out our state laws and other rules.

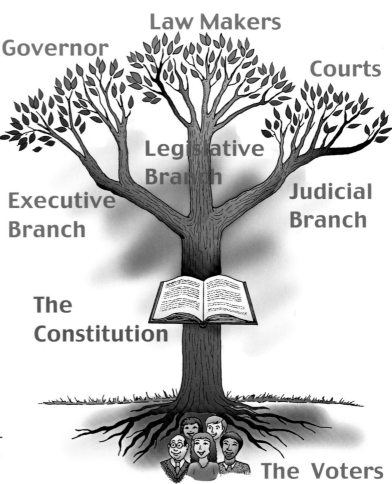

Governor

Law Makers

Courts

Legislative Branch

Executive Branch

Judicial Branch

The Constitution

The Voters

355

The governor oversees many departments that deal with laws and rules. This is why he or she is in this branch. The National Guard is also here. It is under the control of the governor. This is a part of civilian control of the military.

Other Leaders in This Branch

The **attorney general** is also a part of the executive branch. *The attorney general is the lawyer for the state.* This person is elected by the voters of Michigan. He or she helps the state with legal problems. He or she investigates crimes. If there is a phone scam, the attorney general may look into it. Jennifer Granholm was our attorney general before she was elected governor.

The **secretary of state** is another elected leader in this branch. *He or she is in charge of drivers' licenses, elections and signing up voters.*

Many of the services of state government come from the executive branch. The **Department of Transportation** is one example. *It takes care of our main highways. It also deals with airports and trains.*

The Department of Transportation helps with highways, airports and trains.

The Lawmaker's Branch

The second is the **legislative branch**. *This branch can also be called the lawmakers' branch.* Making laws is called legislation. That is how we get the name for this branch.

The men and women in this branch make our state laws. The lawmakers are divided into two groups. One group is called the senate. The other group is called the house. Each group meets in its own large room in Lansing. If you have visited the state capitol building, you probably saw these rooms.

Bruce Caswell is at his desk in the state house. He was a state representative. Photo supplied by Bruce Caswell.

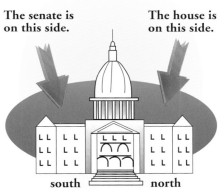

The senate is on this side.

The house is on this side.

south   north

Making a New Law

How do we get new laws? Each begins as an idea. People tell their ideas to the state senator or representative for their district. The lawmaker may also decide to use one of his or her own ideas. The lawmaker will write a **bill**. *A bill is the official wording of the idea for a new law.* The lawmakers will talk about the bill in the house or in the senate. Then they will vote on the bill. If the bill passes, it will go to the other group of lawmakers. Finally, if both groups pass the bill, it goes to the governor.

I am a "Bill"

I may become a new law, if I am passed.

357

Next, the governor can sign the bill. If it is signed, it will become law. If the governor does not like the bill, he or she can veto it. A veto usually keeps it from becoming law.

An Example of Making a Law - The Bottle Bill

Do you remember the "Bottle Bill" from chapter one? The idea for that law started because people complained about empty bottles and cans thrown along our roads. It was a mess! It was felt a deposit would help people to bring the bottles and cans back to the stores. The only way to have a statewide deposit was to pass a state law. That is what took place.

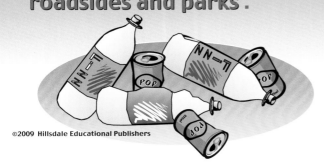

Michigan's Bottle Bill deposit tries to keep junk from roadsides and parks .

©2009 Hillsdale Educational Publishers

This law was been very helpful. Now 96 of every 100 bottles and cans go back to the stores! If you find a bottle or can along the road, look it over. Maybe it came from a state without a deposit. Maybe someone from Ohio tossed it out. They would not get money back for returning it to the store.

The Rule of Law

In our country and state we follow the "**rule of law**." *This means we follow the laws that are passed. We do not ignore them. People do not make up rules as they go.* This is not true in some countries. Their leaders and important people may ignore the laws. They feel they are "above the law." They just do what they please. There is little fairness or justice in those places. The powerful rule everyone. This is not the way we want our nation to work.

The Court's Branch

The third part of state government is the courts. *Judges are in charge of the courts*. Because of this, it can also be called the **judicial branch**.

The courts handle all sorts of disagreements. A local court may have two neighbors upset about a dog that always barks. The state supreme court may have a case that affects everyone in Michigan. It may decide what a state law means.

The Michigan Hall of Justice

Not all government takes place under the big white dome of the capitol building. The state supreme court and some other top courts are in the Michigan Hall of Justice. It is down the street from the capitol.

359

Why Have So Many Parts?

Your mind may be spinning. You may ask, "Why do we need so many parts in government?" Having the three branches divides the power of government. This way no one part has too much power. We call this "**separation of powers**."

When one person or group gets too much power, bad things seem to happen. Then people often lose their freedoms. The core democratic values can be forgotten.

The State Budget

Do you know what a **budget** is? Have you ever heard your parents talking about a family budget? *A budget is the amount of money that will be spent. Budgets are made to see if there will be enough money for the important things.*

Each year Michigan's government makes a budget. It decides how much money it will get from taxes. It decides how this money will be spent. It is a bit like cutting a pie and deciding who gets the big piece and who gets the little piece.

Tough choices are made in the budget. There are opportunity costs. If money is spent on one thing, it will not be there for something else. What will the government need to give up? Should the money go to schools or to highways? Trade-offs are made. Should the state police get less money and the prisons more money?

The amount spent should equal what comes in from taxes and fees. State government is not allowed to spend more than it gets.

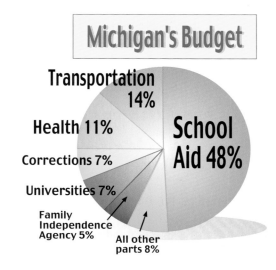

Michigan's Budget

Transportation 14%

Health 11%

Corrections 7%

Universities 7%

Family Independence Agency 5%

All other parts 8%

School Aid 48%

All State Governments are Similar

Michigan works much the same as most other state governments. Governors lead all of them.

Both have 3 branches

The Nation's Government and State Government Are Alike

Our national government in Washington, D.C. also has three branches. These branches work much like they do in Michigan. The biggest difference is the president is in charge, not a governor.

Think About It. Talk About It!

1. Name the three branches of our state government.

2. Explain what each branch does.

3. Why does state government have three branches?

4. Where does the state get the money to pay for its budget?

5. What does the "rule of law" mean?

6. What is the idea for a new law called?

Words In Action

Compare the three branches of government to the three legs of a stool. How does having three branches make our government stronger? Does a stool work with only two legs?

Think Like an Economist

Make an imaginary state budget. Talk about the choices that need to be made. What opportunity costs will there be? What trade-offs will you need to make? How much will you need in taxes to pay for everything?

Take a Stand!

Think about a new law. Should Michigan have a 10 cent deposit on ALL kinds of beverage containers, not just fizzy beverages? This would include water bottles, tea bottles, juice bottles and more. Include any core democratic values that support your stand. Explain the costs and benefits of this change. To find more information, use these Internet sites: www.mucc.org, www.bottlebill.org, www.michigan.gov/deq

Chapter 7 Lesson 6

Ideas To Explore
What happens in a court?

People to Meet
jury - A group of regular people who are asked to come to court and listen to a trial. They decide who is right and who is wrong.

justices - The seven judges on the Michigan State Supreme Court are called justices.

Michigan State Supreme Court - The highest state court. It deals with the most important cases.

Juries decide who is guilty in a trial. Juries are not lawyers or judges.

Places To Discover
courthouse - the building with one or more courts

Words To Welcome
civic responsibility - This is each person doing his or her duty to help government work well and making Michigan a good place to live.

disagreement - This is when two people or groups do not agree. They may not agree on how to solve a public issue.

sue - This happens when people go to court to try to get money which they believe is owed to them by someone else.

Michigan
Social
Studies
GLCES

3C3.0.3
3C3.0.4

Here Comes the Judge!

Think about this question while you read.
Why do we have courts?

This lesson is about the judicial branch. It could be called the judges' or courts' branch too. Our judges work in this branch. What does a judge do? Where do judges work? Why do we have judges?

Judges are in charge of our courts. Most judges work in one of our 83 **courthouses**. *This is where you will find the courts.* The judge makes certain each person in a trial asks the right kind of questions. He or she keeps order in the court. The judge works to make the trial fair for everyone. Often the judge wears a black robe. This is how people can tell who is the judge.

The Midland County courthouse

Photo taken by the author

Courts Settle Disagreements

What happens when there is a **disagreement**? Our courts decide who is right and who is wrong. They settle disagreements. Our state has several kinds of courts. Each one works with a different area.

This is a courtroom. The judge sits in the chair between the two flags.

We Elect Our Judges

The voters elect all of the judges in Michigan. This is not true in some states. Voting for our judges is another way the power rests with the people.

People in the jury listen to the lawyers explain both sides of the case.

The judge is in charge of the trial in each court-room.

What is a Jury?

Most courts also use a **jury**. *Juries help decide who is right or wrong. The people on the jury make the final decision in a trial.* A jury is a group of regular people who are chosen to do this work. They can be anyone who is 18 years old or older. They do not have special training. They may have been on a jury before, or it may be new to them. Jury members are selected from people living in your area. Perhaps one of your parents has served on a jury. Being on a jury is another way we take part in government. Being on a jury is a part of being a responsible citizen. It is a **civic responsibility**.

Many Kinds of Disagreements

Michigan has several courts. Courts deal with many kinds of disagreements. Some are

Picture drawn by
Theresa Deeter.

criminal cases. Someone may be on trial for breaking a law. People may have done crimes and been arrested. It is a crime to rob someone. It is a crime to hurt someone.

In some cases no one has broken a law. These may be times when one person **sues** another person. *This often happens when one person causes damages for another person. These people go to court to settle the disagreement. The court tries to make things right.*

Suppose Frank is driving and accidentally hits Mary's car. Frank was driving without car insurance. Mary will want Frank to pay to fix her car. If he does not do this on his own, Mary might sue him. Frank and Mary will go to court. A judge will run the trial. A jury will decide if Frank should pay or not.

Michigan's Most Important Court

Some cases are very complex. Suppose two groups cannot agree on what a Michigan law means. The **Michigan State Supreme Court** may have a case like that. This court is not like other courts. It deals with only the most important cases. Michigan's seven **justices** decide which cases they will hear. All the justices listen to each case at the same time. There are no juries in this court. The justices all vote to decide each case. This court is in Lansing.

The U. S. Supreme Court decides what the United States constitution means. It also decides what national laws mean. Our state supreme court decides what state laws mean.

A Recent Public Issue

Every place has public issues. These are problems that need to be decided. It is best to think about the common good when deciding public issues. What will be the best for everyone without hurting anyone?

A Real Case

Not long ago the Michigan State Supreme Court had a case about walking along the beaches. Some people said they had the right to walk along any beach on the Great Lakes. Some others owned land along the beach. They said the beach belonged to them. It was a part of their land. They believed they could keep people off the beach if they wanted. Each group wanted to pursue its happiness in different ways. One group wanted privacy on its land. The other group enjoyed walking along the beach.

The Michigan State Supreme Court listened to each side of the case. They thought about what each side said. These judges also looked back at older cases. They reviewed what other judges did in those cases.

367

The Court decided people do have the right to walk along the beaches. They said there were limits, though. People can only walk on the part of the beach that is covered by the highest water. People can not walk over another person's yard.

This only applies to beaches on the Great Lakes. It only applies to the part of the Great Lakes in Michigan. Courts in other states may have different ideas about this same issue.

These are some of the ways our state courts decide disagreements. Remember, each state has many kinds of courts. Each county has a courthouse where it has courts.

Our courts try to solve disagreements in a civilized way. Fighting is not the way to solve problems!

Think About It. Talk About It!

1. Which branch helps settle conflicts and disagreements?

2. Name the person in charge of a court.

3. In a trial, which group decides if a person is guilty?

4. Why is it important to serve on a jury?

5. Which court decides what a law means?

Take a Stand!

Today, Michigan elects its judges. Some people think the governor should choose them instead. Take a stand. Should Michigan's judges be chosen by the governor? Explain your position. Include any core democratic values or constitutional principles you can.

Have Your Own Trial

Pick two students who have an imaginary disagreement. Choose a student to be the judge and 12 others to be on the jury. Choose a lawyer for each side. Use your classroom as the courtroom. The rest of the students can be witnesses for the two sides.

Chapter 7 Lesson 7

Ideas To Explore

responsibilities - These are the things people need to do so our government works well. They are like duties. At home, one of your responsibilities may be to take out the garbage. Once you are 18, one of your responsibilities is to vote.

rights- These are the freedoms given to people in the state and national constitutions.

People to Meet

A citizen

citizen - A citizen is an official member of a country. Often they must be old enough to vote before they are called a citizen.

Democrats - one of the two large political parties in the United States.

political parties - These are groups of people who often think the same way about public issues and government. Usually candidates belong to a political party.

Republicans - one of the two large political parties in the United States.

Words To Welcome

Michigan
Social
Studies
GLCES

3C5.0.1

equal protection - This is giving everyone the same treatment by the government and police.

equality - This means everyone is equal. No one gets special favors.

popular sovereignty - This is the right to vote. It means the people rule.

Doing Your Part

Think about this question while you read.
What should we do to be responsible citizens?

What is your part in our government? Have you ever thought about it? You do have a part even if you are not old enough to vote!

You can think about public issues. You can be informed. Read about the issues. Listen to the issues adults talk about. Share your thoughts with them and with your friends.

You can write letters. You can send e-mails. You can share your stand on issues with government leaders. You can say what you think should be done.

During an election you can find out about the candidates. Talk with your parents about the different candidates. See what they think about them and share your ideas too.

How else can you be a good citizen right now? You already know you can help keep Michigan clean. You can pick up

Alyssa and Grant pick up litter.

litter. You can ask others to pick up after themselves. Being a responsible citizen does not start when you are an adult. Being responsible is a good habit to start right now!

Rights and Freedoms

You know each person in our country has **rights**. Our constitutions list these rights. Look at Michigan's constitution. Here are a few of the rights you can find:

Popular sovereignty. *The power of the government comes from the people.* The people use this power when they vote. (Article 1, section 1)

Equality. *Everyone should get the same treatment.* No person shall be denied **equal protection** by the government. (Article 1, section 2)

Freedom of religion. *This is your right to worship the way you want.* Every person shall be at liberty to worship God as they decide. (Article 1, section 4)

Justice. *All people should be treated fairly. No group should be favored.* The right of trial by jury shall remain. (Article 1, section 14)

Our country is based on core democratic values. We have rights and freedoms people in some countries do not have. Can you name some? We have the freedom of speech. This means we can say what we want about the government. If we do not like something, we can take a stand against it.

Taking a stand against the government in some countries will get you in trouble. A person speaking against the government might be arrested or worse. Even though we can say what we want, we need to be responsible. We must always tell the truth.

Today, some people take a stand on their web sites. They use the Internet to tell what they think. Some countries do not allow this kind of free speech. If a person has a web site the government does not like, it is blocked. No one in that country can see what that site has to say. Countries that do this do not allow free speech.

Another freedom we have is the right to worship as we please. We can go to any place of worship we want, or not go at all. In some countries there is only one religion and no others are allowed.

In a few countries, the government does not allow any religion. In those places, if you want to worship, it has to be done in secret. Maybe people meet in a basement to worship. They might need a lookout to watch in case the police come after them. If they are caught, they can go to jail.

We have many freedoms in our country.

In our country everyone can own property. Your parents can buy a house or a farm. In some countries the government owns all the buildings and all the land. In those countries people must live where the government tells them to live.

Rule of Law

Driving too fast is not thinking of others. There can be negative consequences.

The Democrats have used the donkey as their symbol. The Republicans have used the elephant. Can you find out why?

Responsibilities - Duties

Rights go hand in hand with **responsibilities**. They come with each other. *What are responsibilities? These are things each person must do to make our government work. It is thinking about what is good for everyone.* Responsibilities tie in with the common good. Obeying the laws is one. We believe in the rule of law. Ignoring the law is not a freedom we have. Lawmakers make laws to protect all of us and we need to follow them.

Some people drive faster than the speed limit. They think they are in a hurry. They think the speed laws are for other people. The speed limit is there to keep all drivers safe from accidents. If people drive as fast as they want, there may be many serious accidents.

Each person has a responsibility to pick up litter. Keeping our state clean helps the common good. It is good for everyone and it makes Michigan a better place to live.

Political Parties

People working to be elected belong to a **political party**. This kind of party means a group of people. It is not a place for birthday cake! The members of each party often like the same ideas. They often think alike.

We have two large parties. They are the **Democrats** and the **Republicans**. The Republican Party got its start in Jackson. That took place in

1854. The party was against slavery. Since then, the focus of each party has changed. We also have some other small political parties.

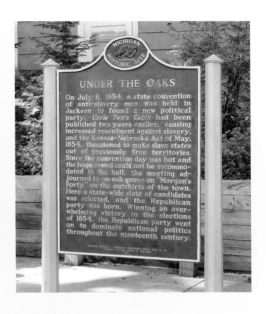

During an election, each party helps its candidates. It helps those who think like it does. They want those candidates elected. People will say this person is a Republican. They will say that person is a Democrat. Sometimes the parties have ideas that are very different. On other issues their ideas are more the same.

The first large meeting of the Republican Party was in Jackson, Michigan.

Voting

It is responsible to vote. It is a duty to vote. Voters are important because the power comes from the people! In the United States, any **citizen** who is 18 years old can vote. *A citizen is anyone born in this country.* People who move here can also become citizens by doing certain things. If they become citizens, they have all the rights of a person born here, except for one. They cannot become President.

People must vote if our government is going to work as it should. If friends asked for your opinion, you would tell them. Maybe they wanted to know if a movie was good. You would think about it and give them a good answer. It would be rude if you did not. Voting is like that. The government is asking for your opinion.

Voting is an opportunity. When you are old enough, vote. Do not let others decide for you.

Tribal Government

There is another part of government that may surprise you. Michigan's Native Americans have their own governments. We have 12 tribes acknowledged by the federal government. From time to time, new tribes are added to this list. These tribes had treaties with the federal government that were made long ago. Go to page 160 to review the treaties.

Each tribe has its own elected leaders. Each has courts and police. Some have other public services like fire departments and schools. They may have health clinics.

Each tribe controls the land in its **reservation**. *A reservation is land that is set aside for the tribes and is controlled by them.* If a crime takes place on a reservation, the tribal police are in charge. If there is a trial, it will be in the tribal court.

Money to pay part of the cost of tribal government may come from the casinos the tribes own. The tribes can have casinos because they can make rules for what happens on their land.

To learn more about how the tribes work, go to the section on tribal government at www.mi.gov.

Think About It. Talk About It!

1. Why is it important for people to vote?

2. Name three rights you have in this country.

3. How does government protect your rights?

4. Think about being a responsible citizen. Name three things you can do.

5. Draw a picture. Have it show a person being a responsible citizen.

6. Name our two large political parties.

Check Out the State Constitution

Find Michigan's constitution on the Internet. Read article 1. Make a list of the 10 rights listed there. Have a class discussion so everyone understands what each right means.

Make a Chart

Make a chart of all the ways you can be a responsible citizen now.

Some Key Events in Michigan Government

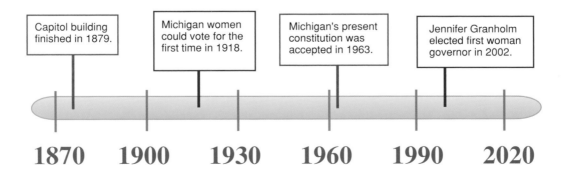

| Capitol building finished in 1879. | Michigan women could vote for the first time in 1918. | Michigan's present constitution was accepted in 1963. | Jennifer Granholm elected first woman governor in 2002. |

1870　1900　1930　1960　1990　2020

Public Issues Facing Michigan Citizens

Chapter 8 Lesson 1

Ideas To Explore

What is a public policy issue? This is an issue or problem that many people are interested in solving. Public means all the people in a place. This is an issue which government may help solve.

different points of view - Not everyone sees things the same way. Each person understands issues the best from his or her own viewpoint. It is harder to understand what other people need if they are quite different from yourself.

Why can people have conflicting views on public issues? This happens because different people pursue their happiness in different ways. It happens because people are not the same and have different ideas on what is best for the common good.

Places To Discover

council chamber- the room in the city hall where the council holds its meetings

Words To Welcome

city ordinance- a law made by a city for the people who live there

public access channel – This is a channel on cable television that is set aside for the public to use. People can make programs and send them out over the cable.

Michigan
Social
Studies
GLCES

3C5.0.1
3P3.1.1
3P3.1.2
3P3.1.3
4H3.0.8

Free to Disagree - A Burning Issue

Think about this question while you read.
What are public policy issues?

There is a Public Issue in the Air!

Ramon woke up one nice, cool spring day and held his nose. He always liked to sleep with his window open. He liked the cool breeze. Usually the spring air was nice and fresh. Today, it was anything but fresh. It smelled like burning garbage. He was sure it was burning garbage! He looked out and there was a haze in the air. At breakfast he talked to his brothers and sisters about the smell. Everyone said it stinks. His mom had already closed all the windows. On his way to school, Ramon tried to see who was burning garbage. He could not find its source. All of his part of town was hazy and smelled bad.

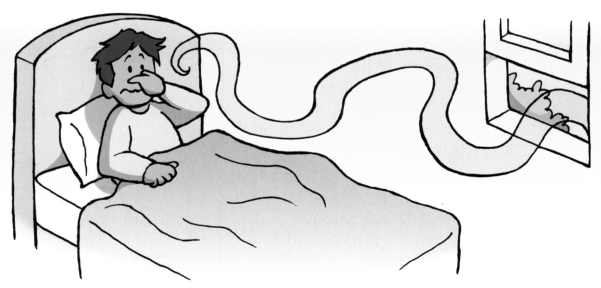

The pictures in this lesson are all drawn by Aaron Zenz.

At school his class discussed public issues. They were making lists of issues their town might have. Ramon said, "What about the bad smell from burning garbage? Is that a public issue?" The other students thought it could be. They added it to their list.

Ramon asked his teacher, Mr. Brown, if it was against the law to burn garbage in town. Mr. Brown said he did not think the town had a law against it. He had seen some people do it before, but not too often.

Why Do People Burn Garbage?

When the class was discussing public issues, they talked about burning garbage. Mr. Brown asked, "Why would someone burn garbage?" Students said to get rid of it.

Someone asked, "Why don't they set it out for the trash pickup?"

Another mentioned, "The pickup costs money. What if the person cannot afford to pay for pickup?"

Is It a Right?

Mr. Brown said, "That is a good point. Students, what do you think? Does the person have the right to burn garbage, especially if they cannot afford to have it picked up?"

They all thought about it. Ramon said, "I think it is against the common good. The whole town smelled bad. It can't be very healthy to breathe that stuff. This person was only thinking about himself or herself. Even if they can't afford to pay for the pickup, I do not think they should do it. I do not feel this person was being a responsible citizen."

Is burning garbage a right?

Is There a Law?

Mr. Brown said, "Many cities have a law or **city ordinance** against burning. *An ordinance is the name for a city law.* They do this so their cities will be better places to live. Maybe we should talk to a member of the city council. What do you think? It may not take very many people burning garbage to affect the whole city. A bad smell is not a good thing for any city. It does not make people feel good about where they live."

Ramon was elected to phone a lady on the city council. He spoke to her to see if the council might pass a law against burning garbage. She said it would be helpful to have some facts. Having facts will make a better stand when the council talks about it. She asked if Ramon's class could find out how many people had burn barrels in the city. It would help to know, she noted.

Gathering Facts

Ramon talked with Mr. Brown at school. Ramon explained

the city council would want as many facts as they can provide. Ramon wondered how they could count the burn barrels. It would take a long time to find all of them.

Mr. Brown had an idea. What if each student checked to see how many barrels were on his or her block. That should not be too hard. Mr. Brown thought they should have other classes help them. Maybe they should e-mail third grade classes in the school across town. Perhaps they could help. They could count burn barrels in their part of town. Ramon's teacher also thought they should see how often the barrels are used. They could make a chart to show the city council.

Soon, all the third grade classes in town were helping. Gathering data is one way people can work together to solve a public issue. Altogether, they found 93 burn barrels. For one month they kept track of when they were used. Fifty-five people used the barrels just once in the month. Twenty-five people used the barrels twice in that month. Ten people used their barrels at least once a week and three did not use them at all. The students also noted that there were times when just one barrel made a bad smell for a large part of the town. This was often true if no wind was blowing.

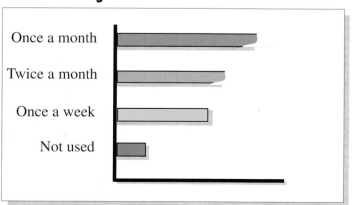

Once a month

Twice a month

Once a week

Not used

At the City Council

Before he knew it, Ramon was at a city council meeting. His class was also there. He could not believe this all started because his bedroom window was open. He had the charts and information the classes had gathered. Then the council asked him to tell them about burn barrels. His mouth was dry and his knees felt weak, but he did a good job. Ramon did not forget to thank his teacher and all the students for their help. Two other students from his class also spoke. Working together to share your stand with government is an important part of solving a public issue.

Discussing the Issue

When he was done, the council talked about the issue. Was it really a problem that needed a new law? One person on the council suggested they ask people not to burn when there is no wind. Another said writing a new law takes time. Some people who burn garbage might get mad at them. One mentioned asking people to burn on the same day, then the city will smell fine on the other six days. That idea got some laughs. The mayor felt that would drive everyone nuts on the day they did burn! One council member talked about the need to balance the rights of a few who want to burn with all those who think it smells bad. She was sure most people thought it smelled bad. Did some people really have a right to burn garbage? Is burning garbage a right?

The city council talks about the issue.

The mayor suggested they check the state constitution. He used his laptop and found the constitution on a web site. He sent the file to the projector in the **council chamber** and scrolled through it. Everyone looked at the rights given people at the beginning of Michigan's constitution. No one could see anything that seemed like a right to burn garbage.

One man on the council said maybe people think it is a part of the right to pursue their happiness. Those who want to burn will not be happy if they must stop. Another person said perhaps the best idea is to let the town vote on the issue. They could write a new law and let people vote at the next election. This would let those who did burn have the chance to speak up and take a stand. That is what the city council decided to do.

Different Points of View

A woman who used a burn barrel wrote a letter to the newspaper. It was in the "Letters to the Editor" section. She disagreed with the idea to stop burning garbage. She wrote,

Stand in my shoes. I am poor. I do not have money to pay for garbage pickup. If you make me do that, I must cut out something else I need. Maybe I will have to skip meals. People

have burned garbage here for years. It has not hurt anyone! I think it is my right to save money any way I can.

View Points

Later, a man also wrote to the newspaper. His letter was printed with the letters to the editor too. He felt the people who burned garbage were not considerate of others. They did not care if it smelled bad. Maybe some people had a bad reaction to the smell. If they were sensitive, it might make them sick. Everyone needs to be thoughtful of others. When people stop thinking about others, new laws are needed to make them behave.

These two letters show **different points of view**. Each person feels his or her view is a good one. They each have good reasons for what they wrote. They do not agree with each other. This does not mean one is a bad person and the other a good person.

Ways to Share Ideas

Will Ramon's class hold meetings to talk about the issue? Will they share their charts and put them in store windows? Will Ramon see if he can be interviewed on a radio program? Do you think the class will make an announcement for the **public access channel on** cable TV? These would be great ways to convince others how to solve this issue. What do you think the vote will be for the new law? Will it pass?

Think About It. Talk About It!

1. What was the public issue Ramon brought to his town's attention?

2. Name two ways people can work together to solve a public issue.

3. Why is it important to use facts and data to back up your stand? Use examples from this story.

4. What is a city ordinance? How can a city ordinance help solve a public issue?

5. Name two ways people can share their stand to help convince others.

6. Give some reasons people have different points of view on issues?

Use a Chart to Help You

Make a chart of the data on burn barrels the students gathered in their town.

Words in Action

Explain how using a core democratic value can help to decide the issue of burning garbage. If we take a stand, why should we use core democratic values?

Is the person who makes the best speech always right? Please explain your answer.

Brain Stretcher

Clean air is a valuable natural resource. Research issues related to air pollution in Michigan. What has been done in the past to try to correct them? What is being done today to protect clean air?

Chapter 8 Lesson 2

Ideas To Explore

fairness - making an honest deal for everyone - Everyone is treated the same and everyone is affected the same.

Places To Discover

Great Lakes Drainage Basin - This is the area of land where all the rivers flow into the Great Lakes. It includes all the states around the Great Lakes and part of Canada too.

Words To Welcome

billion gallons - a 1,000 million is 1 billion. A billion *drops* of water would fill a good sized swimming pool.

cubic mile - This is a cube that is one mile on each side. It is a huge amount of water!

evaporates - water that goes from a lake into the air

freshwater - not ocean water - water that does not have any salt in it

million gallons - 1,000,000 gallons-It takes about this much water to fill 1 1/2 Olympic-sized swimming pools.

Michigan
Social
Studies
GLCES

3G1.0.2
3G2.0.2
3G5.0.1
3C1.0.1
3P3.1.1
3P3.1.2
3P4.2.1
4H3.0.8

387

Using the Great Lakes

Think about this question while you read.
**Why is the issue of how to use
Great Lakes water so important?**

How Fair to Share?

Kim and Tim Jones are very lucky. Their family has a huge swimming pool. They enjoy using it almost every day. They often invite friends to swim with them. The pool is a great place to splash, laugh and have fun.

The pictures in this lesson are all drawn by Aaron Zenz.

A few weeks ago, a neighbor bought a tiny wading pool. Her children wanted to sit in it and keep cool. They were too small to use Kim and Tim's really big pool. The neighbor lady came over and talked to Kim's dad. She said her outside water faucet was broken. Would he let her take some water from their big pool to fill the little pool? Mr. Jones said he was glad to do it. He had so much water; it would not matter to him. He wanted to be a good neighbor!

When to Stop?

A few days later, the neighbor lady stopped by again. She was sorry to bother them. Her dog bit their little pool and all the water leaked out. Now it has been patched. Could they fill it up once more? Mr. Jones said sure they could.

The next week a second neighbor came by to say hello. Then he mentioned that he had a new swimming pool too. He had heard that Kim's dad had helped fill swimming pools for the neighbors. It would be so nice if he could have some water too. His pool was fairly big, but still smaller than the Jones' pool. Mr. Jones gave a little smile. "Okay," he said. "We can give you some water."

It was not long before there were long hoses everywhere. They were sucking water to go over to the neighbors' pools. Kim and Tim saw the water slowly go down in their pool. They had enough, but it was less than before.

Mr. Jones wondered how long it would be before other neighbors might stop over. How much water would they need to "borrow"? He wondered if they would ever give him water if his pool needed more.

How Did They Feel?

Do you think Mr. Jones will continue to give water away? Will Kim and Tim be excited about sharing with everyone who asks? How would you feel if you were Kim and Tim? In a way you are Kim and Tim. You do have a really big pool and it is called the Great Lakes! The Great Lakes have a huge amount of water. Still, there are many people who want to use some of it. Water is a very important natural resource. How much will be left when they are all done? No one knows.

An Important Issue- Water Is Scarce!

This is a public policy issue. The need for water is becoming greater all the time. A *Detroit News* article was written about the growing need for water.

It says 36 states will be short of water in 10 years. Why will this happen? For one thing, we have more people all the time. Our population keeps growing. A town that had enough water for 10,000 people may not have enough for 20,000.

Also, more people have been migrating to warmer states in the South. Often these states are short of water. States like New Mexico are quite dry. Adding more people only makes it worse. A city in Arizona may get 5 inches of rain a year. Detroit may get over 30 inches each year.

Many countries are short of water too. They may be in hot, dry areas like Africa. The populations of these countries keep growing. One study says by 2025 many people in the world will not have enough water. It says half of the people in the world will live in places without the water they need. This data is something to really think about. This is a problem that will need solutions in your lifetime!

Great Lakes Facts

The first thing to do in looking at a public issue is to gather facts. Let us think about all the water in the world. To help us understand how much there is, shrink it into just one gallon. Take out one tablespoonful. This spoonful is how much **freshwater** the earth has. Freshwater is water without salt. It is the water people can drink. Ocean water is salty and people will get sick if they drink it. It cannot be used to water crops. The salt would kill the plants. Looking at our water this way, the Great Lakes is only 1/5 of that tablespoon. Ummm.

The earth has a lot of water, but most of it is salty ocean water. People cannot drink ocean water. Ocean water cannot be used on crops either.

What is the source of the water in the Great Lakes? It comes from rain and snow. Think of the Great Lakes being in a shallow bowl. The bowl is bigger than the Lakes themselves. This bowl is called the **Great Lakes Drainage Basin**. All the rain and snow that fall into it go into the Great Lakes. The rain may not fall into the Lakes at first. It may fall on land, but it is carried by a river into the Great Lakes. Many rivers empty into the Great Lakes. Look at a map of the Great Lakes Drainage Basin.

Great Lakes Water System

The green area is the Great Lakes Drainage Basin.

Water Comes- Water Goes

Each year new water comes into the Great Lakes. It comes from the sky and from rivers. Each year water also leaves the Lakes. How does it do that? The Great Lakes are higher than the Atlantic Ocean. The St. Lawrence River connects the Lakes to the Ocean. Because of this, water flows out the St. Lawrence River. It flows into the Atlantic Ocean.

How much water leaves the Great Lakes? It is 4.5 **billion gallons** a day. Wow!

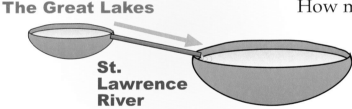

The Great Lakes

St. Lawrence River

The Atlantic Ocean

If you think that is a lot, what about the water that evaporates? The water in the Lakes does not just sit there. As the sun warms it and as the wind blows over it, water is lost. It goes into the air. If you let a bowl of water sit in your classroom, it will evaporate. One day it will be gone.

A cubic mile of water

About 116 billion gallons evaporate every day. That IS a lot of water! That is 38.5 **cubic miles** of water a year. A cubic mile is like a box a mile across and a mile deep. Still, the Great Lakes do not dry up. More water comes in than goes out. We are lucky that nature adds water back into the Great Lakes.

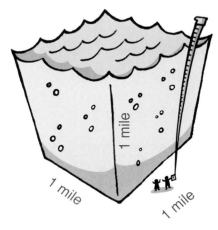

The amount of water is not always the same. Some years there is more rain. Sometimes there is less rain. The water level goes up and down. You might visit a Great Lake and see the water is down compared to the docks.

How Much Water Is In the Great Lakes?
You know the Great Lakes are huge. They have a lot of water, but how much is there? There is so much it is measured in cubic miles. There are about 5,413 cubic miles of water in the Great Lakes. Scientists say this is enough water to cover the 48 states that touch each other! The 4.5 billion gallons that flow out each day make about 1.5 cubic miles a year. So, a very small amount goes out through the St. Lawrence River. The amount that evaporates is more than flows out. Even that is small compared to all the water the Great Lakes hold.

The Great Lakes have enough water to cover all these states.

How Do People Use the Water?

People use the water for many things. Some cities use the water to drink. It goes into their water towers and through their water pipes. Several power plants are along the Great Lakes. They use the water for cooling. Most of that water finds it way back into the Lakes, but some is lost. Many businesses use water. Paper mills use water to make paper. Baby food companies use water to make baby food. Soda pop companies use water to make soda pop. Bottled water companies put it into bottles and sell it. Some farmers water their crops with it. Cows and cattle need water to drink too.

Cows on farms need water too!

Remember, other states use water from the Great Lakes too. Six other states use it along with two provinces from Canada. All of us share the water.

How Much Is Used?

Some people are upset Michigan allows bottled water to be sold. People ask, "Why should we sell our water?" One company bottles 270 **million gallons** a year. This is a lot of water. Of course, companies making soda pop use water too. Should one use be okay and another stopped? Should there be limits on how much is used and who can use it?

How much is used for other things? People use a bit more than 10 billion gallons a day. They drink it. They shower with it. They water their lawns with it. They wash their clothes with it. Businesses use over six billion gallons a day. Farmers use less than half a billion gallons a day. (Do not forget, it takes 1,000 million to equal 1 billion.)

Where the Water Goes Each Day- in Gallons

people	10.0 billion
business	6.0 billion
farms	.5 billion
flows to ocean	4.5 billion
evaporates	116.0 billion

Should We Worry?

There has been talk of building water pipelines from the Great Lakes. The water might be sent far from our borders. It may go to dry states. Or ships could take the water far away. By using ships, it could be exported to places like Africa. Much more water could be bottled and sold.

How many important ways do the people of Michigan use the Great Lakes? What might happen here if there is not enough water? The Great Lakes affect our climate. What might happen if the lack of water changed our climate? The Great Lakes are the main natural characteristic of our region. What might happen to the states around Michigan?

In the past, scarcity of resources elsewhere helped our economy. It brought us jobs. People mined our copper and iron. They cut our trees and sold the lumber. Can the scarcity of water elsewhere help us? Demand for water is going up and the supply is not getting bigger. Would selling water help or hurt our economy? What does Michigan get when a bottle of water is sold?

The Great Lakes states and provinces are working together. These governments are looking at the big picture together. They think it is best to all have the same rules about using Great Lakes water. This makes good sense. If one state had no rules, all the water could be used from it. It would not matter what the others decided to do.

Think About It. Talk About It!

1. Why is the need for water growing?

2. How many states will soon be short of water?

3. Why is using Great Lakes water a public issue?

4. What is the first thing to do when thinking about a public issue?

5. What are three ways people can share with others their ideas about public issues ?

Use a Chart to Help You

Make a chart that shows how water from the Great Lakes is used. Show how much water goes to each use. Use billions of gallons as your measurement.

Words In Action

Take a stand. Do you think we should be worried about using water from the Great Lakes? Give clear reasons for your stand. Use data that backs up your stand. Which core democratic values are involved? Does your stand support the common good for all of Michigan? Please explain.

Would it be hard to solve the problem of using Great Lakes water without the help of government? Please explain your answer.

Internet Research

The Great Lakes are a valuable natural resource. Research what has been done in the past to protect them. Research what is being done to protect them today.

Chapter 8 Lesson 3

Ideas To Explore

recycling - This is to reuse materials. Old items can be ground up or melted to be made into new products. Old glass bottles can be melted and mixed to make new glass.

Words To Welcome

brownfield - This is an old factory building that no one wants anymore. It may be falling down and have toxic waste around it.

carbon dioxide - This is a gas given off when coal, oil and wood are burned. It helps to make the earth warmer.

greenhouse gas - This is any gas like carbon dioxide that helps to make the earth warmer. It makes it warmer like a greenhouse does when the sun hits it.

nuclear power - This is making power by splitting atoms. It is good because it uses just a tiny amount of fuel. It is bad because it leaves radioactive material behind.

eyesore - something that is very ugly

radioactive - This is a material that gives off invisible rays. These rays can harm people and animals.

toxic chemicals - chemicals that are poisonous and can hurt people and animals

water pollution - is caused when bad chemicals get into our water.

Michigan
Social
Studies
GLCES

3P3.1.1
3P3.1.2
3P3.1.3
3P3.3.1
3P4.2.1
3P4.2.2
4H3.0.8

398

Don't Just Sit There- Take a Stand!

Think about this question while you read.
What do you need to do to take a stand on a public issue?

There will always be public issues around us. We need to decide how important each one is. We need to know how these issues will change our lives. We should find out how they will change our town and our state too.

The next step is doing something about these issues. Which ones are the most important to us? Are we willing to take a stand? Are we willing to talk to others and explain our stand? If we are not willing to do this, what is the point in having a stand?

You have already read about an issue in a small town. It was about people burning garbage. You have read about a regional issue. It concerned using water from the Great Lakes. What are some other issues that might be important in Michigan?

Keep the Water Clean
  Water pollution is one. We are in the middle of the Great Lakes. We are surrounded by water and we want it to stay clean. We do not want it to have chemicals in it that hurt us. We do not want things in the water that might hurt the fish that live there.

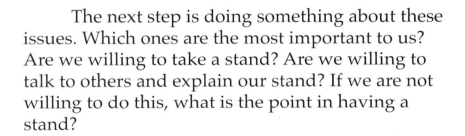

Recycling helps the earth. It means there is less garbage to bury or burn. It helps keep our planet clean.

Recycle

Recycling is important. The more cans, glass, metal, paper and plastic we recycle, the better it is for our planet. Recycling cuts litter. It sends materials back so they can be used again. This cuts energy use. It cuts the amount of resources that need to be mined. It cuts the number of trees that must be cut down. How can we have more people recycle? How should the government help in recycling?

Old Factories and Toxic Chemicals

Have you ever heard of a **brownfield**? This has nothing to do with farming. It often has little to do with fields either. This is a name given to an old factory that is no longer used. It may have **toxic chemicals** there, too. Sometimes companies go out of business because they have no money. Since they have no money, they just leave their buildings. They do not have money to clean up the place.

As the years go by, the buildings begin to fall down. They become dangerous and they do not look good. Everyone wants to get rid of them, but if people think there are toxic chemicals, no one wants to touch them. It can be very expensive to clean up toxic chemicals. No one wants to pay for that. No one wants to pay the cost of removing the old buildings either. The city is left with an **eyesore**.

In recent years, businesses have closed in Michigan. They have moved to places with lower costs. Some of these businesses may become brownfields.

This is a brownfield in Michigan. As businesses close, they may leave behind old buildings and toxic waste.

Who should pay to clean up brownfields? Should the government tax everyone? Should each business pay a tax when it is doing well, to pay to clean up things when it closes? Some old factories have been empty for years. What can be done to get something started?

Nuclear Power Plants

Nuclear power is another issue. Michigan has some very big power plants. They are often along the Great Lakes so they can use the water for cooling. When power plants burn coal, they make a lot of **carbon dioxide**. This is a **greenhouse gas**. At this time, we have 20 power plants that burn coal.

This is a nuclear power plant. Much steam is given off from the large cooling towers. The power is made under the dome.

Nuclear power plants do not give off greenhouse gas. On the other hand, nuclear power can be dangerous if people are careless. At this time, we have four nuclear power plants in Michigan. These four plants give us about one quarter of our state's electricity. Not all the nuclear power plants on the Great Lakes are in our country. Across Lake Huron, Canada has the largest nuclear plant in North America. Some countries use nuclear power to make almost all of their electricity.

With nuclear plants, the used fuel must be recycled. People complain about moving used fuel through their towns. They think it is too dangerous because it is very **radioactive**.

The wind can be a good source of energy in our state.

Nuclear power has good points and bad points. We will need more electricity. Should it come from coal, nuclear or wind? Can we make enough from the sun and the wind to meet our needs?

Here is a chart to help make good decisions.

Making An Informed Decision

What is the public issue?

What are some possible solutions?

Which do you think is the best solution?

Consider core democratic values which go along with this solution.

Write your stand on this issue.

Explain your stand with your reasons.

Take a Stand!

Work in a small group. Choose a public issue that interests your group. Gather more facts about this issue. Use books or the Internet to help you. Then write three possible solutions to this issue.

Part A. Brainstorm with your group. Decide which of these is the best solution to the issue.

Part B. Write out your proposed solution. List data that supports your solution.

Part C. List all core democratic values that connect with your solution.

Part D. Write your stand on this issue. Give your reasons for choosing this solution.

Part E. Each group goes before the class and talks about its issue. Make a list of the different viewpoints students have on each issue. Talk about why students may have different viewpoints.

Part F. Plan two ways you can share your ideas about this issue with others in your school. Talk to your principal for his or her approval. Choose one way and share your stand with your school.

Core Democratic Values

Core- the most important part of anything- like the core of an apple

Democratic- the kind of government run by the people with freedom for all

Values- important beliefs that guide your life

Core democratic values (kor dim oh kra tik val youz) are the main ideas for our kind of government.

∼ Core Democratic Values ∼

The core or center of our government is based on these key values. These are the ideas behind our state and national constitutions.

-Common Good: Working together to make life better for everyone. Not just thinking about ourselves. Example: Girl Scouts picking up trash along the road.

-Diversity: (Diversity sounds like: dih VER seh tee) People having many differences yet working together. Differences are not only allowed, but also accepted. Example: Antonio is Italian American and Giji is Native American, but they still enjoy working on school projects together.

-Equality: (Equality sounds like: ee KWAL uh tee) All people being treated the same. It does not matter how old you are. It does not matter about the color of your skin. It does not matter if you are a girl or a boy. Example: If your teacher only likes to call on girls, this is not showing equality.

-Justice: Everyone being treated the same in our legal system. It should not matter about your race, where you came from, your religion or how much money you have. Everyone has the same legal rights.

-Liberty: Freedom to do as we wish as long as it does not harm anyone else. This is the freedom to do anything that is not against the law. Example: We are free to travel to Lansing any time we wish.

-Life: Our right to live. Each person has the right to his or her life. The government cannot take a person's life unless they have been convicted of a very serious crime.

-Patriotism: (Patriotism sounds like: PAY tree uh tiz em) Love for our country and its values. Standing up for our country and its values. Being willing to protect our freedoms. Examples: People voting or serving in the army.

-Popular Sovereignty: (Sovereignty sounds like: SOV er en tee) People rule through their votes. They have the final say in government. Example: Voters can recall a lawmaker and vote him or her from office.

-Pursuit of Happiness: (Pursuit sounds like: per SOOT) This is the right to go after our goals and dreams. We are allowed to do what makes us happy, as long as it does not harm anyone else or step on his or her rights.

-Truth: Being honest and trustworthy. Our country cannot work well if people do not tell the truth. Not being truthful hurts business and the government. Examples: Always be honest in business deals. Always tell the truth when reporting the news.

∽ *Constitutional principles of the United States* ∽

These are the beliefs or ideas used to build our constitution.

-Checks and Balances: Each of the three branches of government should have equal power. If one branch tries to become too powerful, the other two should check or stop it.

-Civilian control of the military: (civilian sounds like: siv ill yun) The President, not army officers, has final control of the military. The governor is in charge of the state national guard.

-Federalism: (fed er ul izm) This is the sharing of power between the federal government and the state governments. The powers belonging to the federal government are listed in the United States Constitution.

-Freedom of Religion: (Religion sounds like: ree li jun) The right to worship any way you want or not to worship at all. Example: The government cannot say it is against the law to go to church.

-Individual Rights: (Individual sounds like: in di vid yule) This means each citizen has freedoms and rights the government cannot take away. Life, Liberty and Pursuit of Happiness are examples of these rights.

-Representative Government: (Representative sounds like: re pree zin ta tiv) The people vote to elect others to represent them in government.

-Rule of Law: Our nation is ruled by written laws which have been made over many years, not by whims of those in power.

-Separation of Powers: Each of the three branches has its own duties that another branch cannot take over.

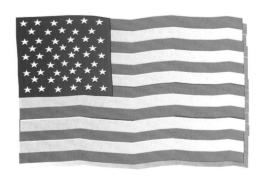

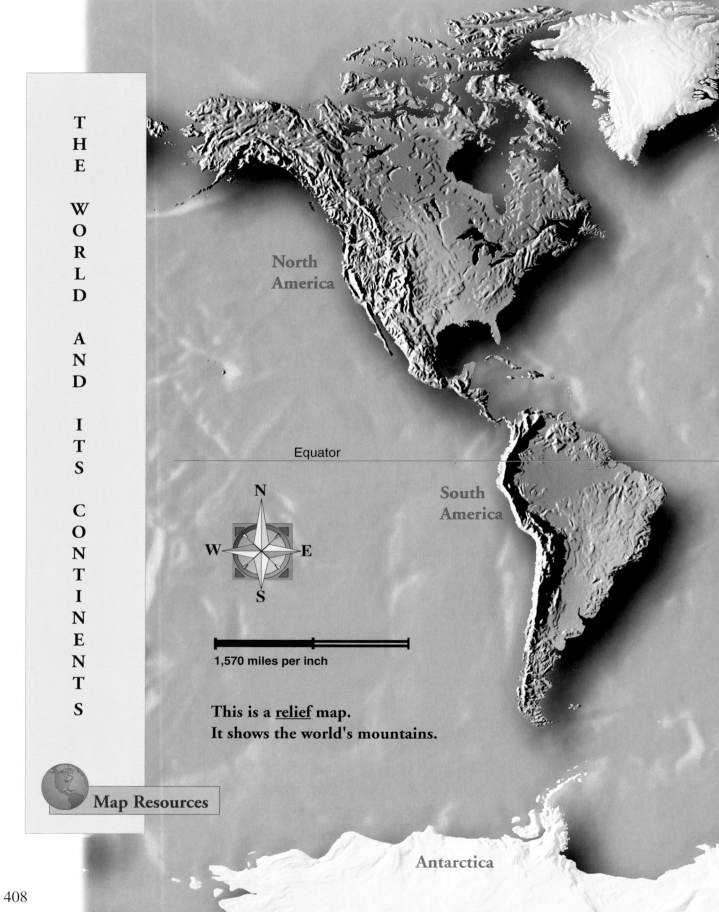

North
America

Equator

South
America

N

W   E

S

1,570 miles per inch

This is a <u>relief</u> map.
It shows the world's mountains.

Map Resources

Antarctica

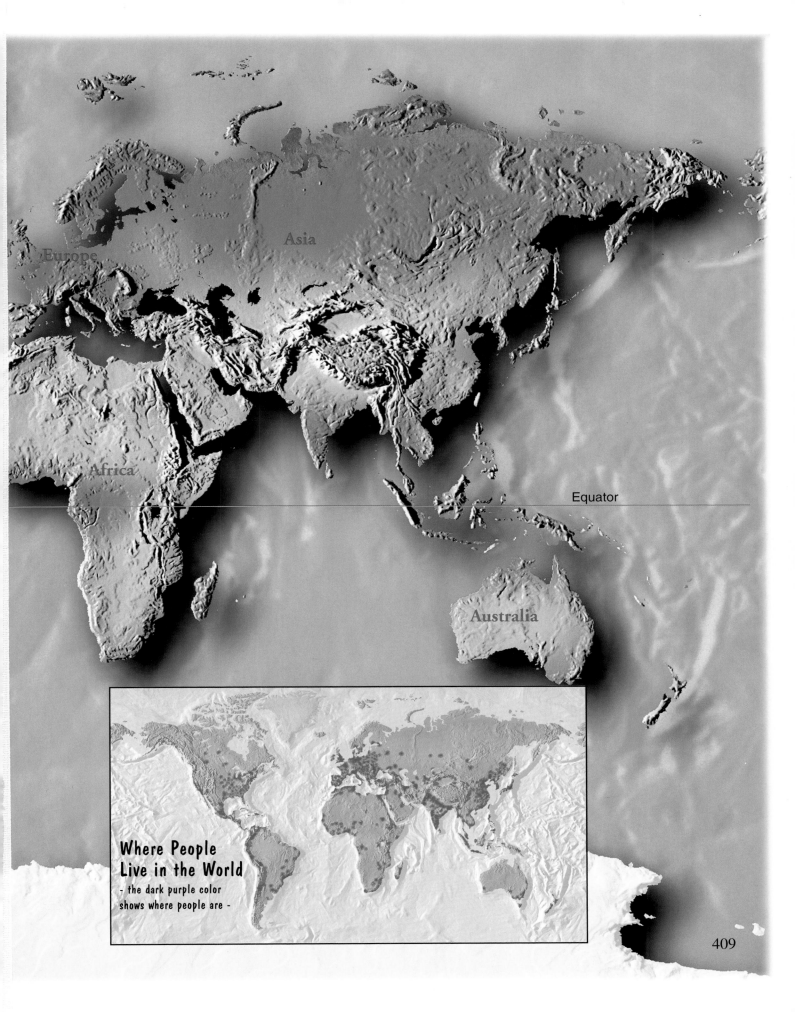

Europe

Asia

Africa

Equator

Australia

Where People Live in the World
- the dark purple color
shows where people are -

409

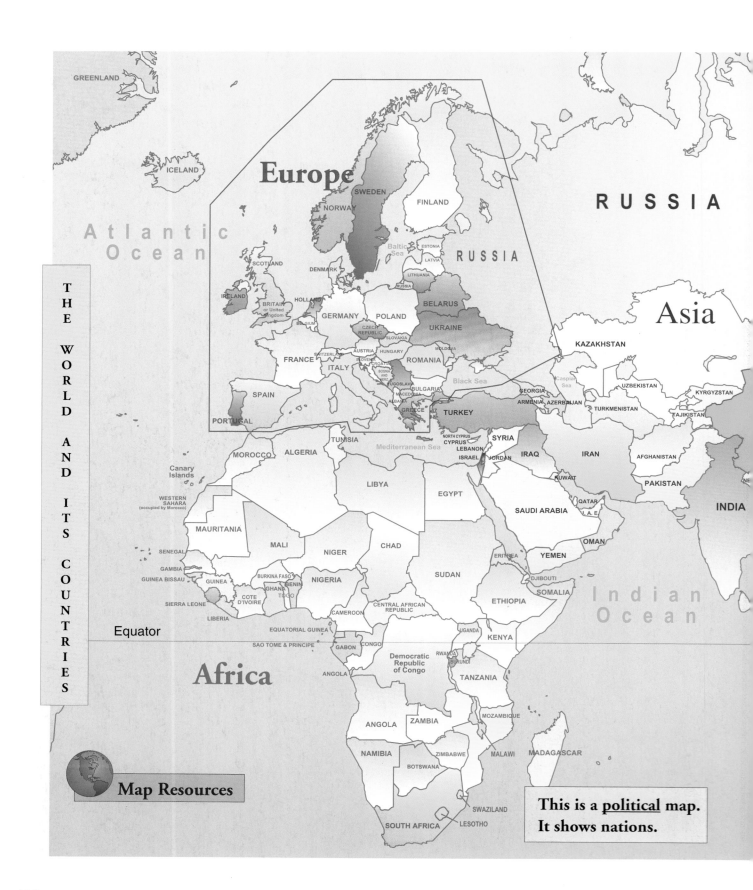

THE WORLD AND ITS COUNTRIES

GREENLAND

ICELAND

Atlantic
Ocean

Europe

SWEDEN

NORWAY

FINLAND

RUSSIA

Baltic
Sea

ESTONIA

LATVIA

SCOTLAND

DENMARK

RUSSIA

Asia

LITHUANIA

IRELAND

BRITAIN
or United
Kingdom

HOLLAND

RUSSIA

BELARUS

KAZAKHSTAN

BELGIUM

GERMANY

POLAND

UKRAINE

CZECH
REPUBLIC

SLOVAKIA

UZBEKISTAN

AUSTRIA

HUNGARY

MOLDOVA

KYRGYZSTAN

FRANCE

SWITZERLAND

SLOVENIA

CROATIA

ROMANIA

GEORGIA

Caspian
Sea

ITALY

BOSNIA
AND
HERZ.

TURKMENISTAN

TAJIKISTAN

SPAIN

YUGOSLAVIA

MACEDONIA

BULGARIA

Black Sea

ARMENIA

AZERBAIJAN

ALBANIA

PORTUGAL

GREECE

TURKEY

TUNISIA

NORTH CYPRUS

CYPRUS

SYRIA

Mediterranean Sea

LEBANON

IRAQ

IRAN

AFGHANISTAN

MOROCCO

ALGERIA

ISRAEL

JORDAN

Canary
Islands

KUWAIT

PAKISTAN

WESTERN
SAHARA
(occupied by Morocco)

LIBYA

EGYPT

QATAR

U.A.E.

INDIA

SAUDI ARABIA

MAURITANIA

OMAN

MALI

NIGER

CHAD

YEMEN

SENEGAL

ERITREA

GAMBIA

BURKINA FASO

SUDAN

DJIBOUTI

GUINEA BISSAU

GUINEA

BENIN

NIGERIA

SOMALIA

Indian
Ocean

SIERRA LEONE

GHANA

TOGO

COTE
D'IVOIRE

CENTRAL AFRICAN
REPUBLIC

ETHIOPIA

LIBERIA

CAMEROON

Equator

EQUATORIAL GUINEA

UGANDA

KENYA

SAO TOME & PRINCIPE

GABON

CONGO

Democratic
Republic
of Congo

RWANDA

BURUNDI

Africa

ANGOLA

TANZANIA

ANGOLA

ZAMBIA

MOZAMBIQUE

NAMIBIA

ZIMBABWE

MALAWI

MADAGASCAR

BOTSWANA

Map Resources

SWAZILAND

SOUTH AFRICA

LESOTHO

This is a **political** map.
It shows nations.

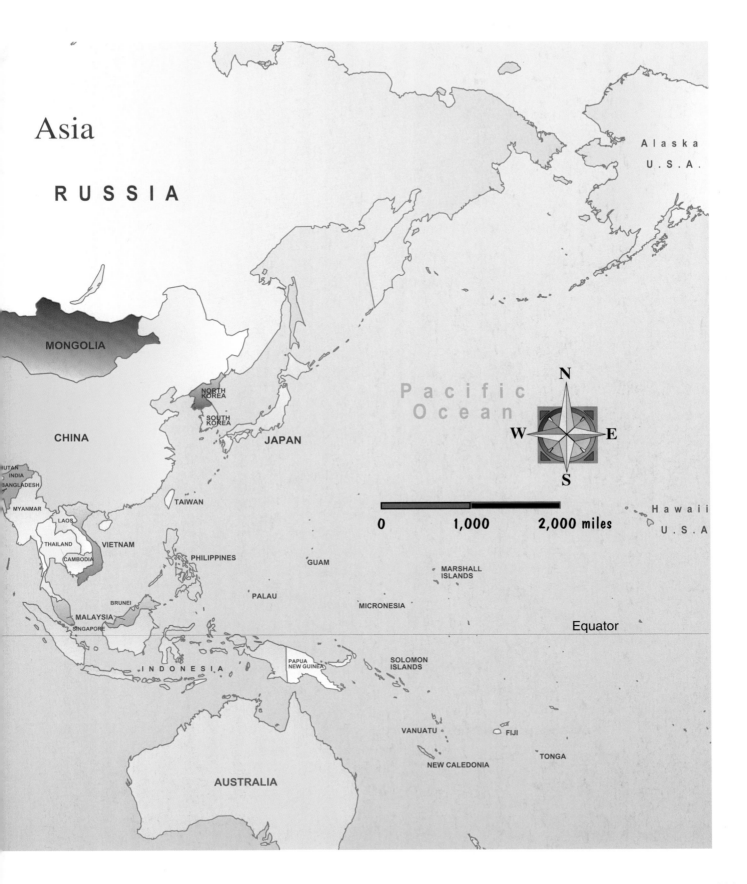

Asia

RUSSIA

MONGOLIA

NORTH
KOREA

SOUTH
KOREA

CHINA

JAPAN

BHUTAN
INDIA
BANGLADESH

MYANMAR

LAOS

THAILAND

CAMBODIA

VIETNAM

TAIWAN

Pacific
Ocean

Alaska
U.S.A.

PHILIPPINES

GUAM

MARSHALL
ISLANDS

Hawaii
U.S.A

N

W   E

S

0   1,000   2,000 miles

BRUNEI

MALAYSIA

SINGAPORE

PALAU

MICRONESIA

INDONESIA

PAPUA
NEW GUINEA

SOLOMON
ISLANDS

Equator

VANUATU

FIJI

NEW CALEDONIA

TONGA

AUSTRALIA

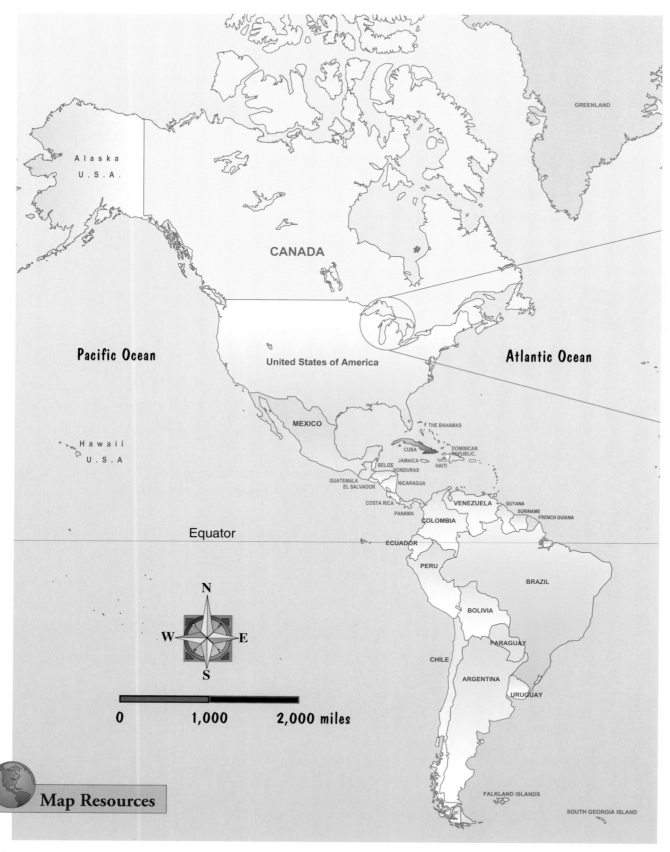

Alaska
U.S.A.

CANADA

Pacific Ocean

United States of America

Atlantic Ocean

GREENLAND

MEXICO

THE BAHAMAS

CUBA

DOMINICAN REPUBLIC.

BELIZE

JAMAICA

HAITI

GUATEMALA

HONDURAS

EL SALVADOR

NICARAGUA

COSTA RICA

VENEZUELA

GUYANA

PANAMA

SURINAME

COLOMBIA

FRENCH GUIANA

Hawaii
U.S.A

Equator

ECUADOR

PERU

BRAZIL

BOLIVIA

N

PARAGUAY

W   E

CHILE

S

ARGENTINA

URUGUAY

0   1,000   2,000 miles

FALKLAND ISLANDS

SOUTH GEORGIA ISLAND

Map Resources

412

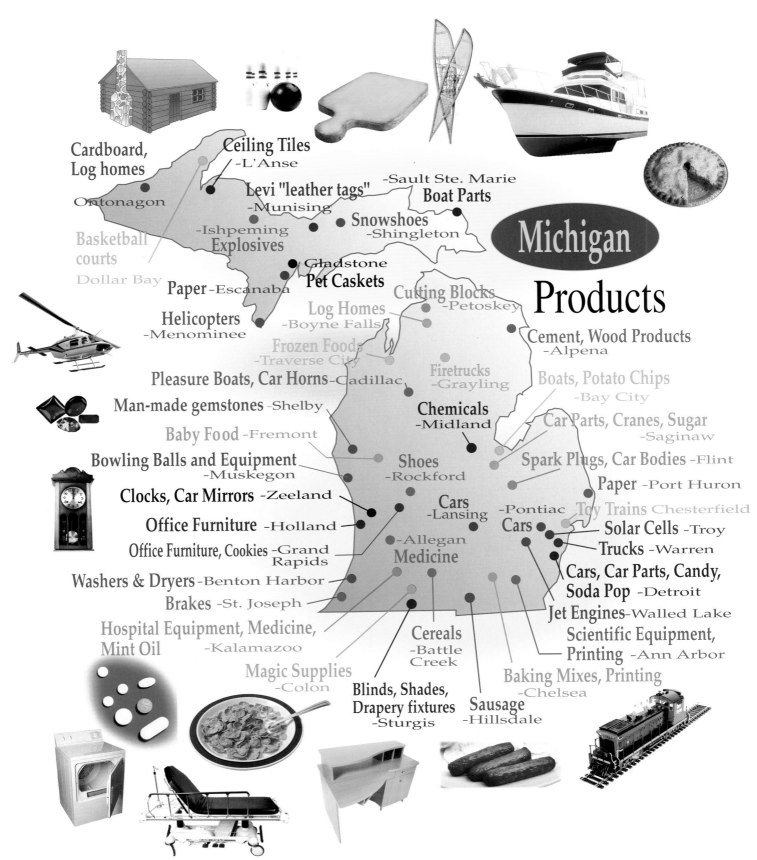

Cardboard, Log homes

Ceiling Tiles -L'Anse

-Sault Ste. Marie
Boat Parts

Levi "leather tags" -Munising

Snowshoes -Shingleton

Ontonagon

Basketball courts

Dollar Bay

-Ishpeming
Explosives

Gladstone
Pet Caskets

Michigan

Paper -Escanaba

Cutting Blocks -Petoskey

Products

Helicopters -Menominee

Log Homes -Boyne Falls

Cement, Wood Products -Alpena

Frozen Foods -Traverse City

Firetrucks -Grayling

Pleasure Boats, Car Horns -Cadillac

Boats, Potato Chips -Bay City

Man-made gemstones -Shelby

Chemicals -Midland

Car Parts, Cranes, Sugar -Saginaw

Baby Food -Fremont

Spark Plugs, Car Bodies -Flint

Bowling Balls and Equipment -Muskegon

Shoes -Rockford

Paper -Port Huron

Clocks, Car Mirrors -Zeeland

Cars -Lansing

-Pontiac Toy Trains Chesterfield

Office Furniture -Holland

Cars

Solar Cells -Troy

Office Furniture, Cookies -Grand Rapids

-Allegan
Medicine

Trucks -Warren

Washers & Dryers -Benton Harbor

Cars, Car Parts, Candy, Soda Pop -Detroit

Brakes -St. Joseph

Jet Engines -Walled Lake

Hospital Equipment, Medicine, Mint Oil -Kalamazoo

Cereals -Battle Creek

Scientific Equipment, Printing -Ann Arbor

Magic Supplies -Colon

Blinds, Shades, Drapery fixtures -Sturgis

Sausage -Hillsdale

Baking Mixes, Printing -Chelsea

Michigan's High & Low Places

- A topographical map -

Our highest point!

Marquette

Sault Ste. Marie

Ironwood

Menominee

Alpena

Traverse City

Cadillac

Saginaw

Grand River

Flint

Port Huron

Grand Rapids

Lansing

Detroit

our lowest point!

St. Joseph

Ann Arbor

Maps which show how high the land is.

The dark browns are highest.

The darker greens are lowest.

N
W E
S

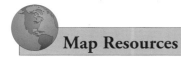

Map Resources

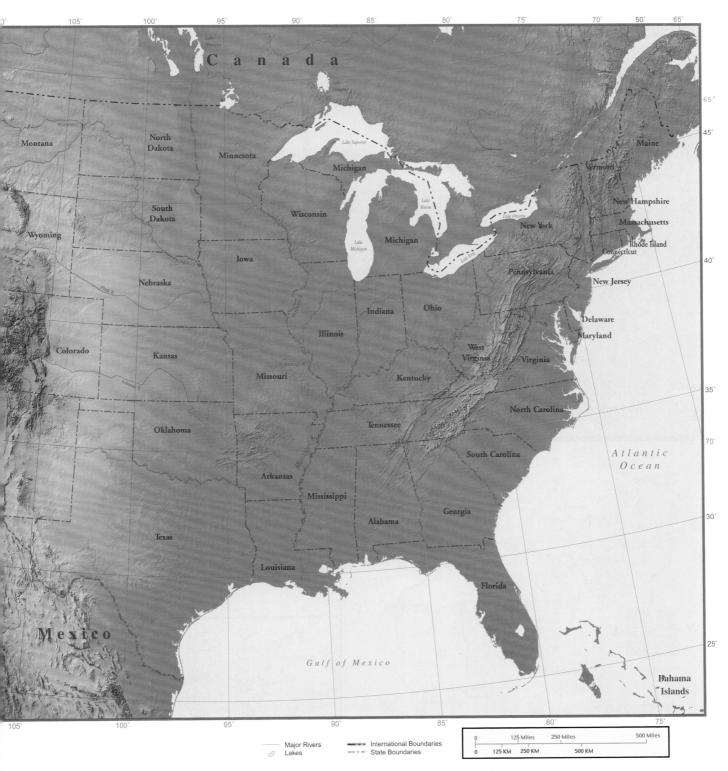

United States of America

shown without Alaska and Hawaii

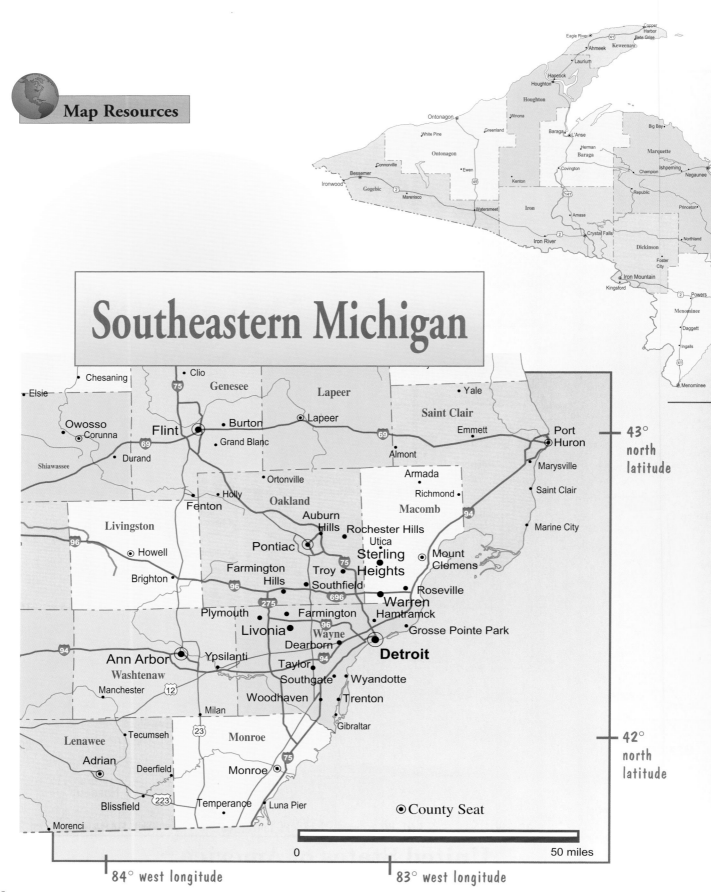

Map Resources

Southeastern Michigan

Chesaning • Clio
Elsie • Genesee Lapeer • Yale
Owosso • Corunna Burton • Lapeer Saint Clair Emmett Port Huron 43° north latitude
Flint • Grand Blanc 69 Almont Marysville
Durand Shiawassee 69 • Ortonville Armada Saint Clair
Holly Oakland Richmond Macomb Marine City
Fenton Livingston Auburn Hills Rochester Hills 94
Howell Pontiac Utica Sterling Heights Mount Clemens
Brighton Farmington Hills 75 Troy Roseville
96 Southfield 696 Warren
Plymouth 275 Farmington Hamtramck Grosse Pointe Park
Livonia 96 Wayne Detroit
Ann Arbor Ypsilanti Dearborn 94
Washtenaw Taylor Wyandotte
Manchester 12 Southgate Trenton
Milan Woodhaven Gibraltar
Lenawee Tecumseh 23 Monroe
Adrian Deerfield Monroe 75 42° north latitude
Blissfield 223 Temperance Luna Pier ◉ County Seat
Morenci

0   50 miles

84° west longitude   83° west longitude

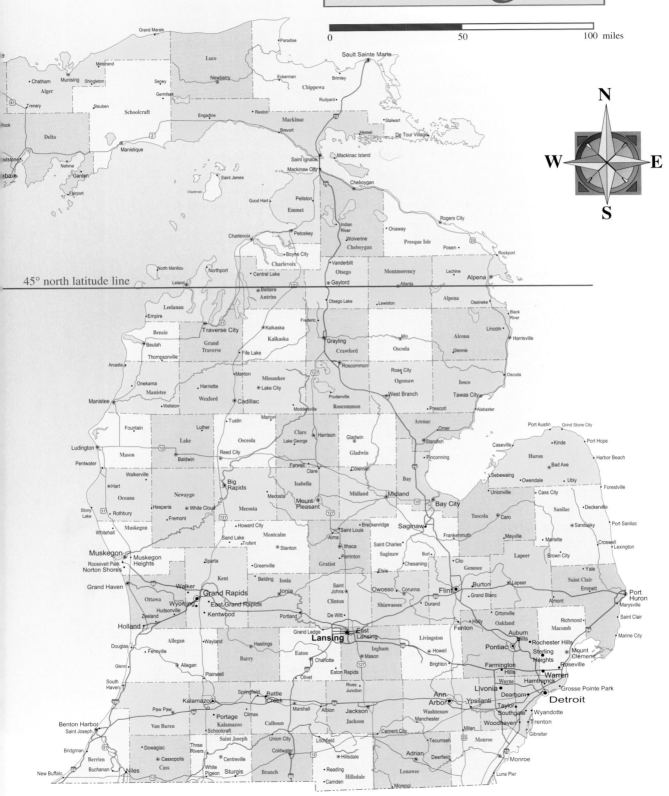

Michigan

0   50   100 miles

N
W   E
S

45° north latitude line

419

Glossary

The meaning of selected vocabulary words and some others that may be helpful

adapting to the environment - changing the way you live to best use what nature and the land provides. p. 51, 147, 157-161, 164-166

advertise – how a business shows and tells customers about its products. You see advertising in newspapers, billboards, television and web sites. You hear it on the radio. p. 291

Africa (AF rih KA)- the world's second largest continent. It is south of Europe. Today, Africa has many countries. Angola, Ghana and Liberia are examples. People from there were brought to America as slaves in the 1700s and early 1800s. p. 269

Alpena (al-pee-na) population about 12,000. The town was started by a fisherman named W.F. Cullings in 1835. Alpena comes from a Native American word for the partridge (a bird). Alpena is on Thunder Bay along Lake Huron. Today, it has one of the world's largest cement making plants. p. 195, 204, 293

amendment (ah mend ment) – a change in the constitution. Michigan's constitution has been amended several times. Since 1963, about 20 changes have been made and about 30 turned down. Amendments must be voted on by the people. p. 352

Anishnabeg (ah NISH nAy beh - the "g" is almost or completely silent) - an Ojibwa name for themselves. It means "the people." It might also be spelled Anishnabek. p. 50, 54

Ann Arbor- population about 101,000. It was started in 1824 by John Allen and Walker Rumsey of New York. It is named after their wives, Ann Allen and Ann Rumsey. The University of Michigan is located there. Many famous people have been students at the university. Much scientific research is done in Ann Arbor. p. 29

Arab Americans – people who came from countries in and around the Arabian Peninsula. Examples are Saudi Arabia, Syria and Lebanon. p. 279-280

artifacts (art eh facts) - things left behind by people who lived long ago. Arrowheads and bones are artifacts. p. 42, 53

automation alley - a nickname for the area around Detroit where many research and technology businesses are located. Automation is using machines to do more work faster and easier with fewer people. p. 316-317

automobile (aw toe moh beel) - another name for a car. It is a French word. Auto means self and mobile means move. The word car comes from Carrus, a Latin word for cart.

ballot - a paper used by each voter to record their choices while voting. p. 231

bargaining –when a union talks with a company to get better pay and working conditions. It is the give and take of reaching an agreement. Deciding what each group will give up and receive. p. 257

Battle Creek – population about 54,000. The town was started in 1831 by J.J. Garnsey. It got its name because two Native Americans and two surveyors had fought there near a small creek. Known as the Cereal City. It is famous for making breakfast cereal. p. 234, 237-239, 323

bill - the idea for a new law in the state house or senate. p. 357

borders (bor ders) - where one state ends and the next state or country begins. Borders are usually printed on maps. p. 3

branches of government – how our government is divided. There are three branches. They are the executive (governor or president), the legislative (law makers) and the judicial (courts). p. 355-361

Britain (brit an) – also known as England. It is an island country in Europe. The people from this country are called British. Britain controlled Michigan for a short time. It took control of New France in 1760. People from Britain started the 13 colonies, like Virginia, which became the first states in the United States. We fought the War for Independence against Britain in order to start the

United States. p. 88, 115-124, 127-132. 140-141

brownfield - land with an old factory building that no one wants anymore. It may be falling down and have toxic waste around it. p. 400-401

budget – an amount of money that can be spent. In state government, balancing the money coming in from taxes and the money going out to pay for projects. p. 360-361

Cadillac, Antoine (ahn TWAHN • KAD el ak) - [1658-1730]- French explorer and fur trader. In charge of French fort at Mackinac in 1694. He started Detroit in 1701. He was told to return to France 1711. He became governor of Louisiana 1713-1716 and then went back to France. p. 106-112

Cadillac, Marie-Therese (ma REE TEH rez • KAD el ak) - [1671-1740]- wife of Antoine Cadillac. One of the first French women to come to Detroit. p. 109

Canada (KAN uh duh) - the large country mostly north of Michigan. It has slightly more land than the U.S. It was settled by the British and French. Both languages are spoken there today. The capital is Ottawa. It has ten provinces and two territories instead of states. About 30 million people live there and most of them live near its southern border. p. 19, 292, 295

candidates - people who want to hold an office, such as mayor. The voters will choose one of the candidates. p. 325

capital resource - tools, machines and equipment used in a business. p. 150, 208, 286-287

capitol building - a building with a white dome in Lansing where laws are made. p. 180

Cass, Lewis - [1782-1866]- governor of Michigan Territory for 18 years (1813-1831). He suggested the state motto and designed the state seal. He made land treaties with the Indians and helped explore the land. p. 172

cause and effect - In history, where one event leads to a second event happening later. The first event is the cause. The second event is the effect. p. 124, 162, 178, 199, 251

Chrysler, Walter (cry sler)- [1875-1940] In 1905 he bought a very expensive car and the first thing he did was to take it apart and put it back together! He quickly moved up in the growing car business. Started his own company in 1924. p. 249

citizen (sit eh zin) - anyone born in a country. People who move here can also become citizens after taking a test and swearing to uphold the Constitution and to defend the country. Often people must be old enough to vote before they are called a citizen. p. 371

civic responsibility - each person doing his or her duty to help government work well and making Michigan a good place to live. p. 365

Civil War (1861-1865) - when the United States broke into two parts that fought each other. A civil war is a war between parts of the same country. The United States had a civil war (1861-1865) between the northern states which were against slavery and the southern states which were for slavery. The war started when the southern states tried to form their own country called the Confederate States of America. p. 232- 234

climate (kli mit) - the pattern of weather in a region over a long time. Here are two climate questions. How much snow is there usually in December? How hot is it usually in June? The climate of northern Michigan is colder than the climate of southern Michigan. p. 20, 30, 299

common good - what is best for everyone, not just yourself. p. 13, 143, 206, 210, 223, 322-323

conflicting views – when people have different ideas about what is the best thing to do. It happens because people are not the same. They come from different backgrounds. They see things differently. They may not agree on what is best for themselves and for the common good. p. 378

Glossary

Congress (kon gres) – the law makers in our national government in Washington, D.C. p. 169

consequences - things that happen because of an event. Consequences can be good (positive) or they can be bad (negative). p. 326

conservation (kon ser va shun) - not wasting resources, leaving some to use later. p. 199

constitution - a rule book for government. It tells what the government can do and what it cannot do. It lists the rights that people have. p. 349, 352-353

continent - a large land with many countries. p. 269

copper - a reddish colored metal. It is flexible and a good conductor of electricity. It is often used to make electric wire. Copper mining was a big industry in Michigan from the 1840s to 1920s. p. 33, 205-209

core democratic values - key values or ideas of the people in this country. Our government and constitution are based on these values. Examples are liberty, justice, equality, the right to vote and religious freedom. See the list on pages 405-406.

counties (KOUN tees) - many Michigan counties are shown as square boxes on maps. Michigan has 83 counties and each one is like a small state government. p. 33, 340-342, maps 76, 341

Couzens, James - (KUZ zins) [1872-1936] - a hard-working executive and investor in the Ford Motor Company. He was the mayor of Detroit and later a U.S. Senator (1922-1936). During the Great Depression he gave 10 million dollars to help needy children in Michigan. p. 251

credit (kred it) - using someone else's money to buy something. A loan from a bank is one kind. Using a credit card is another kind of credit. It must be paid back with interest. p. 148

culture - all the different ways a group lives. Culture includes their food, homes, jobs, beliefs, government and more. p. 164, 265-282

customs (kus tums) - the usual ways of doing things among a group of people. Like traditions or habits. Her family has the custom of getting a white pine for their Christmas tree. p. 62, 265-282

de Baptiste, George [1815-1875] – born in Virginia. Once the valet of President Harrison; a helper on the Underground Railroad who lived in Detroit from 1846 to 1875. p. 230

de Sable, Jean (jHAN day-SAW-bul) - [1745-1818]- He was born in Haiti. He went to school in France. He was one of the first African Americans in the Michigan area. As a fur trader, he started the city of Chicago in 1779. During the War for Independence, he was captured by the British. Later, he was a trader at Port Huron, MI. p. 124

de Tonty, Anne -(day TAHN tee) - came to Michigan in 1701. The first Italian woman here. Wife of Alphonse de Tonty and the mother of the first European child born in Michigan. p. 110

de troit (the French said- day twaw) - French words meaning "strait," a narrow river connecting two lakes. These words became the name of Michigan's largest city, Detroit. The way the words are spoken has changed. p. 107

Dearborn - population about 90,000. It was started in 1795 and named for General Henry Dearborn, a leader in the War of 1812. It is the home of the Ford Motor Company, The Henry Ford and Fairlane (Henry Ford's home built in 1915). It also has the Automotive Hall of Fame. p. 29, 159

democracy (dem oc rass ee) –the kind of government where the voters have the final say in what happens. p. 328

Detroit (dee TROYt) - Michigan's largest city with almost one million people. It is in Wayne County. It was started in 1701 by Cadillac, a Frenchman. It grew rapidly between 1830 and 1860 and again between 1910 and 1920. It is port to Great Lakes ships. Many car companies are in or near Detroit. It is called Motor Town or Motown. p. 28, 105, 105-112 and others

diversity (dih VER seh tee) - when different kinds of people live and work together. Accepting the idea that a place is better with many different kinds of people is a core democratic value. p. 44, 405

Durant, Billy (DUR ant)- [1861-1947]- In 1886, he started a company that made horse-drawn buggies. Because of this, his hometown of Flint was called the "Vehicle City." In 1908, he started General Motors which became one of the world's largest companies. p. 249

Dutch - the people of the country of the Netherlands, also called Holland. Many Dutch people moved to western Michigan in the 1840s and 1850s. They helped start cities like Holland and Zeeland. p. 275

economy - everything that is a part of producing and consuming products and services. It includes what businesses, stores and factories make and sell. It includes workers and what they earn. It includes consumers and what they buy. p. 182, 207

election - when people vote and decide which person will hold each office. Elections are held for governor, mayor, lawmakers, judges and others. p. 324

entrepreneur (on tray pren ur) - a person who takes the risks to start and run a business. Henry Ford was an entrepreneur when he began his car business. p. 149, 245

Erie Canal (ear ee • can al) – a 363 mile man-made river that crosses New York state. It connects Albany, New York with Lake Erie. It opened in 1825. Using it, people could travel from New York City to Detroit. Many pioneer settlers used the canal in the 1800s. p. 155-159

ethnic group. (eth nik) - people who once lived together in another land. They have the same ancestors. In the past, they spoke the same language and had the same customs. p. 264-283

Europe (your up) - the continent that is across the Atlantic Ocean from North America. It has several countries. Some them are: Britain, Finland, France, Holland, Germany, Italy, Norway, Poland and Sweden. p. 55 and others

executive branch - the part of state government headed by the governor. p. 355

export (ex port) - something that is sent to another country (exported) and sold. p. 147, 292, 294-295

federal government - another name for the national government in Washington, D.C. The President is the leader. It prints our money. It controls the army, navy and air force. It makes treaties with other countries. p. 344, 361

Flint - population about 130,000. Flint was started in 1819 by a trader named Jacob Smith. The city is named after the Flint River which goes through it. Flint was known for the making of wagons and buggies before cars were invented. The General Motors company started in Flint. p. 30, 259

Ford, Gerald [1913-2006] - became the 38th President of the United States in 1974. He replaced President Nixon when he resigned that year. He is the only person from Michigan to be President. He is the only U.S. President who was not elected to office. He served in the U. S. House of Representatives for many years before he became Vice President. p.307

Ford, Henry [1863-1947] - a man whose dream was to make a practical car almost anyone could afford. In 1903 he started the Ford Motor Company. He helped start the idea of the moving assembly line for factories. This idea made cars and many other products cost less. In 1914 he offered workers a wage of $5.00 a day. Ford became one of the world's first billionaires. p. 240, 243-252, 273

Fort Michilimackinac (MISH ill eh MACK in aw) – the French fort built in 1715 across from Mackinac Island in the Lower Peninsula. p. 120, 309

fossil (fos el) - once a living thing that has changed to stone. p. 11

Glossary

France - A country in Europe whose people speak French. The capital city is Paris. The first Europeans in Michigan were from France. The French controlled Michigan and a large part of North American for over 100 years. The British forced them out in 1760. p. 80-117, 281

French and Indian War - between 1754 and 1760 the British attacked the French areas of North America. Native American warriors often helped the French. The French lost the war and had to leave much of North America. p. 116

freshwater - not ocean water - water that does not have any salt in it. p. 391

fruit belt - the land along Lake Michigan that is very good for growing fruit. The lake helps keep the temperature just right. p. 298-299

glacier (glay sher) - a thick cover of ice that does not melt in summer. Long ago glaciers moved slowly over Michigan pushing dirt and rocks along with it. p. 21

government (gov ern ment) - (national, state and local)- the system which rules a country, state or city. It makes the laws, collects taxes, operates the courts, police, military forces and so forth. It provides services for us which we cannot do by ourselves. p. 3, 320-377

Grand Rapids - population about 190,000. It is the second largest city in Michigan. Louis Campau arrived in 1826 and started a trading post. He bought the land which became most of the downtown area for $90! It has been called the Furniture City. Much home furniture was made here beginning in the late 1850s. It is on the Grand River at a small rapids. Many people in and around Grand Rapids have ancestors form the country of Holland. p. 29, 192, 291-292

Grand River - Michigan's longest river. It starts in Hillsdale County and flows through Lansing and Grand Rapids into Lake Michigan at Grand Haven. About 260 miles long. It drains about 10 percent of the state. p. 21, 146, 234

Great Depression (dee PRESH en) - the years from 1929 until about 1939 when there was a great business slowdown. Banks closed. Companies went out of business. Millions of people were out of work and out of money. p. 255

Great Lakes Region (REE jun) - the land around the five Great Lakes. It usually includes Michigan, Ohio, Wisconsin, Minnesota, Illinois, Indiana and sometimes Ontario. These places are grouped together because they all share the Great Lakes. This gives them much in common. p. 35-36

Great Lakes Drainage Basin - the area of land where all the rivers flow into the Great Lakes. It includes all the states around the Great Lakes and part of Canada too.   p. 392

Great Migration (my gray shun) - the time beginning about 1910 and lasting through the 1940s when poor people from the South moved north to find better jobs. p. 270

greenhouse gas - any gas like carbon dioxide that helps to make the earth warmer. It makes it warmer like a greenhouse does when the sun hits it. p. 401

Haviland, Laura [1807-1898] - She and her husband had one of the first U.S. schools for African American children. This was near Adrian. She also helped escaped slaves through the Underground Railroad. p. 230

heritage (HAIR uh tij) - the history of a group of people. It includes foods and language. It includes the old ways of doing things. It includes the old customs and festivals. p. 265-282

Hiawatha (HI eh WA tha) - a Native American hero in the poem "The Song of the Hiawatha." The name means "he makes rivers." p. 70-72

Hispanic (hiss pan ik) - the prefix "his" of this word means "relating to". In this case, Hispanic means relating to Spain. Hispanic people are those from Central and South America which were once controlled by Spain. People from Mexico, Puerto Rico and Cuba are often called Hispanic. p. 276

historians (hiss tor ee ans) – people who study clues from the past to learn what really happened. p. 45, 123

Hopewell people (hope well) - a group of Native Americans who came before the time of the tribes that we know today. They are named after Captain Mordecai C. Hopewell, a farmer from Ohio. Mounds on his farm were dug up in 1892. The Hopewell are also known as mound builders because they often buried their dead in large mounds of dirt. They lived as far south as Alabama and west to St. Louis. Most mounds were removed to make room for towns and farms. p. 41-42

Houghton, Douglass (HO tun) -[1809-1845]- interested in science and medicine. Michigan's first state geologist. To do this job, he traveled all over Michigan. He wrote about the minerals and natural resources he found. One of these reports told about large copper deposits in the U.P. This started the copper industry in the 1840s. He drowned when his boat flipped over in a Lake Superior storm. p. 206

Hull, William [1753-1825]- first governor of the Michigan Territory from 1805-1812. Following the War of 1812, he was court-martialed. He was sentenced to be shot for his surrender of Detroit. President Madison, however, gave him a pardon. p. 136-138

human resource - the people who provide their skill's and energy to work in a business. p. 149, 286

human characteristic (hu man • kar ak ter iz tik) - things made by people. Cities and highways are two human characteristics of Michigan. p. 12, 34, 39

Huron (hYOUR on) tribe or Wyandotte (WY-n-dot) - one of the smaller tribes living in the Lower Peninsula. p. 63

import (em port) – a product people buy that was made in another country. p. 147, 295

incentive - a reward for doing a certain action. p. 209

income tax - the part of the money people earn that goes to pay for government. p. 335

independence (in dee pend ense) - not to be ruled by someone else. p. 127

Indians (in de yuns) another name for Native Americans or the first people to live here. Some of the early explorers became lost and thought they had reached India. So, the first people they saw were named Indians.

interdependence - people depending on each other for products they each need. p. 296

iron – a heavy metal used to make steel, frying pans, cars and other products. It is attracted by magnets. Iron is mined in the Upper Peninsula near Marquette. Many big ships on the Great Lakes carry iron ore. It is an important natural resource. p. 33

Iroquois (ear uh koy) – a group of tribes who lived along Lakes Erie and Ontario and disliked the French. p. 93

judicial branch - the part of government with our courts and judges. p. 355, 359, 364-368

jury - A group of regular people asked to come to court and listen to a trial. They decide who is right and who is wrong. p. 365

justices - the seven judges on the Michigan State Supreme Court. p. 366

Kalamazoo (kal ah mah zoo) - population about 80,000. A city in west Michigan. The name means "boiling water." Started in 1829 by Titus Bronson. It is now the home of Western Michigan University and Kalamazoo College. Known for making medical equipment and medicine. p. 74-75, 234, 289

Kellogg, Dr. John Harvey [1852-1943]- head of a large hospital in Battle Creek. In 1876 he developed granola as a health food. He was not a part of the Kellogg Company. He did not think it was proper for a doctor to be involved with a business. p. 237

Kellogg, William Keith [1850-1951] - started the Battle Creek Toasted Corn Flake Company in 1906. Charles Post started making breakfast cereals with his ideas before Kellogg did. p. 237, 239

key events - events that are the reason something happens later. p. 127, 180, 210, 251, 377

King George III (III means third) [1738-1820] - one of the kings of Britain. He was the king during the War for Independence. p. 127

LaFramboise, Madeline [1780-1846] - name means raspberry. A French and Native American Ottawa woman. She and her husband were successful fur traders in West Michigan. Today she is buried on Mackinac Island. p. 145

lake effect (ee fect) - effects of weather in Michigan because of the Great Lakes. It helps keep the land cooler in the summer and warmer in the winter. p. 20

Lake Erie (EAR ree) - farther south than the other Great Lakes and is the most shallow. Lake Erie only touches a small part of Michigan. It holds 116 cubic miles of water. Its length is 241 miles. p. 19

Lake Huron (hYOUR on) - second largest Great Lake and was named after an Indian tribe who once lived along its shore. Lake Huron has the most islands of the Great Lakes. It holds 849 cubic miles of water. Its length is 205 miles p. 19, 209

Lake Michigan (MISH ah gun) - the only Great Lake completely inside the United States. There are many huge sand dunes on the Lower Peninsula side of Lake Michigan. It holds 1,180 cubic miles of water. Its length is 307 miles. p. 19

Lake Ontario (ON tair ee oh) - one of the five Great Lakes located farthest east. It is the only Great Lake that does not touch Michigan. It holds 393 cubic miles of water. Its length is 193 miles. p. 18

Lake Superior (SUP EAR ee or) - the largest, coldest and deepest of the Great Lakes. It is over 1,300 feet deep. It is the largest fresh water lake in the world by area, but not by volume. It is farther north than any other Great Lake. It holds 2,935 cubic miles of water. It is 350 miles long. p. 19, 209

Lambert, William – [1817-1890] - a leader in the Detroit Underground Railroad. p. 230

Lansing (lan sing) - population about 128,000. Michigan's state capitol. Started in 1835. It grew very little until the capital was moved there in 1848. Named after the city, Lansing, New York. Once known for making Oldsmobile cars. p. 10, 308, 312, 331, 338

legislative branch – one of the three branches of government- the lawmakers. p. 357

legislators (lej es lay tors) - our state lawmakers. The men and women elected to serve as members of the state house and senate. Michigan has 148 legislators. They meet in the capitol building in Lansing. p. 170

liberty (lib er tee) - to do what you wish as long as it does not hurt anyone. It is the freedom to do anything that is not against the law. p. 128

loan - borrowing money for some purpose. Loans must be paid back plus some extra money, which is called interest. p. 318

lock - A way to raise and lower ships. Locks and canals are often used together. p. 209

Lower Peninsula (pen in soo la)- the southern part of Michigan where nearly nine million people live. It is shaped like a mitten on the map. It has Michigan's largest cities. p. 5, 22, 30-33, 38

Mackinac Island (MACK in aw • EYE land) - a small island in Lake Huron. It was a fur trading center during the 1700s and early 1800s. Today it is a popular tourist stop. Thousands of people

visit it each summer, but only a few hundred stay in the winter. No cars are allowed on the island. p. 74-75, 309-310

Marquette (mar KETT) - largest city in the Upper Peninsula. It was started in 1849 and called Iron Bay at first. Robert Graveraet (GRAY ver et) bought the first land. The county and city are named after Father Marquette. Population about 22,000. p. 30, 117, 216

Marquette, Jacques (jHAK • mar KETT) [1637-1675]- French missionary who started Sault Ste. Marie in 1668 and St. Ignace in 1671. He was excited to tell the Native Americans about his God. In 1673 he explored the Mississippi River. p. 97-102

Mason, Stevens T. [1811-1843]- Michigan's first state governor, was known as the 'Boy Governor' since he was only twenty-three years old. He was the youngest man to be governor. He was governor until 1840. His work as governor was not easy. He had to deal with the border conflict called the Toledo War with Ohio. Later, he moved to New York and died at an early age due to illness. p. 174-178

Menominee River (meh NOM eh nee) - a river much used in logging days. It also goes through a rich iron mining area. The Brulé River and the Michigamme Rivers come together to form the Menominee River. It flows into Lake Michigan. Forms part of the border between Michigan and Wisconsin. p. 22

Menominee (meh NOM eh nee) tribe - Means "wild rice people." Wild rice was an important food for them. Their customs were much like those of the Ojibwa who lived nearby They lived in the Upper Peninsula. p. 62, 74-75

Mexico (MEX eh co) - the large country located south of the United States. Many Hispanic people come from Mexico to the United States and Michigan. Many imports and exports flow between Mexico and the United States. p. 51, 276, 292, 295

Michigan - the name comes from the Native American words mishi gami. They mean big lake or big water. p. 6

Midwest - Michigan and states around it. This land was once in the middle of the western part of our country. That was when the United States was smaller than it is today. p. 154

migrate (mi grate) - moving from place to place. To move a long way to start a new home. p. 60, 221, 267

Model T - a simple, but popular car built by Henry Ford from 1908 to 1927. p. 246-248, 252

modify the environment - people changing their surroundings to meet their wants and needs. p. 60, 187

moving assembly line - This idea helps people do more work in factories. The product moves along as the workers put it together. p. 247

Mt. Arvon (Mt. stands for mount, like mountain) (ar von) - the highest point in Michigan. It is 1,979 feet above sea level. It is in the north central U.P. p. 32

Murphy, Frank (mur fee)- [1890-1949] born in Harbor Beach, MI. He went to law school at the University of Michigan. Mayor of Detroit 1930-1933; Governor General of the Philippine Islands (1935-1936); Governor of Michigan 1936-1938;United States Attorney General 1939-1940; Justice of the U.S. Supreme Court 1940-1949. p. 259

Muskegon (mus KEE gon) - name means "marsh." Population about 40,000. It started as a trading post in 1834. It became a lumber town and busy port city. It was once called the "Lumber Queen of the World." p. 74-75

Muskegon River - a long river starting at Houghton Lake in the Lower Peninsula. It was once a

famous river used to carry logs to the sawmills of the city of Muskegon. p. 195

national government – also federal government- The United States government led by the President in Washington, D.C. p. 173, 344, 361

Native Americans (nay tiv • am air uh kins)- native means first. First people in America. Sometimes called Indians. p. 42-76, 159-163

natural characteristic - part of nature - the outdoors. p. 10-11, 34 , 39

natural resource - something found in nature that is used to meet people's needs.   Resources used to make or grow things. p. 33, 164-166, 184-216, 234-240

negative consequences (kon see quin siss) - the bad things that happen because of an event or decision. p. 200

New France - the land of Canada and the Great Lakes, including Michigan, claimed by France. p. 91, 115-117

North America - The continent where Canada, the United States and Mexico are found. The world is divided into six or seven continents depending on the definition used. p. 51

Northwest Ordinance (or den anse) - A law passed by the national government in 1787. It told how a large piece of land in the Great Lakes area was to be governed. It told how the land could be made into states. p. 170-171

Northwest Territory (tear eh tor ee) - former United States frontier land that included the present states of Illinois, Indiana, Michigan, Ohio, Wisconsin, and part of Minnesota. It was formed in 1787. p. 169-174

nuclear power - This is making power by splitting atoms. It is good because it uses just a tiny amount of fuel. It is bad because it leaves radioactive material behind. p. 401

Odawa or Ottawa (oh DA wa), (ott uh wa) - the name means to trade. A tribe of the northwest Lower Peninsula. The Ojibwa and Ottawa were related. Many of their ways of living and doing things were also alike. p. 50

Ojibwa, Ojibway or Chippewa (oh jib way) - a large tribe living in and around the northern Great Lakes area. Probably the largest Michigan tribe. They shared the Upper Peninsula with the Menominee. p. 50, 59

Olds, Ransom [1864-1950]- started the first Michigan automobile company in 1897. In 1901 he moved the company to Lansing. He left that company in 1904 and started one called REO (after his own initials). This was also in Lansing. After he died in 1950, his home was torn down to make room for a freeway! p. 243

opinion - your ideas and thoughts about a subject. p. 15

opportunity cost - (ah por tune uh tee) a person gives up this to get what is better. The one you do not choose, your second choice, is your opportunity cost. p. 85, 326

Parks, Rosa [1913-2005]- born in Tuskegee, Alabama. She is known as the Mother of the Civil Rights Movement. In 1955 she refused to give up her seat on an Alabama bus to a white person. This broke an Alabama law and she was arrested. She moved to Detroit, MI in 1957. In 1999 she was awarded the Presidential Medal of Freedom for her accomplishments. p. 270

peninsula (pen in su la) - A peninsula is land with water on three sides. Michigan is made of two large peninsulas. p. 5

Pere Marquette River (peer • mar KETT) - Pere means "Father." A river in the Lower Peninsula named in honor of Father Jacques Marquette. p. 102

Perry, Oliver Hazard (ol eh ver • haz ard • pear ee) [1785-1819]- American naval officer. He fought the British on Lake Erie during the War of 1812. p. 139

persuasive essay (per sway siv • es say) - writing down what you believe to get others to see your point of view. p. 24

pioneers – what we call the first people to come to Michigan in the 1800s. Another name for early settlers. p. 153-166, 183-188

plank road - an early kind of road made by laying down wooden boards or planks. They were very bumpy and soon rotted. They were used because the modern ways of making roads had not been invented. There was no concrete or asphalt. p. 224

point of view – how each person sees issues. p. 384-385

Pontiac (PON tee ak) [1720-1769] – an Odawa leader. He was probably born in Ohio. He helped the tribes try to drive the British out of the Great Lakes Region in 1763. He organized the longest attack by Native Americans on a fort (Detroit). Later, he left the Michigan area. He was murdered by other Native Americans near St. Louis, Missouri in 1769. p. 75, 118

popular sovereignty – the peoples' right to vote. It means the people rule. p. 372, 375, 405

population (pop. you lay shun) - it is how many people live in a place. p. 156, 179, 279

port - a city on a lake or ocean where ships can dock. p. 221

Potawatomi (POT a WAT oh me) – a tribe who settled in southern Michigan by the 1750s. The name comes from Ojibwa words for fire. They probably got this name because they burned the grassland before planting their crops. p. 50, 60

Pow Wow - a special get-together or meeting of Native Americans. Pow Wows have dancing, singing and eating. p. 265

priests (preests) - religious leaders similar to a pastor or minister, often in the Catholic church. p. 90

primary source (pri mary • sorse) – any record from the actual time of an event. It can be a book or diary written by a person who was there. A photograph taken when an event took place. p. 96, 100, 140-141, 157-159

proclamation (prok la may shun) – another name for a law. p. 123

producers - the people and businesses that make products. p. 285, 287

profit - the amount of money a business has left after paying its costs. p. 88, 149

property tax - a tax based on the value of homes, offices and farms. It goes to pay for the cost of government. p. 335

public access channel - a channel on cable television that is set aside for the public to use. People can make programs and send them out over the cable. p. 385

public policy issue - an issue or problem that many people are interested in solving. Public means all the people in a place. An issue which government may help solve. p. 24, 378-403

public services - services government does for us. Supplying city water is a public service. p. 322-323, 339

pursuit of happiness (pur soot) – Pursue means to go after something you want. To let people do what they want. Let them be happy as long as it does not bother someone else. p. 123, 384, 405

radioactive - a material that gives off invisible rays that can harm people and animals. p. 402

rebellion (ree bell yun) - a fight against a government or those in charge. p. 122

recycling - to reuse materials. Old items can be ground up or melted to be made into new products. Old glass bottles can be melted and mixed to make new glass. p. 400

region (REE jun) - an area of land or sometimes water. All parts of a region have something in common. p. 34-36, 154

representative government – a kind of government where others take our place to make laws. Those people represent us in government. p. 331, 407

representatives - the people who take our places in government. p. 331

republic - a kind of government where people use their power by voting. It comes from old words meaning "people matter." p. 331

Republicans - one of the two large political parties in the United States. p. 374

responsibilities - the things people need to do as a part of working with others. They are like duties. At home, one of your responsibilities may be to take out the garbage. Once you are 18, one of your responsibilities is to vote. p. 371-375

Reuther, Walter (ROO ther) [1907-1970]- came to Detroit in 1927 to work making cars. He and his brothers, Roy and Victor, helped start labor unions. He was the president of the United Auto Workers Union from 1946 to 1970. In May 1970 he and his wife died in a small plane crash. p. 257

rights - the freedoms given to people in the state and national constitutions. p. 322-373, 380-381

rule of law - following our laws and not doing whatever we want. p. 358, 374, 407

Saginaw (SAG en aw) - population 69,500. A city started by the trader Louis Campau in 1816. The name means "place of the Sauks." The Sauk tribe once lived in the area. It became a main lumbering and ship building center. It is located on the Saginaw River near Saginaw Bay. p. 75

Saginaw River - a river that flows between Bay City and Saginaw. At one time, there were 112 sawmills along this river. The river is short, but it helps drain about 40 percent of the state. p. 195

sales tax - an extra amount added to the cost of most things bought in stores which helps pay for the government. At this time, it is six cents on each dollar spent. p. 335

Sault Ste. Marie (soo SAYnt MAR ee) - Ste. stands for Saint. Population about 15,000. The oldest city in Michigan. It was started by Father Marquette in 1668. Located in the eastern Upper Peninsula (between Lake Superior and Lake Huron). It has the Soo Locks, the world's busiest locks. It is across the river from a Canadian city with the same name. p. 30, 208, 310-312

scarce - something hard to find or in short supply. Scarce things are usually more valuable. People are willing to pay more to get them. p. 59

scarcity (skair seh tee) – scarcity of resources in one place often leads to jobs related to those things someplace else. Scarcity of copper, iron and trees in some places led to logging and mining jobs in Michigan.   p. 52, 83, 153,183, 192, 390-396

Schoolcraft, Henry [1793-1864] - an Upper Peninsula Indian agent. He married an Ojibway woman. He wrote down many of the Indian legends. He also named many of the counties in Michigan. p. 70

Schoolcraft, Jane [1800-1842] - Ojibway wife of Henry Schoolcraft. She gathered legends from her tribe and recorded them so they would not be lost. p. 70

separation of powers (sep er a shun)- dividing government into 3 main parts so no part can become too powerful. p. 360, 407

service jobs - Doctors, nurses and teachers do jobs that are services. You cannot usually hold a service in your hand like a product. p. 305

settlers (set lers) - another name for pioneers. People who moved to Michigan in the 1800s to start farms or new homes. p. 122, 140, 153-166, 183-188

shanty boys (shan tee) - another name for the loggers or lumberjacks. They had this name because they slept in simple rough cabins called shanties. p. 194

sit-down strike - a strike were workers do not leave the factory to force the business to bargain. p. 258

slavery - the practice where some people own other people. Slaves were forced to do hard work without any pay. Slaves were bought and sold without their permission. Their families could be broken up and the children taken away. Many countries ended slavery in the 1800s. Our country said it was to end at the start of 1863, but it went on until 1865 in the South. p. 170, 229-230

Soo Locks - locks at Sault Ste. Marie that raise and lower ships between Lake Huron and Lake Superior. The first locks were finished in 1855. Lake Superior is about 18 feet higher. p. 210

specialization (spesh el iz a shun) - each person or group learns to do one job. They become very good in doing this one thing. p. 94

St. Lawrence River (St. stands for Saint which sounds like SAYnt. Lawrence sounds like LOR ents) - (SAYnt LOR ents)- the long, large river which drains the Great Lakes. Water from the Great Lakes flows through this river into the Atlantic Ocean. It was an important water route for the French and British. It separates Canada and the United States. p. 90

strike - when a group of workers decide to stop working to bargain for better pay. p. 257

supply and demand – the balance between how much there is (the supply) and how much people want (the demand). When the supply of something is big and the demand is small, it means there is more than people want. In this case, the price is usually low. When the demand goes up, the price usually goes up too. p. 153

supreme court - the highest court in a state or country. It chooses the cases that go before it. It may decide what a law means. p. 351, 367

Tahquamenon Falls (TAH KWA meh non) - Michigan's biggest waterfall. It is in the eastern Upper Peninsula. It has two parts, an upper and a lower falls. One of the largest and most beautiful falls in the eastern United States. p. 23, 311

tax - the money people and businesses pay for the cost of government. Taxes pay for the salary of government workers and supplies. They pay for roads and schools. p. 325

tax breaks - incentives from the government for people or businesses to do things. p. 318

Tecumseh (Ta KUM see) [1768?-1813] - powerful Shawnee Native American leader during the War of 1812. For a time he lived near Detroit. He fought with the British to keep American settlers out of the Great Lakes area. p. 140-141

term limits - not letting the same person have the same government job many times in a row. It limits the number of times he or she can be elected. p. 352

territory (tear eh tor ee) - land that is a part of the United States, but not yet a state. p. 135, 169

time line- a way to show the order of key events from history. It shows which happened first, second, third and so forth. Time lines may be divided into groups of years. John made a time line marked every ten years. See the index for page numbers.

Toledo War (toe lee doe) [1835] – a time of arguing between people in Michigan and Ohio. They disagreed over the border between them. Originally, Toledo was in Michigan. Michigan gave up Toledo and a few miles of land on the south for the western part of the Upper Peninsula. p. 177

Glossary

Three Fires tribes - The Potawatomi, Ojibway and Odawa tribes as they are related and have similar languages. p. 60

trade - exchanging something you have more of than you need for something you do not have. In the fur trade, the tribes had more furs than they needed. They exchanged them for products from France that they did not have and wanted. p. 59

Traverse City (trav erss) - population about 14,500. The name comes from the French who made the "long crossing" or *la grande traverse* across the bay in their canoes. Started in 1847 by Captain Boardman who built a sawmill. More sawmills followed. It is the largest city in the area and is a center for business and tourists. It is known as the "Cherry Capital of the World." p. 117, 195

Truth, Sojourner [1797 -1883] - a former slave whose real name was Isabella Baumfree. She was born in New York. She moved to Battle Creek in 1858. She traveled throughout the northern states speaking against slavery. She is buried in Battle Creek. p. 230

Underground Railroad – people who helped escaped slaves. The slaves were trying to reach Canada. It was not underground and not a railroad. It was called underground because it was secret. It was called a railroad because it was moving people from place to place. The members used railway words like conductor and station. p. 230-231, 269

union - workers who come together as a group to bargain for better conditions and pay. p. 257

United Auto Workers or U.A.W. - a powerful labor union. It was started in Detroit in 1935 to help auto workers. The Reuther brothers were early leaders of the U.A.W. Today it has thousands of members. p. 257

Upper Peninsula (pen in soo la) or U.P.- the northern part of Michigan. It is south of Lake Superior and north of Lake Michigan. It borders the state of Wisconsin. It is famous for copper and iron mining. The U.P. has about one third of Michigan's land. p. 5, 23, 30-32, 38 and others

voters – people who can vote. They are at least 18 years old. They must also be a citizen of the United States. p. 326

War for Independence [1775-1783] – a fight by the American colonies to be free from British rule. The American colonies won with the help of the French. The colonies formed the United States after the war ended. p. 127-129

War of 1812 [1812-1815] – a war started by the United States in 1812 to stop the British from bothering our country. The U.S. also had hopes of taking over part of Canada. The only battles ever fought in or near Michigan were during this war. The British and tribes tried to take over Michigan, but they failed. Michigan became safely a part of the United States once the war ended. p. 136-141

Warren (war in) - Michigan's third largest city. It has about 140,000 people. Warren was started in the 1830s. It is named for General Joseph Warren who fought in the American War for Independence. Known for making army tanks and car parts. p. 29

Wayne, General Anthony (an thon ee wayn) [1745-1796] - led American soldiers against the tribes and the British at the Battle of "Fallen Timbers" in Ohio. This allowed the United States government to take control of Michigan. General Wayne made a treaty with the Native Americans for a large part of Ohio and some of Michigan. The Michigan county with the most people is named after him. p. 130

wolverine (wool ver een) - a wild animal known for its bad temper and bad smell. It is sometimes called a "skunk-bear." It is now a nickname for our state. p. 177

Index